Remarks on the Phonological Evolution of Russian in Comparison with the Other Slavic Languages

Remarks on the Phonological Evolution of Russian in Comparison with the Other Slavic Languages

Roman Jakobson
Translated and annotated by Ronald F. Feldstein

The MIT Press
Cambridge, Massachusetts
London, England

This book was set in Times LT Std by Toppan Best-set Premedia Limited. Printed and bound in the United States of America.

Library of Congress Cataloging-in-Publication Data

Names: Jakobson, Roman, 1896–1982 author. | Feldstein, Ronald F. translator.
Title: Remarks on the phonological evolution of Russian in comparison with the other Slavic languages / Roman Jakobson ; translated by Ronald F. Feldstein.
Description: Cambridge, MA : The MIT Press, 2018. | Based on the French translation of the original Russian text, which was never published. The only known copy of the Russian original was destroyed during the German invasion of Brno in 1939. | Includes bibliographical references and index.
Identifiers: LCCN 2018007480 | ISBN 9780262038690 (hardcover : alk. paper)
Subjects: LCSH: Russian language--Phonology. | Slavic languages--Phonology, Comparative.
Classification: LCC PG2131 .J313 2018 | DDC 491.71/5--dc23 LC record available at https://lccn.loc.gov/2018007480

10   9   8   7   6   5   4   3   2   1

Every linguistic fact is part of a whole in which everything is connected to everything else. One detail must not be linked to another detail, but one linguistic system to another system.
—A. Meillet

The history of a language ... should not be restricted to the study of isolated changes, but should try to deal with them on the basis of their place in the system that experiences them.
—Resolution of the First International Congress of Linguists at The Hague

One must guard against attributing to separation that which can be explained without it.
—F. de Saussure

Contents

Appendix A: Author's Transcription 169

Appendix B: On Cyrillic Transliteration 171

Appendix C: Major *Jakan'e* Types 177

Translator's Foreword: The Significance of Roman Jakobson's *Remarks on the Phonological Evolution of Russian in Comparison with the Other Slavic Languages*

Preliminary

Remarks on the Phonological Evolution of Russian in Comparison with the Other Slavic Languages (henceforth *Remarks*) is uniquely interesting in many ways. It was the first linguistics monograph by Roman Jakobson, one of the greatest scholars of the twentieth century in the fields of both literature and linguistics. Originally written in Russian, this groundbreaking book on the subject of historical phonology was never published in that form, and, unfortunately, the only known copy of the Russian original "perished under the German invasion of Brno in 1939" (Trubetzkoy and Jakobson 1975, 147). Until now, the only surviving edition has been the French translation by Louis Brun. Consequently, this new, annotated English edition represents the first opportunity for many linguists to become acquainted with a major early work by Jakobson, filling a long-standing, unfortunate gap in the linguistic literature.

Jakobson's Purpose

The subject of the book is as unique as its history. It was written as part of the new Prague School structural approach to linguistics and was published as the second volume of the Prague School series, *Travaux du Cercle Linguistique de Prague*. A look at the first three titles that were reprinted in the first volume of Jakobson's *Selected Writings* (1962, 1–116) offers some insight into the history of *Remarks.* These three entries form a kind of trilogy. The first two are short papers on the "sound law and the teleological criterion" (Jakobson 1928/1962a, 1–2) and how best to "completely and practically present the phonological data of any language" (Jakobson 1928/1962b, 3–6). They set forth a programmatic plan for a new type of teleological historical phonology. The third entry is a reprint of the 1929 French translated edition of this book (with some small textual changes and corrections of misprints). A teleological study implies that phonological history is purposeful, moving toward a goal, rather than haphazard and accidental, and this is precisely what Jakobson had in mind. This book is a reaction to previous descriptions of diachronic (i.e., historical) phonology, which record sound changes, but which consider them to be "fortuitous and blind" (Jakobson 1928/1962a, 2, quoting Ferdinand de Saussure) rather than systematic and motivated. Jakobson's new methodology was primarily intended as a corrective to the historical work of both the Neo-grammarians of the nineteenth century (see Halle 1986, 36) and Saussure's *Course in General Linguistics* (see Joseph 2000, 170–173).

The Neogrammarian school was known for presenting sound changes in an isolated manner that did not account for systematic phonological properties. On the other hand, Saussure's *Course in General Linguistics* displayed a true understanding of the phonological system, in the context of a given synchronic state of a language. In fact, Jakobson greatly admired the famous Saussurean analogy between a synchronic phonological system and a game of chess, refer-ring to it as "Saussure's brilliant comparison between the play of language and a game of chess" (*Remarks*, section 2.2). However, Saussure felt that diachrony was different from synchrony and that the chess analogy did not apply to historical evolution, since "language premeditates nothing," but "the chess player *intends*" to make changes (Saussure 1959, 89). This notion was contrary to Jakobson's approach and it led him to conclude that Saussure never managed to escape the "Neogrammarian rut" (*Remarks*, section 2.2; Joseph 2000, 172). I might add that *Remarks* has been very controversial among adherents of Saussurean linguistics. Čermák (1997, 32) and Harris (2001, 94) have gone so far as to say that Jakobson did not properly understand Saussure. However, one can also argue that Jakobson accurately cited specific passages from Sau-ssure's *Course in General Linguistics* and clearly demonstrated that the history of Slavic phonology is not "fortuitous and blind."

The Jakobson-Trubetzkoy Dialogue about *Remarks*

Thanks to the publication of Nikolai Trubetzkoy's letters to Jakobson about the publication of *Remarks* (e.g., Trubetzkoy and Jakobson 1975, 144–149), we have an opportunity to see how the book was discussed behind the scenes. Trubetzkoy agreed completely with the basic idea of the book, that linguistic universals and phonological patterns can influence the direction of sound change, and he praised it as "remarkable" in his letters to Jakobson (Trubetz-koy and Jakobson 1975, 144). However, he felt that Jakobson's book was too difficult for the average linguist to read, because of its style and the fact that it was translated into French, rather than in the original Russian. In one of his letters to Jakobson, he stated that the difficulties were "the result of haste and not enough restraint when you deal with an extremely strong torrent of ideas" (1975, 147). In a written response to Trubetzkoy, Jakobson agreed that his style was difficult, but he said that it was the result not of haste but of the fact that he kept adding more and more detail as he worked on each chapter (1975, 148).

There are two possible sources of difficulty in reading this work. First, Jakobson assumes a basic knowledge of the history of Slavic phonology; to explore this topic, see an introductory work such as Townsend and Janda 1996, 21–119, Lunt 2001, 181–221, or Jakobson 1955. Second, Jakobson frequently uses metaphors that relate to the potential juxtaposition or avoidance of incompatible phonological features in a given dialect zone. Terms such as "struggle" and "conflict" refer to a system that must deal with the simultaneous presence of incompatible phonological features by eliminating one or both of them. On the other hand, if the presence of incompatible features is avoided, Jakobson sometimes says that the conflict was "prearranged" or that the dialect used a "prepared formula" or "model" for dealing with it. As explained in the annotations to the various chapters, the Slavic dialect zones differ mainly in the chronological order in which the various rules applied as a reaction to the loss of the weak high short vowels, known as *jers*, and this can be understood in terms of isoglosses passing through different zones at different rates of speed, which could create a different phonological result in each zone.

Jakobson's Methodology

Jakobson's methodology represents one of the earliest uses of the concept of the distinctive feature, although Jakobson did not use this term, and he did not develop distinctive feature theory fully until two or three decades after the 1929 publication of *Remarks* (see Jakobson and Halle 1956). In 1929, Jakobson had not yet been able to treat all of the features as binary. In *Remarks*, he refers to series of binary feature oppositions as *correlations*, and to isolated binary pairs and nonbinary oppositions as *disjunctive*. A decade later (see Jakobson 1938/1962), he had revised the disjunctive features, such as the opposition of the various places of consonant articulation (labial, dental, palatal, velar), and also treated them as binary features (ultimately *grave-acute* and *compact-diffuse*; see Jakobson and Halle 1956, 29–31). This led to a disagreement between Jakobson and Trubetzkoy in 1936, since Trubetzkoy was not in favor of treating all features as binary (Eramian 1978, 280–281). In any case, Jakobson is able to avoid the piecemeal treatment of individual sounds in *Remarks* by focusing on their common denominator at the feature level. He starts by establishing pairs of distinctive features that either are incompatible and unable to cooccur in phonological systems or have to occur together. For example (sections 2.5, 6.3):

1. Phonemic pitch must cooccur with phonemic vowel quantity. Since phonemic pitch was viewed as a tonal curve across the two moras of a long syllable, pitch implied quantity.

2. A phonemic intensity accent cannot cooccur with phonemic vowel quantity. If accent is truly phonemic and free, it will occur on either mora of long syllables within a system of phonemic quantity, producing a system of phonemic pitch rather than an atonal intensity accent.

3. If there is no opposition between pitch and unaccented syllables, there is also no phonemic opposition between two types of pitch (e.g., rising vs. falling).

4. The features of phonemic pitch and phonemic consonant palatalization cannot cooccur. Although this applies both to the Slavic languages and to other language families, Jakobson does not present it as a universal law, due to Polivanov's Japanese data (see *Remarks*, section 6.3 and note 2 of chapter 6).

On the basis of these four rules of inclusion or exclusion, Jakobson traces the reaction of each Slavic dialect zone to the loss of *jers*. Dialects could either anticipate the potential development of incompatible features due to *jer* loss and modify the system prior to the loss of *jers*, or fail to anticipate the incompatibility and face a conflict of two phonological features, which often led to the loss of both. Each zone reacted in its own way as *jer* loss progressed from the extreme southwest of the Slavic territory (Slovene and Serbo-Croatian) toward the east (Bulgarian) and the northwest (East Slavic).

Russian Unaccented Vowel Systems

After discussing the phonological systems that resulted after the loss of *jers*, Jakobson goes into considerable detail about the various Russian phonological systems of unaccented vowels (chapter 9). Russian dialects typically have a smaller inventory of vowels outside accent and a larger inventory of accented vowels. This means that certain oppositions can occur under accent but are neutralized in unaccented position and that the different vowel systems can serve as redundant signals of accent. The Russian word commonly used for a generic type of vowel reduction is *akan'e*, which literally refers to the merger of /a/ and /o/ outside accent. Jakobson examines many contemporary analyses of this dialect feature and its origin and places the developments in their proper historical context, as well as providing a teleological analysis of how the interplay of inherent and prosodic sonority led to the system of vowel reduction. He also demonstrates that the change could only have proceeded from south to north, since the non-*akan'e* dialects require only a simple rule of merger to undergo it, but the *akan'e* dialects would require a complex set of rules to reverse it and revert to a non-*akan'e* (*okan'e*) system.

Since the neutralization of vowels in unaccented positions usually causes the merger of two vowel heights in those positions, Jakobson examines the relation between inherent sonority (i.e., vowel height) and prosodic sonority (i.e., accent vs. absence of accent). Again, he provides a masterful analysis of distinctive features, analogous to his analysis of the interrelationship of inherent and prosodic tonality features (i.e., consonant palatalization and phonemic pitch), which are incompatible in the Slavic languages. Such analyses constitute some of the great achievements of *Remarks*, which were far ahead of their time and prefigure linguistic work undertaken many decades after the book's first appearance in print.

Conclusion

Jakobson ends *Remarks* by placing his study in the context of the exciting structural developments of the early twentieth century, including Einstein's theories and modern biology. Indeed, Jakobson's study of evolving systems, rather than of individual sounds, was an outstanding linguistic achievement. I am pleased to make it available here in English.

I would like to dedicate this translation to the memory of two sadly departed but unforgettable colleagues, who were of immense help to me in my studies and in my teaching career: Charles Townsend, who taught me the basics of Slavic and Jakobsonian linguistics, and Kees van Schooneveld, who gave me the opportunity to teach the contents of this book.

Notes on Early Common Slavic to Late Common Slavic

As Roman Jakobson states at the beginning of his preface, *Remarks* presumes a knowledge of Slavic languages that is usually found in textbooks. I would recommend Townsend and Janda 1996, 21–119, Lunt 2001, 181–221, and Jakobson 1955 as introductions to the history of Slavic phonology and a supplement to this book. Explanatory information is also presented in the annotations that follow each chapter. The notes in this section provide a bare outline of the most salient facts about the history of Slavic.

Two terms are frequently used to refer to the early history of the Slavic languages: *Proto-Slavic* and *Common Slavic*. They overlap to some extent, but have different emphases. *Proto-Slavic* refers to the unattested and reconstructed language that was the ancestor of the modern Slavic languages. *Common Slavic* refers to a period when the Slavic dialects were mutually comprehensible and could still be considered a common language. (Of course, the linguistic definition of a single language with several dialects, as opposed to several related languages, is not precise.) Traditionally, the first attested Slavic writing, copies of Evangelical texts written in Old Church Slavonic, is viewed as early South Slavic, rather than Late Common Slavic, because it displays several marked South Slavic dialect features characteristic of Macedonian and Bulgarian, such as the change of the $\widehat{or}/\widehat{ol}$ diphthongs to *ra*/*la* sequences. Under this view, the last manifestation of Common Slavic is the period preceding these texts. While the traditional view of Common Slavic places it before the first appearance of Old Church Slavonic texts due to the above-mentioned South Slavic features, Trubetzkoy held the view that the Common Slavic period lasted until the loss of mutual comprehensibility. Since he identified this loss with the fall of the weak *jer* vowels, he famously termed *jer*-fall as "the last event of Common Slavic" (quoted by Jakobson in section 6.1). Jakobson's *Remarks* is one of the best and most detailed treatments of the events that transformed Late Common Slavic into the separate Slavic languages.

Two main phonological tendencies preceded the loss of *jers* in the period between Early Common Slavic and Late Common Slavic. Both tendencies related to the pattern of the individual syllable. Inherent phonological features are often classed as either sonority or tonality features (Jakobson and Halle 1956, 29), depending on whether a given feature is related to levels of energy or frequency, respectively. It happens that there was a particular Common Slavic direction of phonological evolution in both areas, which may clarify the pattern as a whole.

The trend in sonority was toward the open syllable or *rising sonority*, meaning an ideal syllable that started with the least sonorous obstruents, continued with sonorants such as liquids, nasals, and glides, and ended with the most sonorous sounds—the vowels. Since Common Slavic inherited a pattern that was not rising in sonority, a number of changes were required to bring the system into alignment with the new syllabic pattern of rising sonority. Word-final consonants had to be deleted or incorporated into vowels that preceded them; for example, some nasal consonants underwent the latter process, giving rise to nasal vowels. Syllable-final consonants could be deleted or join the following syllable. Diphthongs with falling sonority also changed to fit the rising-sonority model. When low vowels were followed by high, new monophthongs resulted. When vowels were followed by nasal consonants, new nasal vowels resulted. When vowels were followed by the liquids *r* and *l*, in the so-called liquid diphthongs, the Slavic modification to rising sonority was late enough to produce different results in the various zones, which Jakobson treats in detail (see section 3.7 for general discussion of Proto-Slavic diphthongs). The result of all of these changes was a syllable that usually ended in a vowel (i.e., an open syllable). In this connection, one might recall the language universal that all languages have open syllables, but only a subset has closed syllables.

The corresponding trend in tonality split all syllables into a high-tonality type, which were of a higher frequency and contained either palatal, palatalized, or front-vowel components, and a low-tonality type, which lacked any of the high-tonality elements. Since the result was a syllable with uniform tonality, the term *syllabic synharmony* is used to describe this trend. The direction of change caused lower-tonality elements to change to higher tonality. Thus, whenever a nonpalatal or nonpalatalized consonant was followed by a front vowel, it was subject to change. Jakobson uses terms typical of the Slavic linguistic tradition for high-tonality consonants (palatal and palatalized) and for low-tonality consonants (nonpalatal and nonpalatalized): *soft* and *hard*, respectively. The various types of palatalization arose because of the tendency toward syllabic synharmony; since new front vowels could enter the language as diphthongs changed to monophthongs, there were several waves of palatalizations, both regressive and progressive. Much debate has ensued about the relative chronology of these palatalizations. It also should be noted that the term *palatalization* itself is ambiguous, since it can mean the change of a sound either to a palatal consonant (with a single palatal point of articulation) or to a palatalized consonant (with a primary point of articulation and a simultaneous secondary palatalization).

In reading *Remarks*, it will be helpful to keep both major tendencies in mind: rising sonority and syllabic synharmony. These two phonological patterns, and their interruption by the coming process of *jer*-loss at the very end of the Common Slavic period, go a long way toward explaining the many individual changes that they subsume under these major headings.

Author's Preface

I avoid presenting detailed facts of Russian and other Slavic languages that are described in textbooks. A number of issues have had to be presented without argumentation, or at least without detailed argumentation; that task is for specialized studies. Raising them in the present sketch would run the risk of failing to see the forest for the trees. The bibliographical references and critical notes are not intended to exhaust the current literature on the subject, nor to cover the "history of the question."

I am pleased to thank professors L. Brun, F. Dominois, N. Durnovo, O. Hujer, S. Karcevskij, O. Kraus, V. Mathesius, and N. Trubetzkoy for their advice, guidance, and personal cooperation in this work.

Without the insightful research of the latter in the field of the prehistory of Slavic languages, this work would have been impossible. This research, built on a broad and fruitful application of the principle of relative chronology, strives to account for the facts of language through intrinsic linguistic factors and to derive a series of changes from the same initial principle; in short, to discover the internal logic of linguistic evolution (a methodology previously indicated by the Russian linguistic tradition). It was N. S. Trubetzkoy who created the necessary foundation for moving from the history of facts to the history of the evolution of the system.

It is to him that I respectfully dedicate this essay.

Finally, it is my pleasant duty to recall everything that I owe to the thought-provoking works of A. Meillet, which have sought and successfully established the characteristic tendencies of language evolution.

1 Basic Principles

1.1 Phonological System: The Phoneme

By the *phonological system* of a language, I refer to the inventory, proper to that language, of the "meaningful distinctions" that exist among the concepts of acoustic-motor units—that is, the inventory of oppositions that can be linked to differences in meaning (inventory of *phonological oppositions*). All phonological oppositions that cannot be broken down into smaller oppositions are referred to as *phonemes*.[1]

For practical reasons, in the present work I restrict the use of the term "phonological system" by convention: I use it only to refer to the system of meaningful oppositions that is realized within the confines of the word; that is, I ignore the system of oppositions that is manifested only within sequences of words, which serve to express syntactic rather than lexical and morphological meanings. The latter is a separate system, though linked with the former. The nature of this linkage could be translated into a series of precise formulas. The phonological elements of word sequences are, for example, intonation, pauses, accent as a sign of the unity of the phrase, the hierarchy of accents (sentence accent), and so on.

In the Slavic languages, the system of meaningful elements realized within the word is unitary and not subdivided into linked subsystems with specialized functions. However, this is an individual case. Certain other languages exhibit greater functional specialization of phonological elements. Thus, in the Semitic languages the vowel system is morphologized and serves exclusively to express internal root inflection. In most of the Germanic languages, accent as a meaningful element is realized not within the word but only in compound words, where it serves to mark the reciprocal relation of the constituents.

The well-known definition of a phonological system as a "collection of sound concepts" has involuntarily concentrated our attention on the acoustic-motor units themselves. Their types of interrelations have not been subjected to the required analysis; however, it is within them that the essence of the phonological system resides. The sign itself is fortuitous and arbitrary.

1.2   Types of Phonological Oppositions: Correlations

The phonological system presents two basic types of oppositions:

1. Oppositions of *correlative* phonemes, and

2. Oppositions of *disjunctive* phonemes[2]

The first type of opposition manifests a consciousness of the correlation of opposed phonemes, defined by the existence of a series of binary oppositions of the same type within a given phonological system, which I will conventionally refer to as "correlated pairs." The basis for classication (*principium divisionis*) is abstracted by the linguistic consciousness; the common properties are identified and then can be conceived of in the abstract, outside of the specific pairs that are being opposed.[3] On the other hand, of course, one can also abstract the common elements that unite the two members of an opposition, and this substratum is a kind of real unity within the phonological system. The grammatical alternation of two members of an opposition (i.e., the morphological use of this opposition) can be an important concomitant factor that helps us to discern both the substratum and the basis for classification (*principium divisionis*). However, neither this grammatical alternation nor the articulatory relationship can be abstractly conceived of alone and autonomously, as defined above, when a given phonological opposition is isolated in the language. As a result, certain phonemes can be opposed to each other as a correlation within one phonological system, if there exists a system of parallel oppositions; however, in the absence of such a system, within another phonological system the very same phonemes can function as disjunctive. For example, within phonological systems where an entire series of vowels can be both long and short (e.g., Czech, Hungarian, and Ancient Greek), the long and short entities constitute a correlation. On the other hand, where the short vs. long opposition is sporadic (e.g., Abkhaz ā, ă; see Jakovlev, *a* 59), the phonological elements are disjunctive.[4]

The phonological system of Russian has the following correlations:

1. Voiced ~ voiceless consonants (presence or absence of voice)[5]

2. Soft ~ hard consonants (degree of height of the inherent tonality)

3. Intensity accent ~ unaccented vowels (degree of loudness of the voice)[6]

Correlations of the Czech phonological system:

1. Voiced ~ voiceless consonants
2. Length ~ shortness (quantity) of vowels

   Correlations of the literary Serbian phonological system:

1. Voiced ~ voiceless consonants
2. Length ~ shortness of vowels
3. Pitch accent ~ unaccented vowels (degree of voice pitch)
4. One ~ another structure of syllabic intonation

1.3   Paired and Unpaired Phonemes

When considering a correlation, besides the pairs of the existing correlation A_1—A_2, B_1—B_2, C_1—C_2, …, one takes into account phonemes that do not have a partner (i.e., a correlative phoneme)—D_1, E_1, …, F_2, G_2, …—and that are more or less associated with the features of existing correlational pairs (D_1, E_1, … with A_1, B_1, C_1, …; F_2, G_2, … with A_2, B_2, C_2, …), because the content of the correlation, the basis for classification (*principium divisionis*), is to some extent abstracted and thought of by itself. From the perspective of a given correlation, we conventionally refer to phonemes of the type A_1—A_2 as *"paired" phonemes*, and those of the D_1—F_2 type as *"unpaired" phonemes*. For example, if we consider the correlation "voiced ~ voiceless consonants," we distinguish the "paired" voiced consonants, which have "paired" voiceless consonants as correlatives, from the "unpaired" voiced consonants, which lack voiceless partners, and the "unpaired" voiceless consonants, which lack voiced partners.

1.4   Relations between Disjunctive and Correlative Units

In analyzing the phonological system, it would be dangerously illogical to project both correlations and oppositions of disjunctive phonemes onto the same plane and to deal with them without taking into account the essential difference between the two categories, as well as their specific features.

It is not only the correlations and the relationships between disjunctive phonemes that are incommensurable; the terms of the two types of oppositions themselves do not always coincide in number. Thus, in contemporary literary Russian, the categories of the "voiced ~ voiceless" correlation are only opposed to each other preceding unpaired voiced phonemes. To be realized, the opposition of the "accented ~ unaccented" correlation requires at least a disyllabic sequence. In precisely the same way, it is only in a combination of phonemes that the Czech opposition of "length ~ shortness" is fully realized, because, first, the quantity of the vowel has a relative duration that oscillates outside the framework of a determined "tempo," and second, in the final syllable of the word, quantitative relations are distorted and tend to fade.

However, while the phonemes as such constitute the terms of the correlations in the examples cited, one can conceive of cases where the phonological system presents entire sequences of phonemes that are opposed to each other inseparably. For example, several Turkic languages (Kazakh[-kirgiz], [Kara-] kirgiz, Turkmen, Tatar, Bashkir) manifest the so-called *synharmonic law*, as stated by Jakovlev: "Both vowels and paired hard and soft consonants can only be either all hard or all soft within the boundaries of a single word in a language of this type; conversely, within the limits of a single word there cannot be both hard and soft vowels or paired consonants" (Jakovlev, *a* 61ff.; see also Šaraf 97ff.). Setting aside the synharmony of the word, which serves to distinguish words as wholes within the flow of speech and thus is a fact of "syntactic phonology," I emphasize the synharmony of the syllable—that is, the phonological opposition neither of "soft consonant ~ hard consonant" nor of "front vowel ~ back vowel"—separately, but, rather, of "soft group ~ hard group." In written form, the sign indicating softness could apply to the entire syllable (or the entire word) and treat it as a whole, a practice followed in some Latinized Turkic alphabets (Šaraf, 101).

1.5   The Archiphoneme and Its Variants

Taking the delimitation of concepts set forth above as our starting point, we can establish a new entity, essential to phonology: the *archiphoneme*. On the one hand, the archiphoneme cannot be subdivided into smaller disjunctive phonemic oppositions, and, on the other, it cannot share with another archiphoneme a common substratum that can be isolated by the linguistic consciousness; that is to say, one archiphoneme cannot be a correlative of another archiphoneme.[7] The archiphoneme is a generic concept, an abstract unit that can join one or more pairs of correlated variants (correlative phonemes). Just as the extragrammatical variants united within a phoneme can be *combinatory* or *autonomous* (*stylistic* variants),[8] the correlative variants of archiphonemes (correlative phonemes) can likewise be either autonomous or combinatory themselves. The *combinatory correlative variants* of an archiphoneme are correlative variants that manifest themselves only in combination with the correlative variants of another archiphoneme, which are equally combinatory. That is, none of these pairs of correlative combinatory variants is a paired correlation; instead, each is only a *fraction* of a pair. A correlation of phonemic pairs is possible only if these pairs are inseparable.

Let us suppose that the pair A + B is opposed to the pair $A_1 + B_1$. In such a case, A and A_1 can be opposed to each other independently, outside of their combination with B and B_1, while the opposition of B and B_1 is impossible outside of their combination with A and A_1. In this case, it is A and A_1, and neither (A + B) nor ($A_1 + B_1$), which are the basis of the correlation, while B and B_1 are merely extragrammatical variants. The opposition of B and B_1 is one of the types of *concomitant extragrammatical difference* attached to a correlation; the phonological difference that exists between A_1 and A_2 is accompanied by combinatory extragrammatical differences between these phonemes. For example, the Russian phonological opposition "intensity accent ~ unaccented" is accompanied by the extragrammatical differences "pitch accent—unaccented" and "length—shortness." Only one of the acoustic-motor oppositions constitutes the content of the correlation, and it is this opposition that is least distorted in emotive speech, while the combinatory extragrammatical elements are usually also utilized as stylistic differences.[9] Nevertheless, the boundary between the phonological content of the correlation and the concomitant extragrammatical differences is usually fluid, and it can happen that these roles are reversed, so that the concomitant extragrammatical difference becomes the phonological content of the correlation, and its former phonological content becomes a concomitant extragrammatical difference and is seen to be utilized as a stylistic difference.

1.6 Phonological System of Literary Russian

To illustrate what I have said about the archiphonemes and their phonological content, I will give an overview of the inventory of the archiphonemes of contemporary literary Russian (see figure 1.1). Correlative phonemes united into an archiphoneme are shown in parentheses.[10]

The correlation "length ~ shortness of consonants" does not exist in literary Russian. One encounters long consonants only at morphological boundaries, that is, where one part of the long consonant belongs to the root and the other part to an affix: for example, *ras-sadit'* 'offer seats', *vin-nyj* 'wine'. Such long consonants are felt to be a sequence of two short ones. The long soft husher consonants (<*žž, šč*) are independent phonemes; they are not the correlatives of the short hard hushers, since hard hushers can occur in the environment where hard paired consonants cannot (before *i* and *e*). The [long soft and short hard husher—RF] consonants *ž̄'—ž, š̄'—š* (*ščit* 'shield'— *sšit* 'sewn') are also not correlatives since literary Russian does have long hard hushers as single phonological units.

Isn't there a reason to consider the velars of the Russian phonological system as hard unpaired, since the corresponding softs appear only before

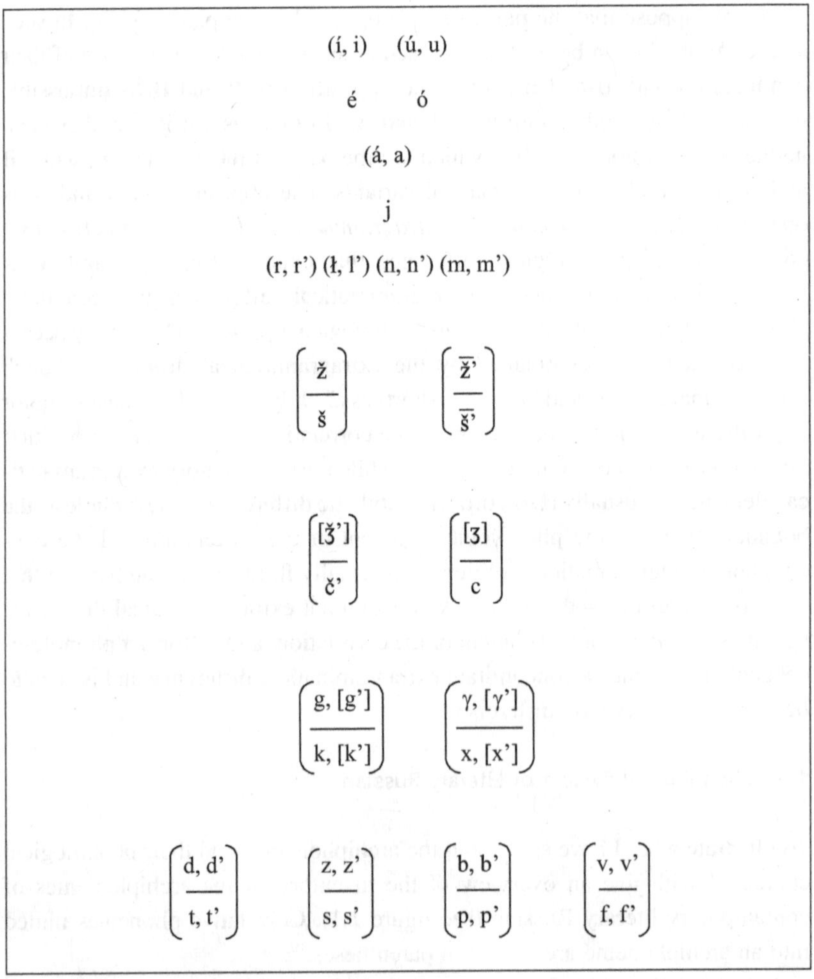

$$(\text{í, i}) \quad (\text{ú, u})$$

$$\text{é} \qquad \text{ó}$$

$$(\text{á, a})$$

$$\text{j}$$

$$(\text{r, r'}) \, (\text{ł, l'}) \, (\text{n, n'}) \, (\text{m, m'})$$

$$\left[\frac{\check{z}}{\check{s}} \right] \qquad \left[\frac{\bar{\check{z}}'}{\bar{\check{s}}'} \right]$$

$$\left[\frac{[\check{3}']}{\check{c}'} \right] \qquad \left[\frac{[\text{3}]}{\text{c}} \right]$$

$$\left[\frac{\text{g, [g']}}{\text{k, [k']}} \right] \qquad \left[\frac{\gamma, [\gamma']}{\text{x, [x']}} \right]$$

$$\left[\frac{\text{d, d'}}{\text{t, t'}} \right] \quad \left[\frac{\text{z, z'}}{\text{s, s'}} \right] \quad \left[\frac{\text{b, b'}}{\text{p, p'}} \right] \quad \left[\frac{\text{v, v'}}{\text{f, f'}} \right]$$

Figure 1.1
Russian phonological system

front-vowel phonemes—that is, strictly speaking, in the role of combinatory extragrammatical variants? We could recognize such a variant for voiced affricates as well, and speak of unpaired voiceless affricates in a similar way. However, the presence of the correlations "soft ~ hard consonant" and "voiced ~ voiceless consonant" permits the relationships *k'*—*k*, *ž*—*č*, and so on, to be interpreted on the basis of the pairs of these correlations. I will refer to phonemes that are identified in this way as *imaginary* or *supplementary* phonemes (in square brackets in figure 1.1). These phonemes occupy a place intermediate between the basic paired phonemes and the combinatory extragrammatical variants.[11]

1.7 Relations between Phonemic Variants and Archiphonemes

I use the term *basic variant* of a phoneme (or of an archiphoneme) to refer to the particular combinatory extragrammatical variant of the phoneme (or archiphoneme) that is the least dependent on extrinsic conditions and that is realized in the most numerous and clearest conditions for phonemes (or archiphonemes) of the language (cf. Jakovlev, *b* 69ff.). The variant that is found to be least dependent on extrinsic conditions is the one that is found in the most varied environments, while the variant that is always associated with just one environment acquires the value of a *secondary variant*—that is, of a combinatory variant in the true sense of the term. For example, if the vocalism of the accented syllable manifests a larger number of phonological differences than that of the unaccented syllable, or if, for the same number of phonological elements, the accented syllable is differentiated with greater phonetic clarity, the basic variants of vocalic archiphonemes are drawn precisely from within the inventory of the accented vowels. If the long vowels have a larger number of phonological elements than the shorts, the basic variants of the archiphonemes are the long vowels; in the opposite case, the basic variants are the shorts. If one variant of a vocalic phoneme occurs only after a hard consonant and word-initially, and a second variant is found only after a soft consonant, the difference is viewed roughly as follows: the second variant is conditioned by the position after a soft consonant, while the first occurs everywhere other than after a soft consonant, that is, in all other environments; in other words, the first variant is the basic one and the second, the secondary one. However, if the first variant occurs only after a hard consonant, while the second one occurs both in word-initial position and after a soft consonant, then, naturally, the second variant is the basic one. If the vocalic phoneme is represented by a total of two combinatory variants and if one is conditioned by a preceding hard consonant and the other by a preceding soft, with no other occurrences in other environments, the two variants are considered to be equipollent. The Russian accented *e* is high before a soft consonant and low in all other positions, that is, before a hard consonant and in final position. Therefore, the low *e* is the basic variant of the *e* phoneme.

The trend toward unification of a phoneme (or archiphoneme)—that is, toward phonetic approximation or merging into a single variant for variants that are markedly differentiated—is particularly strong when there is a basic variant of the phoneme (or archiphoneme), but it is also not uncommon for equipollent variants to result. Where a basic variant exists, the tendency to unify the phoneme (or archiphoneme) occurs most often in the secondary- to basic-variant direction.

The basic variant tends to represent a phoneme (or archiphoneme) in the linguistic consciousness. In the Russian literary language, accented vowels after soft consonants are distinguished from accented vowels in all other environments, that is, after hard consonants and word-initially; accented vowels before soft consonants are distinguished from accented vowels before hard consonants and in word-final position. The basic variants of Russian vowels are accented vowels not adjacent to a soft consonant.

Annotations to Chapter 1, Basic Principles

1.1 Phonological System: The Phoneme

In a 1959 lecture, Jakobson criticized the two theses that he viewed as the "basic principles" of Saussure's *Course on General Linguistics*: "arbitrariness of the sign" and linearity (Jakobson 1985, 28–29). Specifically, he called linearity a "dangerous simplification." However, in 1979 he described his own definition of the phoneme as related to this concept, as presented in the *Course*. Along with coauthor Linda Waugh (1979, 18), he cited his early definition of phonemes as "oppositions that cannot be dissociated into smaller oppositions." The authors claimed that this view was a "corollary" of Saussure's view of linearity and that it was typical of analyses in the 1920s, "which did not go beyond the successive segments of the sound sequence." They contrasted this claim, that there were no oppositions smaller than the linear segment, with the later view of phonemes as being composed of simultaneous distinctive features.

In the first endnote of this book, Jakobson specifically refers to Saussure's view of the "phoneme." Harris (2001, 94–95) later criticized Jakobson for misinterpreting Saussure on several points, including the fact that the term "phoneme" was due not to Saussure himself but to the editors of the *Course*. In the transcript of a 1963 lecture, published in 1989, Jakobson mentioned the fact that Saussure used the term "phoneme" in another sense (e.g., Jakobson 1989, 28), namely, "an invariant in the past," or the invariant of a protoform, in contrast to all the different reflexes in the daughter languages. However, this may not have been as clear to Jakobson at the time *Remarks* was written in the 1920s.

For these reasons, it should be noted that the juxtaposition of Jakobson's and Saussure's views of the phoneme has a long and complicated history in linguistics.

1.2 Types of Phonological Oppositions: Correlations

Correlations are binary and based on a single feature. Jakobson uses the term "correlation" with the symbol ~ to indicate a series of oppositions that differ only by a single binary feature: for example, palatalized vs. nonpalatalized consonants (usually called "soft ~ hard consonants" by Jakobson), length vs. shortness of vowels, voiced vs. voiceless consonants. Note that there is good reason to use the terms "soft" and "hard," rather than "palatalized" and "nonpalatalized," since Russian treats certain palatals (with a primary palatal articulation) and palatalized consonants (with a secondary palatalization) similarly, and one of the most convenient ways of referring to both types at once is to call them "soft" and "hard," or perhaps "high tonality" and "low tonality." Traditional linguists have often confused the terminology and referred to both palatals and palatalized consonants with the same word, but Jakobson and Horace Lunt (1956, 306–307; 1966, 87) often pointed this out as an error. Thus, it is not merely the Russian linguistic tradition that motivates Jakobson's use of the terms "hard" and "soft."

The term "disjunction" was used by Jakobson in the 1920s for oppositions other than correlations—that is, those that could not be expressed as a binary series. Later (1938/1962, 272–279), however, he adopted new types of binary features and thus eliminated the concept of disjunction from his phonology. For example, he modified the features for consonantal places of articulation from the nonbinary labial-dental-palatal-velar to the binary compact/diffuse and grave/acute. Trubetzkoy took a different route. He refined the concept of disjunction to include many different types of opposition, but retained various nonbinary types, such as the places of articulation for consonants, in contrast to Jakobson's approach. (For more details, see Eramian 1978, 275–288.)

For Jakobson, a "correlation" must not only be binary—it must also be found in more than just one binary pair. His precise definition, published in French (1928/1962b, 3) and cited by Eramian (1978, 275), reads as follows (translation mine): "A phonological correlation consists of a series of binary oppositions, defined by a common principle that can be conceived of independently of each pair of opposed terms." Thus, Abkhaz long and short *a* (i.e., *ā*, *ă*) have the binary opposition of length, but form a disjunction, rather than a correlation, since *a* is the only Abkhaz vowel that exhibits the quantity opposition; in this, Abkhaz contrasts with languages like Czech and Hungarian, where a large series of vowels displays a quantity opposition. Jakobson's thinking is that if more than one pair displays a binary opposition, the abstract distinctive feature itself can be thought of as an abstract entity in the speaker's linguistic knowledge and is not bound to a single phonological pair.

In this section, Jakobson presents the oppositions found in Russian, Czech, and Serbian. This choice reflects the fact that these languages represent the three major branches of Slavic. One can assume that Jakobson used the combinations of cooccurring phonological oppositions in the Slavic branches to deduce which features could cooccur in the evolution of Slavic and which could not. For example, he knew that languages with the pitch opposition (in the southwest of Slavic) never have phonemic palatalization, whereas the languages in the Northeast display the opposite situation. Additionally, languages geographically located between these zones (e.g., Czech, Slovak, Macedonian, Western Bulgarian) often lack both features.

1.3   Paired and Unpaired Phonemes

In this section, Jakobson introduces the notions "paired" and "unpaired." Paired phonemes participate in a binary opposition: for example, a "soft" (palatalized) paired phoneme is opposed to another phoneme that agrees with it in all of its phonological features, except for the fact that it is "hard" (non-palatalized). An unpaired hard or soft phoneme participates in no such binary opposition on the basis of palatalization.

1.4   Relations between Disjunctive and Correlative Units

Jakobson cautions against equating correlations and disjunctions and states that all oppositions must be qualified in terms of various environmental restrictions that apply to them. For example, the accent opposition requires at least two syllables for its realization; the Russian voicing opposition occurs only in a specified environment. Sometimes sequences of phonemes function together, as in vowel harmony or as in Common Slavic synharmonic syllables, where the entire syllable, including both vowels and consonants, was either a high-tonality "soft" or a low-tonality "hard" syllable.

1.5   The Archiphoneme and Its Variants

In this section, Jakobson introduces the concept of "archiphoneme": the set of features common to two paired phonemes, which differ by a single binary feature. Thus, in certain positions of neutralization, when the single opposing feature is suspended (as with voicing in word-final position), the occurring sound, which lacks the binary distinction, can be considered equivalent to the "archiphoneme." Both phonemes and archiphonemes can have both "combinatory" and "autonomous" variants. Combinatory variants are similar to allophones, which are predictable from the phonological environment.

Autonomous variants are stylistic variants (called "optional" by Baudouin de Courtenay).

Jakobson also mentions concomitant extragrammatical features. In contrast to distinctive differences, which always differentiate two phonemes, concomitant extragrammatical features occur only under certain conditions, related to stylistic and other factors. Unlike distinctive features, they are predictable; for example, pitch distinctions can accompany Russian accent, but—unlike the distinctive feature of intensity—they are a concomitant extragrammatical feature that is not necessarily present. Jakobson also refers to vowel quantity as a concomitant extragrammatical feature of accent. Finally, he points out that distinctive and extragrammatical features can switch roles in the history of a language.

Note that Jakobson uses the symbol ~ to indicate the distinctive difference between phonemes and the symbol — to identify concomitant extragrammatical features: for example, "intensity accent ~ unaccented," but "pitch accent—unaccented," in the case of Russian.

1.6 Phonological System of Literary Russian

Jakobson presents the phonemic system of Russian in chart form. Correlations that constitute archiphonemes (i.e., differ by a single binary feature) appear in parentheses. (Note that in Jakobson's later system of distinctive features, phonemic oppositions such as /p/ vs. /k/ and /p/ vs. /t/ are also binary.) In a note, Jakobson discusses the unusual status of the variants [i] and [y] of the phoneme /i/.

Jakobson addresses the question of palatalized velars in terms of hard ~ soft pairedness. Since this correlation exists for other phonemes but is a predictable, combinatory extragrammatical feature for velars, he assigns it the status of an "imaginary" or "supplementary" phoneme, placed in square brackets in his chart.

1.7 Relations between Phonemic Variants and Archiphonemes

In the case of multiple combinatory variants, the one that occurs most widely and independently, and is the least dependent on extrinsic conditions, is considered to be the "basic variant." For example, basic variants of Russian vowels are drawn from the inventory of accented vowels, rather than unaccented. Russian /e/ has both higher and lower variants, but the lower variant is basic since the higher one occurs only before a soft consonant and the lower one occurs elsewhere.

This section has been plagued by misprints in various editions. The 1929 edition had two misprints or erroneous translations into French. The first error, which was corrected in the 1962 edition, used the word "before" (French *devant*) instead of "after" (*après*) in the sentence "the second variant is conditioned by the position after a soft consonant, while the first occurs everywhere other than after a soft consonant." The second error has not been corrected in any previous edition of which I am aware. The word I have translated as "soft" originally appeared as the word "hard" (French *dure*) in the sentence "However, if the first variant occurs only after a hard consonant, while the second one occurs both in word-initial position and after a *soft* consonant, then, naturally, the second variant is the basic one." In other words, it would not make sense to refer to both vocalic variants as occurring after hard consonants, as the French text reads; if that were the case, the two consonants would not be variants (allophones) in complementary distribution.

2 Remarks on Current Issues of Comparative Historical Phonology

2.1 Extending the Use of Comparative Historical Methodology

The traditional object of comparative grammar is the reconstruction of an "initial common language," carried out by comparing related languages. Once this goal was achieved and once historians of these related languages were given a point of departure, it seemed that the comparativist's task was completed. However, in this case the most one could say was that the first chapter of the comparative grammar was completed. The operational framework needed to be expanded. It is not only a question of the common inheritance from the mother language by the daughter languages; rather, the evolution of the related languages after the disintegration of the "common language" ought equally to be the object of comparative study. The fundamental differences and convergences within the independent evolution of the related languages ought to be identified and compared; it is only in this way that one can shed light on the basic tendencies of the evolution of these languages and connect the historical episodes of their evolution, which at first glance are dissimilar and aimless, in order to establish a complete cycle of changes aimed at reaching a goal.

2.2 Contradiction (Antinomy) between Synchronic and Diachronic Linguistics and Ways of Overcoming It

The cornerstone of the contemporary theory of language is Saussure's thesis that language is a system of relative values, which should be considered from the viewpoint of the functions they fulfill. This thesis is more or less accepted in synchronic linguistics (although we have not yet completely understood all of its particular consequences). On the other hand, diachronic linguistics remains in the Neogrammarian rut. In his interpretation of diachrony, Saussure is closely connected to the scientific traditions of the nineteenth century. For him, changes occur without any intention; they are fortuitous and involuntary, and certain elements are altered without regard for the unity that links them to the whole. Consequently, they can only be studied outside the system. Changes in a system occur under the influence not only of events that are alien to it, but also of events that are isolated and do not themselves constitute a system. Thus, there is a huge gulf between diachronic and synchronic linguistics. Saussure's brilliant comparison between the play of language and a game of chess loses its persuasive force if one adopts Saussure's view that language does not anticipate anything and that its parts move by accident. From this standpoint, the history of the sounds of a given language would be the result of turmoil and blind deterioration, caused by extrinsic factors. From the point of view of the phonological system, these disordered actions would be nothing but unfortunate burglaries, totally devoid of purpose.

Schleicher reconciled a recognition of the internal and functional sense of the linguistic system, provided by direct experience, with the idea of senselessness and blind chance in the evolution of language. He did so by interpreting the internal and functional sense as a remnant of an original state of perfection of the system. From this point of view, changes are reduced to disintegration and destruction. Once the romantic myth of a Common Indo-European epoch as a golden age of the language had been removed from science, the contradiction was exposed. German Neogrammarians postponed this extralinguistic contradiction, by stating that the science of language is limited to its history (cf. Paul §10). For Saussure, who rehabilitated synchronic linguistics, the contradiction becomes blatant and built on dogma.

By contaminating both the concept of diachrony in question and the teleological method of dealing with synchronic phonology, Saussure's doctrine only allows the speech community to find meaning in the state of disorder in which they find themselves at a given moment, by interpreting it as an ordered system. However, in reality, the role of the speech community is much more active, while the scope of "phonetic damage" in the history of the language is much more limited. In particular, wherever a destructive process has taken place, it has necessarily been followed by an active reaction. And, just as the loss of a piece in a game of chess often provokes a series of moves by the threatened player, in order to restore balance, similarly a given language needs a series of innovations aimed at restoring the phonological system's stability and balance. It happens that both the speech community and the chess player resort to procedures that, while saving the situation at one point, risk precipitating disastrous consequences at other points of the system. Saussure's analogy between language and a game of chess can be pushed to its limit. Like movements of pawns on the chessboard, many linguistic changes have "the intention of influencing the system."

Gilliéron and his successors assign a considerable role to verbal therapy in the life of a language. But, in any case, phonological therapy is no less essential. In the event of damage, the language tries to support and restore sharpness and flexibility, not only to the vocabulary, but also directly to the phonological system—the instrument for differentiating words.

However, the activity of the linguistic system is not restricted to reacting to blows that come from outside and healing its wounds. In the course of its evolution, a language resolves internal problems. It would be an error to represent a linguistic system left to its own devices as condemned to stagnation and unable to evolve. The structural elements of the language are used like the parts of any structure and mechanism. Repairs are necessary to renew efficiency. For example, elements of emotive language become automatic, lose their emotional value, and change their function. Consequently, emotive language creates a new inventory of means of expression. In addition, there may be a change in the attitude of speakers toward the language, a change in the dominant linguistic styles, and a modification of the hierarchy of functions. An essential point within a given speech community is the relative role of emotive language and intellectual language, poetic language and the language of communication, theoretical language and practical language, and internal and overt speech. The concepts that have been introduced in literary studies by the Russian "Formalist School," of "form going beyond its original function" and a "redirection of functions," can clearly be applied to the history of language. For example, a given function will have created numerous means of expression that eventually become excessive. These means then seek out a new function, adapt to it, and so on.

I have emphasized that linguistic changes cannot be understood as detached from the system, but neither can the system be regarded as excluding changes. What is a synchronic system? It is a system existing at a given moment in the linguistic consciousness of a speech community and constituting an indispensable premise for speech. It is precisely on this point that one must consider changes as falling into the domain of synchrony. The most characteristic form taken by the projection of diachrony within synchrony is the assignment of a different function to the two terms of a change; thus, two phonological stages are evaluated like two functionally different dialects, like two "styles." Conversely, the characteristic form taken by the projection of synchrony within diachrony is the generalization of a style; two styles become two stages of the language (cf. §10.2). However, a mutation may be a fact of synchrony itself, even without transposition into specifically synchronic categories; at a given moment, a mutation can be conceived of as such by the speech community. There are styles of pronunciation, grammatical variants, words, turns of phrase, which are interpreted by the speech community as belonging to and suitable for the older generation, and conversely, others that are considered to be the prerogative of youth or the latest word in fashion, in which case it is a question not only of different ready-made inventories, but also of stylistic tendencies seen as being very modern. Nevertheless, the issue cannot be reduced to the mere coexistence, perceived by the speech community, of peculiarities of expression used by different generations; one and the same person can use the existing variants of the language; thus, for example, a speaker of the young generation can be in solidarity with the speech of the elderly and consciously archaize his style of speech. Thus, one does not have the right to claim that the succession of linguistic facts over time is invariably nonexistent for the speech community.

What is an archaism in the synchronic sense of the term? It is a part of our language that we view as transplanted from the language of the older generation or even earlier times, while an archaism from the diachronic perspective is an active remnant of a bygone era. It is in this sense that we say, for example, that the forms of the dual in Slovene are an archaism. The two concepts do not overlap, and facts felt to be archaic may not be, and vice versa. The relationship between archaisms from the synchronic and diachronic points of view is roughly the same as that between folk etymology and historical etymology. What are productive forms in comparison to nonproductive? Productive forms are those that we feel can serve in the formation or inflection of neologisms (cf. Karcevskij 48ff.); that is, these are forms to which we attribute a future. From the synchronic point of view, one has no reason to deny the existence of a difference between productive and nonproductive forms, nor to exclude the notion of archaisms from synchronic linguistics.

The object of synchronic linguistics is not the facts sensed by the speech community as simultaneous among its individual speakers, but the facts that are simultaneously sensed by it as a unit—in other words, the facts that constitute the linguistic consciousness at a given moment in time. For the consciousness of the speech community, some of these facts can be strictly linked to the present, while others, as we have seen, can refer to the past or gravitate toward the future.

The contradiction that exists between a synchronic and a diachronic characteristic of the sound system of a language would be eliminated once these changes are considered in relation to the function of the phonological system that undergoes them. Historical phonetics would thus be transformed into a history of the evolution of a phonological system.[1]

2.3 Typology of Changes

It is impossible to characterize sound changes while ignoring what changes: phonological elements or extragrammatical elements. But this boundary itself is insufficient; in dealing with the change of phonological elements, linguistics cannot avoid accounting for the specific differences that exist between changes that affect the oppositions of disjunctive and correlative elements or, finally, correlations taken as a whole.

The speech community's attitude to these different types of oppositions is not uniform. Thus, for example, it is not at all rare to see a language abandon the differences between disjunctive phonemes in the name of conserving differences between correlatives. Equally essential is the very difference of the roles played by the change of phonological elements. Some of them cause an existing distinction to disappear (A merges with B); others reduce two existing differences to a single one (A merges with C and B with D), give rise to a new phonological opposition (A splits into A_1 and A_2), modify the content of an existing distinction (the distinctive mark of A and B is no longer the same)— or, finally, the difference is preserved, but with a change in the sphere in which the elements of the opposition are used (A and B are preserved, but some instances of A are changed to B). In a word, a typology of changes is indispensable.

2.4 Phonetic "Laws"

It is not by abandoning the notion of a "sound law" that one would go beyond the Neogrammarian tradition; rather, it is by abandoning the mechanical nature of this concept and interpreting it teleologically. The comparative analysis of phonological systems and their evolution allows one to approach the central problem of general phonology: the exploration of the structure of phonological systems. The concept of a phonological system as a chance collection of elements must be abandoned. The inventory of permissible combinations of phonemes that form words is linked to other facts of the phonological system; the length of the word is linked to the number of phonemes (e.g., the more phonemes in the language, the smaller is the permitted range of word lengths). There are facts about incompatibility and, conversely, about inseparability, in the inventory of both correlations and disjunctive elements.

2.5 Laws of Reciprocal Relations of Correlations

There are correlations that coexist in certain phonological systems, but not in others. Such is the case, for example, for the correlation "voiced ~ voiceless consonant" in its relations with other correlations previously enumerated. However, certain correlations obey rigorous laws:

1. *If a exists, then b also exists.* Such is the relation between the correlations "one ~ another structure of syllabic intonation" and "length ~ shortness of vowel."[2] If the first of these two correlations is found in a given phonological system, the second must inevitably also occur. However, the converse is not true.

2. *If a exists, then b is absent.* Such is the relation between the correlation "intensity accent ~ unaccented" and that of "length ~ shortness of vowel."[3] Logically, it also means that if *b* exists, then *a* is absent. However, this does not mean that *a* must be present if *b* is absent and vice versa.

3. *If a is absent, then b is also absent.* This logically also means that if *b* exists, then *a* also exists, but it does not mean that if *b* is absent, then *a* must also be absent, nor that if *a* exists, *b* must also exist. This is the relation that obtains between the correlations "one ~ another structure of syllabic intonation" and "pitch accent ~ unaccented."[4]

The confrontation of these relationships permits us to calculate several derived relations: when the correlation "one ~ another structure of syllabic intonation" exists, the correlation "length ~ shortness of vowel" also exists. When the correlation "one ~ another structure of syllabic intonation" exists, the correlation "intensity accent ~ unaccented" is absent.[5] When we have the correlation "pitch accent ~ unaccented," we do not have the correlation "intensity accent ~ unaccented."

One of the current problems of comparative phonology is that of clarifying the other lawful relationships between the correlations of the phonological system.[6] These relationships, which have the inevitable value of laws, are one of the most important factors in phonological change. The loss or appearance of a new correlation (e.g., the transformation of the basis for classification (*principium divisionis*) of a correlation, or the replacement of one correlation by another) often leads inevitably to an essential rebuilding of the phonological system, in view of the rigidity of the relationships that have just been examined and the correlations between them.

In a word, the variety of structural types of the phonological system is limited, just like the variety of structural types in the syntactic and morphological systems; it is also probable that the multiplicity of relationships between the phonological, morphological, and syntactic systems is also limited. By establishing the laws of general phonology, we acquire the opportunity to control actual attempts to reconstruct the sound system of a language at a particular historical period.

2.6   Importance of Acoustics for Historical Phonology

Just as issues of sound production are being replaced by questions about the tendencies and goals of phonology, so the physiology of language sounds, in its role of interpreting the external and material aspect of these phenomena, will have to yield more and more to the primacy of acoustics, since it is precisely the acoustic and not the motor image that is envisioned by the speaker and constitutes the social fact.[7]

Annotations to Chapter 2, Remarks on Current Issues of Comparative Historical Phonology

2.1 Extending the Use of Comparative Historical Methodology

The traditional object of comparative historical phonology has been the reconstruction of the protolanguage. This should be just the beginning of research into how the system changed into the various daughter languages. One should ask how the process was systemic and rule-based, rather than haphazard and accidental.

2.2 Contradiction (Antinomy) between Synchronic and Diachronic Linguistics and Ways of Overcoming It

Saussure's thesis of the synchronic system of language is the basis of modern phonology. However, Saussure continued to treat the historical development of language (diachrony) as accidental and unsystematic, in contrast to synchrony (the current language system). Jakobson's main thrust in this book is to show that diachrony is just as systematic as synchrony, but that it requires research into how systems change and which combinations of phonological features are compatible. Saussure once analogized synchrony to a game of chess, in which every piece is related to the others in some way, just as phonemes are relational and based on opposition. Jakobson feels that Saussure was mistaken in not extending this analogy to diachrony, since the loss of a chess piece requires a systematic evaluation of each new position and a strategy for continuing, just as changing linguistic systems do, in Jakobson's opinion. The bulk of this book is devoted to illustrating this principle—the notion that diachronic linguistics should be the study of successive systems and how they evolve.

2.3 Typology of Changes

In this section, Jakobson treats changes in correlations and disjunctions. There are many possible ways that phonemic oppositions can change. A typology of phonological mergers, splits, and so on, should be established.

2.4 Phonetic "Laws"

Jakobson introduces the concept of teleology into language change. Changes in language systems are not totally accidental; rather, there are limitations on the ways systems can change. *Teleology* refers to striving toward a particular end, in accord with general principles of language systems. For example, if two features in a language are incompatible, this fact determines that one or both must be lost; this loss is not an accident, but arises from an inherent property of language in general.

Instead of just mechanically recording which sounds change to others, one should establish permissible and impermissible combinations of phonological features and oppositions. One should show how the historical evolution of a language eliminates some features in favor of others within the phonological inventory.

2.5 Laws of Reciprocal Relations of Correlations

Jakobson lists three rules about how two features can imply or exclude each other, and he gives examples of each. To illustrate the first rule, he cites the relationships between vowel intonation, quantity, and accent. Note that the correlation "one ~ another structure of syllabic intonation" refers to a pitch opposition between two different tones, such as the rising and falling tones of Slovene, Serbian, and Croatian. The notion that a pitch opposition requires vowel quantity refers to the interpretation of long vowels as two units, called moras, while a short vowel is just one mora in length. Rising tone is interpreted as a type of accent on the second of a long vowel's two moras, while falling tone is interpreted as an accent on the first. Therefore, Jakobson states that the pitch opposition requires vowel quantity.

Jakobson's example of the second rule of implication states that the nontonal intensity accent excludes phonemic quantity. The reasoning behind this rule is not so obvious, but the following explanation can be offered. In the case of free intensity accent, the accent may fall on any syllable of a word, as in Russian and English. If there is no phonemic quantity, each vowel is treated as a single unit and any such unit can bear the accent. However, since Jakobson treats long-vowel quantity as consisting of two moras, truly free accent in a quantitative system with moras would create a phonemic pitch accent, rather than a nontonal intensity accent. In order for phonemic nontonal intensity accent to coexist with phonemic vowel quantity, a somewhat anomalous system would be required: accent would be free to occur on any vowel, but it would always have to occur on the same mora, because free accent on any mora would imply a pitch opposition, rather than intensity accent. So, Jakobson treats a system of free intensity accent on any syllable but fixed accent on any given two-mora combination as an impermissible combination of intensity accent and phonemic quantity. Ivić (2001/1965, 73) mentions that several South Slavic dialects, in Montenegro and elsewhere, violate this rule, although it holds for the majority of Slavic languages and dialects. We can assume that Jakobson was not aware of the exceptions when he was writing this book in the 1920s.

Jakobson's example of the third rule of implication also refers to the prosodic feature of pitch; he states that the absence of an opposition between two pitch accents (e.g., rising vs. falling) implies the absence of an opposition between the pitch accent and an unaccented syllable. In other words, the pitch opposition can oppose both two different tones to each other and a tonal accent to an unaccented syllable.

Note that all three of Jakobson's examples are drawn from the domain of prosodic features.

2.6   Importance of Acoustics for Historical Phonology

This section emphasizes the importance of acoustics over articulatory phonetics for historical linguistics. This view can be directly related to Jakobson 1938, in which the acoustic interpretation of the places of consonant articulation solved the problem of how to treat many disjunctive oppositions as binary. As long as the basis for classification had been strictly articulatory, these oppositions could not easily be interpreted as binary. Later work by Jakobson and others (particularly Jakobson, Fant, and Halle 1951 and Jakobson and Halle 1956) continued to pursue the acoustic analysis of phonological systems, which was especially important for establishing the system of distinctive features.

3 Remarks on the Evolution of the Phonological System of Proto-Slavic

3.1 First and Second Velar Palatalizations

At the beginning of the independent existence of Proto-Slavic, the phonological system of the language had, among other correlations, that of "palatal ~ labiovelar vowel." There was a tendency to labialize consonants before rounded vowels (cf. Šaxmatov, c §111). Nonlabialized velars were going to be eliminated: thus, k, g, x before front vowels first changed to the palatals $č$, $ž$ (probably $ǯ$ at first), $š$ (a change called the "first velar palatalization"); next, the weakly labialized velars (i.e., the velars before long or short o and before short u) lost their labialization when following long or short i and their articulation moved toward the front (a process called the "second velar palatalization"). (Cf. Trubetzkoy, c 230.) We do not have reliable data to establish the original products of the second palatalization, which I indicate with the symbols k_1, g_1, x_1. In West Slavic, the reflex of x_1 is different than it is in the other Slavic zones, and since the isoglosses specifically common to West Slavic are evidently a relatively late fact, one could equally consider the current Slavic reflexes of x_1 as late. Similarly, one cannot claim that c, $ʒ$ have come from k, g without an intermediary. It is very possible that the intermediate stage, or the final intermediate stage between k, g, x and c, $ʒ$, $s/š$, was a palatal stop or a corresponding back husher.

Originally, $č$, $ž$ (or $ǯ$), $š$, along with k_1, g_1, x_1, were extragrammatical combinatory variants of the phonemes k, g, x. The variants $č$, $ž$ (or $ǯ$), $š$ could occur only before front vowels; k_1, g_1, x_1 occurred between i and a weakly labialized back vowel; k, g, x occurred in all other environments, that is, always before a strongly labialized back vowel, and before a weakly labialized back vowel only if not preceded by i.

This was the situation on the eve of the period that was marked by the beginning of the dialect differentiation of Proto-Slavic (cf. Trubetzkoy, c 218ff.). The main facts of the Russian phonological system cannot be historically clarified without first describing the most important events of that period, which brought a number of important innovations to the phonological structure of Proto-Slavic.

3.2   Influence of Palatal Consonants on Following Vowels

One of the tendencies that runs like a thread throughout the entire period under consideration is the standardization of the syllable. Gradually, a harmony of sounds gets established within the syllable (syllabic synharmony; cf. §1.5), and two types of syllables become crystallized—soft and hard. The tendency in question is realized by means of both regressive and progressive assimilation.

The latter type, progressive assimilation, is manifested in the form of the influence of palatal sounds on the nonpalatals of the same syllable.

The first realization of this principle was the law that specified that back vowels after palatal consonants became fronted (Meillet, *c* 78; Trubetzkoy, *c* 221–224). Trubetzkoy introduced the following reservation to this law: in palatalizing, tense vowels remain rounded ($\bar{u} > \bar{\ddot{u}}, \bar{\varrho} > \bar{\ddot{\varrho}}, \varrho > \ddot{\varrho}$), while nontense vowels lose their rounding ($u > i, \bar{o} > \bar{e}, o > e$). However, we do not have any data that would make us suppose that the Common Slavic reflex of $\bar{u}$ after a palatal—$\bar{\imath}$—only arose in the period of the unrounding of long vowels and that between $\bar{u}$ and $\bar{\imath}$ there was an intermediate phase of $\bar{\ddot{u}}$. The hypothesis of $\bar{\ddot{u}}$ substitutes a triple series $\bar{\imath}$—$\bar{\ddot{u}}$—$\bar{u}$ for the binary opposition $\bar{\imath}$—$\bar{u}$, but such an entity would have been an isolated fact for Proto-Slavic, contradicting the entire structure of the phonological system of this language. It is more likely that the "unpaired" back vowels kept their rounding when they were fronted: that is, $\bar{\varrho} > \bar{\ddot{\varrho}}, \varrho > \ddot{\varrho}$, but $\bar{u} > \bar{\imath}$, the same as $u > i$.

After the fronting of back vowels, the Proto-Slavic vowel system found itself reduced to the following oppositions:

i—u

$\ddot{\varrho}$—ϱ

e—o

(Each vowel occurred in two correlative variants, long and short.)

3.3   Reciprocal Influence of Vowels and Liquids inside Diphthongs

The second manifestation of progressive assimilation was the softening of the consonant in the diphthongs consisting of an unrounded front vowel plus a sonorant consonant: $\widehat{er}, \widehat{el}, \widehat{en}, \widehat{ir}, \widehat{il}, \widehat{in} > \widehat{er'}, \widehat{el'}, \widehat{en'}, \widehat{ir'}, \widehat{il'}, \widehat{in'}$ (Šaxmatov, *c* §§80–83; Trubetzkoy, *g* 670ff.). Shortly before this process, front vowels before *l* in the same syllable had rounded, subject to different dialectal conditions, but preserving their front-vowel quality after a palatal consonant (since back vowels were not admitted after palatal consonants); in other environments, they became back vowels in the process of rounding (e.g., *dilgu* > *dulgu*, *žiltu* > *žültu*).

In the East Slavic dialect, the front vowels of the diphthong ending in *l* were rounded, regardless of what preceded; in the dialects that eventually resulted in Polish, Czecho-Slovak, and the South Slavic languages, the rounding occurred only after labial consonants.[1] It seems that the obstacle to rounding, at least under certain conditions, had been a front vowel in the following syllable. Thus, in Russian one finds several words that preserved the *l* of the diphthong $\widehat{el}$, followed by a syllable with a front vowel: cf. *oželedica, oželed'* 'ice sheet'; *pelevnja* (but *polovy*) 'threshing barn'; *peleščutsja* (but *poloskat'sja*) 'bathe with splashing'; *veleten'* (but *volot*) 'giant'; *selezen'* 'drake', *selezenka* 'spleen'; *lebed'* 'swan' (but *lebeda*, variant *loboda* 'saltbush, Atriplex, genus Chenopodium').

Perhaps the form *dlъžě* 'long, loc. sg.', found in Zographensis, should also be explained in terms of the front vowel of the following syllable. In all likelihood, doublets such as Old Church Slavonic *žlado̧, žlasti* and *žlědo̧, žlěsti* 'atone', Slovene and Czech *član* and *člen* 'member', Czech *žlab* and *žleb* 'trough' can all be explained by two diverse, nonphonetic generalizations; in one case, what generalized was the vowel that originally existed only when the following syllable had been hard; by contrast, in the other case, what generalized was the vowel that had phonetically occurred only before a soft syllable: for example, *člen*, instead of the expected form *član*, under the influence of the locative and vocative, and so forth. We are not so clear about whether there was a labiovelarization of a neutral *l* in the diphthongs consisting of a front rounded vowel plus *l*, or whether Polish *złób* 'trough', *żółty* 'yellow', and Russian *žëlob* 'trough', *žëltyj* 'yellow', etc., are the result of a later dialect change of *l* to *ł*.

If one considers the velarization of *l* in a diphthong after a rounded vowel as a fact of Proto-Slavic, it would then be necessary to explain forms such as *žlab*, from a Czech text that has still preserved the particular phoneme *ł* (cf. Gebauer, I 360), as a contamination of the forms *žłab* and *žleb*. (Cf. *žluč* (op. cit. 361) in the same text, which may be a contamination of *žlutý* 'yellow' and *žlč* 'bile'.)

The diphthongs $\widehat{ol}, \widehat{ül}$ (or $\widehat{ół}, \widehat{ül}$?) were the only violation of "synharmony"— a soft syllable that ended with a nonsoft consonant. However, the diphthongs in question were indivisible entities in the phonological system and the front vowel correlative of the diphthong $\widehat{ol}$ was the diphthong represented by the two extragrammatical combinatory variants $\widehat{öl}$ (or $\widehat{öł}$?) and $\widehat{el}$', while that of the diphthong $\widehat{uł}$ was the diphthong represented by the combinatory variants $\widehat{ül}$ (or $\widehat{üł}$?) and $\widehat{il}$'. The variant $\widehat{il}$', and also, partially, $\widehat{el}$', are absent in many Slavic languages. During the change of $\widehat{öl}$ by means of metathesis, the $ö$ after nonpalatalized l was naturally replaced by the sound o (and, in parallel fashion, dialectal $\bar{\bar{o}}$ by $\bar{o}$). During the process of eliminating the diphthong $\widehat{öl}$ by changing it into a disyllabic group, $ö$ was in an open syllable and was naturally replaced by the sound e.

3.4 Influence of Vowels on Preceding Consonants

Regressive assimilation was equally utilized as a vehicle for creating syllabic "synharmony": consonants adapted the level of their tonality to that of the following vowel phoneme within the same syllable. Consonants became palatalized before front vowels ($ti > t^i i$, $te > t^e e$, etc.). We are not able to state the precise relative chronology of this process. Transformations such as $\widehat{tel} > \widehat{tol}$ do not permit us to infer that these consonants preceding e were still hard at the time of this change. If the law of consonant assimilation to the inherent tonality of the following vowel had continued to apply, $t^e el$ should have given rise to $\widehat{tol}$, and not to $t^e \widehat{ol}$.

3.5 Unification of the Syllable

Generalizing, one can formulate the law of the realization of syllabic "synharmony" as follows: vowels caused the assimilation of the adjacent consonants of the same syllable ($te > t^e e$, $er > er^e$, etc.) on the basis of their tonality; in cases where the consonants did not lend themselves to such assimilation (palatal consonants), the opposite occurred, with the vowels assimilating to the palatal consonants ($jo > je$, etc.).

3.6 Ultimate Fate of the Products of Velar Palatalizations

After the fronting of back vowels when they were preceded by palatal consonants, the products of the first and second velar palatalizations acquired a modified status within the phonological system. The products of the second palatalization were found only before a front vowel; that is, both k_l, g_l, x_l and $č$, $ž$, $š$ could occur in the same environment (between i and a front vowel). The position before a back vowel became a specific feature of k, g, x; on the one hand, neither $č$, $ž$, $š$ nor k_l, g_l, x_l could occur in that environment and, on the other hand, no other vowel could occur after k, g, x. All vowels, including i, could precede k, g, x. Thus, the preceding vowel no longer determined the choice of consonant. Just like $č$, $ž$, $š$, the consonants k_1, g_1, x_1 could be characterized as combinatory variants in relation to k, g, x, conditioned by the pre-front-vowel environment. However, since $č$, $ž$, $š$ and k_1, g_1, x_1 were themselves not environmentally restricted, they tended to be opposed to each other phonologically, and one of these two groups had to become phonologically emancipated. Given that k—k_1, g—g_1, x—x_1 participated in grammatical alternations more frequently than did k—$č$, g—$ž$, x—$š$, it was precisely $č$, $ž$, $š$ that assumed the role of independent phonemes, as a consequence of the change of phonological values, while k_1, g_1, x_1 continued to be evaluated as extragrammatical variants of k, g, x. In cases that arose later, the softening of velars continued to be carried out in the form of a change to k_1, g_1, x_1: before $\widehat{ie} < \widehat{oi}$, and dialectally before palatalized v.

When regressive assimilation created t', as an extragrammatical variant of t, conditioned by the position before a front vowel (where t represents dentals and labials), this led to the unique proportional equivalence of $t':t = k_1:k$. This proportion is real only in the sense that both t' and k_1 were the only permissible variants of t and k in the pre-front-vowel environment. However, despite this common property, there were essential differences between the relations $t':t$ and $k_1:k$. First, from the acoustic point of view t' and t differed only in their inherent tonality, while k_1 and k were directly opposed to each other by their sound quality; second, the grammatical alternations that accompanied the t'—t variants were not parallel to those that accompanied the k_1—k variants.

3.7 Diphthongs of Proto-Slavic

Proto-Slavic did not preserve the quantitative feature of the components that made up the Indo-European diphthongs. From the quantitative point of view, in the Proto-Slavic system diphthongs were equivalent to long vowels. Length and tone were borne by the diphthong as a whole. The diphthongal relations of quantity were determined by the tone. In accord with Trubetzkoy's hypothesis, the first component was longer than the second in a diphthong with acute tone, but shorter in a diphthong with circumflex tone. Diphthongs met different fates depending on the relationship of their components. In this regard, they can be divided into three categories:

1. Diphthongs made up of the most homogeneous elements, that is, vowels from the same vertical row ($\widehat{ou}$, $\widehat{ọü}$, $\widehat{ei}$).

2. Diphthongs with a nasal consonant as the second component; the nasal consonant exerted a nasalizing influence on the first component and itself was very susceptible to reduction; these are the diphthongs *ǫn, ạn* (cf. §3.9), *ǫ̈n'*, *en'* (cf. §3.9), *ǭn, ǭ̈n'*, where the vowel length is a Proto-Slavic innovation.

3. The other diphthongs, with the most heterogeneous components: *o͡i*, and the combinations of *o, e, u, i* with a liquid.

In Proto-Slavic, the following processes of diphthongal evolution can be distinguished for category 3:

A. In word-initial position, the *o* of the diphthong (there are no reliable examples for *e*) is lengthened to the quantity of a long vowel in the groups under acute tone; in groups with circumflex tone, one assumes that, as a parallel development, the vowel assumes the normal short quantity, while the second diphthongal element now ceases to participate in the syllabic melody.

B. In South Slavic and Czecho-Slovak dialects, the function of the bearer of length and tone became dominant in one of the elements of liquid diphthongs. If the first diphthongal component was more perceptible and less rapid in nature (*o, e*), the lengthening of this vowel made it equal to a long and it assumed the dominant role; if the first element was less perceptible and more rapid in nature (*u, i*), the liquid assumed the syllabic role and dominated the quantity and tone, and the vowel became reduced (*tort > tōrt, turt > tr̥̄t*).

In Czech, process A preceded B, while the South Slavic dialects and Slovak (more precisely, the ancestor of the Central Slovak dialect) underwent process B before A, such that the latter had no effect. Thus, along with Serbian *lâni, zlâto*, Bulgarian *láni, zláto*, Slovak *lani, zlato*, we have Czech *loni, zlato*, etc.

C. The monosyllabic groups *oi, or, ol, er', el'* (independently of all quantitative and tonal considerations) underwent a metathesis, preserving the quantity of each component and the tone of the entire sequence.

   o͡r, o͡l, e͡r', e͡l' > r͡o, l͡o, r͡e, l͡e

   ōr, ōl > rō, lō

   ŏr, ŏl > rŏ, lŏ

   o͡i > i͡o > i͡e (assimilatory effect)

   ōi > iō (subsequently *i > j, ō > ā*)

The *ŏi* construct has no reliable examples.

D. In the dialects that preserved the "vowel + liquid" groups with the ability to bear vowel length and tone (i.e., in the dialects that did not undergo process B—Slavic dialects of the Northwest and East), a process opposite to that of B occurred after process A. While the latter is characterized by an enrichment of the strongest component, to the detriment of the weakest one, the opposite happens in the Slavic dialects of the Northwest and East, where the weakest components become reinforced, perhaps in the course of assuming a part of the syllabic tone. In the combinations of *o, e* with a liquid, the weakest element was the liquid itself, and the liquids were transformed either into a group consisting of a nonsyllabic liquid and a fully syllabic liquid, or into one consisting of a nonsyllabic liquid and a *svarabhakti* vowel. Parallel to this, in the "*u, i* + liquid" groups, the weakest components, with a tendency toward reduction (i.e., *u, i*) were quantitatively reinforced and, as a result, we see the later preservation of their reflexes even in environments where the reflexes of *u, i* outside diphthongs were lost.

In the East Slavic dialect, process D preceded process C; conversely, D followed C in the Northwest. That is why in East Slavic we have the group *tort* > *torịt* or *tor·t*, but *tort* > *tŗrot*, or *t·rot* in the Northwest. The initial *ort* group was not able to split into two syllables, since the liquid had previously left the syllabic melody.

In East Slavic, the syllabic liquid (or neutral *svarabhakti* vowel) was later changed into a vowel of the same degree as the preceding vowel, in the course of which the choice of frontness or backness was determined by the liquid's inherent tonality level. Thus, for example, *el'* finally became *el'e, oł* > *oło, öl* (or *öł*) > *eło*, etc. In the dialects of the Northwest, we have reason to assume the presence of a secondary irrational vowel, later deleted just like original weak ъ and ь, with strengthening of ъ and ь located in the preceding syllable (again, as for weak ъ and ь) (cf. Rozwadowski, *b* and *a* 164).[2]

In some dialects of the Northwest (Polabian and Pomeranian), the *o* of the *or* diphthong changed to *u*, due to reduction, after process C but before D (Trubetzkoy).

3.8   Elimination of Homogeneous Diphthongs

The second group to be affected by the change was the group of diphthongs consisting of vowels of the same front-back row. The first component was assimilated to the second and the diphthongs became long monophthongs: *ou* > *ū, öü* > *ǖ, ei* > *ī* (Trubetzkoy, *c* 225).

3.9   Evolution of Nasal Diphthongs

Finally, nasal diphthongs were modified. The vowels *o* and *e* combined with a tautosyllabic nasal consonant underwent the nasalizing influence of the latter.

The characteristic tonality of nasal vowels is slightly lower than that of the corresponding pure vowels (cf. Thomson, *b* 174, 185). Thus, *o* in such a combination was a higher vowel in Proto-Slavic than *o* preceding other consonants (*ǫ* and, likewise, *ö̲*; Trubetzkoy, *c* 223). In parallel fashion, *e* in this environment was lower than the normal *e* (*ę*).

Along with the pair *ön'*—*ǫn*, the majority of Proto-Slavic dialects also had the pair *en'*—*ǝn*. The latter diphthong was found in the ending of the present active participle of verbs in conjugation classes I, II, and V. It was only in Old Church Slavonic that the corresponding participles ended in *-y*, a fact attested by the probable absence of a symbol for the phoneme *ǝ* in the earliest Slavic alphabets and by the absolute predominance of forms in *-y* in Old Church Slavonic texts. However, Old Church Slavonic did have a dialect with the phoneme *ǝ*, which is attested by the special grapheme used to render it, found in Zographensis and Marianus, and which is conventionally rendered in Cyrillic transcription by the symbol ѧ. (For a list of forms with this grapheme in both texts, see Torbiörnsson, *a* 208ff.) In all the Slavic languages, the diphthong *ǝn* has reflexes that are related to *en'* just as *ǫn* and *ön'* are related; cf. Russian *nesa* 'carry, pres. act. part.', Czech *nesa* (*ön'*, *ǫn* > *ü, u*; *en'*, *ǝn* > *ä*, *a*), Serbian *nese* (*ön'* > *ǫn*, *ǝn* > *en*); Middle Bulgarian *nesǫ* (fusion of *ǝn* with *ǫn*, parallel to that of *ön'* with *en'*), Polish *niosą*.[3]

The Slavic languages reflect two different types of nasal diphthong evolution.

1. Implementation of the process of lengthening the vowel and the reduction of the nasal consonant: the vowel takes on the quantity that had been that of the entire diphthong (cf. the fate of *o, e* in the *or, er* diphthongs in the South Slavic and Czecho-Slovak dialects), the nasal consonant is lost, and the assimilative nasalization of the vowel is lost at the same time. The lengthening of the vowel is accompanied by a new lowering of its tonality (*ö̲* > *ü*, *ǫ* > *u*, *ę* > *ä*, *ǝ* > *a*), at a time when there were no phonological impediments to this change.

2. The first component is shortened in favor of the second. The vowels *ǫ, ę* of the diphthongs in question are merged with the vowels that are intrinsically the shortest, namely, the reflexes of *u, i* (Trubetzkoy, *f* 37). Cf. the fate of *o* in the Polabian *or* diphthong (§3.7).

In §3.18, I attempt to identify what other phonological factor enters into the choice between these two possible evolutions.

3.10 Fundamental Tendency of Diphthongal Evolution

Summing up the evolution of falling diphthongs in Proto-Slavic, we can establish a fundamental tendency: the quantitative syllable cannot exceed the length of a long vowel. Solutions that excluded the consonant from the syllabic melody turned out to be an insufficient measure and, ultimately, closed syllables containing *o* or *e* plus a consonantal sonorant were all eliminated.

The means used for this elimination are metathesis, the reduplication of the diphthong into two syllables, the assimilation of the first component of the diphthong to the second, the suppression of the second component, and, finally, the reduction of *o, e*. The combinations of *u, i* plus consonant did not exceed long vowels in length and, in the majority of cases, there were no reasons causing them to be deleted. This serves as a corrective to current assertions that Proto-Slavic was dominated by the tendency to open syllables.

3.11 Qualitative Differentiation of Long and Short Vowels

The metathesis of liquid diphthongs was followed by changes in the vowel system that tended to separate the quality of the long and corresponding short vowels, and to reinforce the qualitative differences that accompanied the quantitative differences.

1. Before the monophthongization of diphthongs that contained vowels from the same front-back row, long rounded vowels had become unrounded (Trubetzkoy, *c* 223), while the shorts had preserved their rounding. Thus, the following series of the correlation "length ~ shortness of vowels" changed in this manner: $\bar{u}$—*u* > $\bar{y}$—*u*, $\bar{o}$—*o* > $\bar{a}$—*o*, $\bar{o}^n$—*ǫn* > $\bar{ə}^n$—*ǫn*, $\bar{ö}^{n'}$—*ön'* > $\bar{ę}^{n'}$—*ön'*.

2. Simultaneously, $\bar{e}$ changed into $\bar{a}$ in the environment following *j, č, ž* (or *ǯ*), *š, k₁, g₁, x₁*.

This condition, which limited the change, can easily be explained from the phonological point of view, if one starts from the premise that the palatalization of consonants before front vowels precedes this change.

The qualitative differentiation of long and short vowels removed the former clarity of the opposition of front and back vowels. Rounding ceased to be a distinctive feature that always accompanied back vowels. The *i*—*y* opposition itself was less sharp than that of *i*—*u*. In a related development, the extragrammatical opposition "soft—hard character of consonants," which accompanied the correlation "front ~ back vowel," acquired a greater value than it previously had. The inherent tonality of the consonant, as we have already noted, corresponded to the tonality of the following vowel. Compared with the clear opposition $t^i i$—ty, the opposition $t^d \ddot{a}$—ta would have been much less determinate. This circumstance impeded the change of $\bar{e}$ to $\ddot{\bar{a}}$ after soft dentals and labials, while the same change proceeded easily when $\bar{e}$ was preceded by a consonant that did not have a doublet in the language that was susceptible of being opposed solely on the basis of its inherent tonality.

The appearance of groups such as $k_1 \ddot{\bar{a}}$ contributed to the realization of the process of phonologically emancipating k_1, g_1, x_1 from k, g, x.

3. When the vowel $\bar{e}$ did not change to $\ddot{\bar{a}}$, it became a rising diphthong and was assimilated to the reflex of $\widehat{oi}$ ($\bar{e} > ie$).

4. The monophthongization of homogeneous diphthongs was followed by the reappearance of the quantitative opposition $\bar{u}$—u, not accompanied by a significant difference in quality. The qualitative differentiation was achieved by means of lowering and a novel weakening of the rounding of u ($u > ъ$). A parallel change of i to $ь$ took place. Did this qualitative differentiation of $\bar{i}$ and i take place at the same time as the change of u to $ъ$, or even earlier, at the time of the first manifestations of the tendency to qualitatively differentiate long vowels from short vowels? I am inclined to favor the former hypothesis—first, because of the parallel evolution of u and i, and second, because the qualitative differentiation of long and short vowels is manifested in its first stage (developments 1, 2, 3), in the transformation of the long correlatives. It is possible that the first stage of the differentiation did not see the qualitative change of long vowels, with the pair $\bar{i}$—i remaining outside of this modification, and that the change occurred only after the monophthongization of homogeneous diphthongs, when $\bar{i}$ had become a more frequent phoneme than it had previously been, and when a new u had appeared, that the rest of the differentiation took place, this time by means of transforming the short correlatives.

To be precise, this change only accented a very old qualitative difference. Prior to this (as demonstrated by a comparison with Baltic languages), i was differentiated from $\bar{i}$ (along with the pair u and $\bar{u}$) by being a lower vowel. However, the qualitative difference became palpable and was reevaluated when i and u were transformed into $ь$ and $ъ$—reduced *mid* vowels.

3.12   Evolution of "Long Vowel + n" Diphthongs

The fate of the Proto-Slavic diphthongs of the type "long vowel + n" requires clarification. These diphthongs came into existence after the loss of the Indo-European quantitative differences within diphthongs. The nasal component of these diphthongs underwent an early reduction: $\bar{o}^n$, $\bar{\varrho}^{n'}$ (Trubetzkoy, c 223). The evolution of the two diphthongs is parallel: unrounding of the first component, followed by a lowering of the tonality of the vowel ($\bar{o}^n > \bar{e}^n > \bar{y}^n; \bar{\bar{o}}^{n'} > \bar{e}^{n'} > \bar{e}^{n'}$). The new $\bar{e}$ was no longer changed to $\bar{a}$, since the change of $\bar{e}$ to $\bar{a}$, contemporaneous with the change of $\bar{\bar{o}}$ to $\bar{e}$, was no longer current at the moment of the change of $\bar{e}$ to $\bar{e}$. The diphthongs of the type "long vowel + n" were maintained when the first component was a vowel unknown to the language outside diphthongs ($\bar{o}$, $\bar{\bar{o}}$). However, when the first diphthongal components were changed into vowels that also existed in the language outside diphthongs ($\bar{y}$, $\bar{e}$), the change was followed by the disappearance of the category "diphthong with long component."

In the phonological system of the South Slavic dialects, the diphthong $\bar{e}^{n'}$ was assimilated to the corresponding diphthong with a short first component ($e^{n'}$), and the diphthong $\bar{y}^n$ lost its nasal component. This difference in evolution can be explained by the fact that there was no diphthong with a short first component that corresponded to the diphthong $\bar{y}^n$. In the other Slavic languages (West and East), it was not only the group $\bar{y}^n$ that lost its nasal component, but also the group $\bar{e}^{n'}$, or, more precisely, the reflex of $\bar{e}^{n'}$. It is most probable to assume that in West and East Slavic, $\bar{e}$ had already become diphthongized before the loss of "long vowel + n" diphthongs ($\bar{e}^{n'} > i\bar{e}^{n'} > ie$), while, in the South Slavic dialects, the elimination of the "long vowel + n" diphthongs had preceded the diphthongization of $\bar{e}$. Thus, one can formulate the following law, as applicable to the whole of Slavic: "long vowel + n" diphthongs assimilated to the corresponding diphthongs with a short first component, if the corresponding diphthong existed in the language; if the converse was true, then "long vowel + n" diphthongs lost their second component. In general, "long vowel + n" diphthongs have assimilated to the elements closest to them in the phonological system.

3.13 Restructuring of Quantitative Relations

The final result of the gradual qualitative differentiation of long and short vowels and of the monophthongization of homogeneous diphthongs was the loss of the old correlation "length ~ shortness of vowel" (cf., e.g., the change of $\widehat{o\ddot{u}}$ to $\bar{u}$ without a short correlative phoneme). Quantity was transformed into a secondary, extragrammatical mark for both high and low vowels (i, y, $\ddot{u}$, u, $\ddot{a}$, a) and diphthongs ($\widehat{ie}$, groups of jer with liquid, and diphthongs ending in a nasal); shortness became transformed into a similar mark for mid vowels, both lower-mid (e, o) and higher-mid ($ь$, $ъ$). The loss of the correlation "length ~ shortness of vowel" threatened to result in the removal of tonal distinctions from the phonological system (cf. §2.5), but the language hastened to reestablish the correlation "short ~ long vowel" and thus escaped the risk of a new loss. The aforementioned correlation was reestablished by means of a change of certain tonal distinctions to differences of quantity, and it was partly Common Slavic and partly dialectal. The shortening of long vowels under certain tonal conditions gave long vowels short correlatives, and thus length survived to restore its phonological status. As to the mid vowels, some acquired long correlatives (which actually were lengthened, from the standpoint of their original shortness); some changed from the phonological category of extra-grammatical shorts to that of unpaired shorts. I believe that many points in the accentological evolution of Proto-Slavic will become less obscure and less ambiguous when one considers this evolution within the entirety of the evolution of Proto-Slavic phonology. In particular, an explanation is needed for the fact that the Slavic languages that regularly preserved length under circumflex tone are the only ones that preserved tonal distinctions. (Cf. Serbian and Slovene on the one hand vs. all of West Slavic, on the other.)

3.14   Redistribution of Prothetic Consonants and Its Consequences

Since a soft consonant was the only possible one before a front vowel, as was a hard consonant before a back vowel, and since the unrounding of long vowels had increased the weight of the opposition "soft—hard consonant," the opposite generalization was easy to establish: a front vowel was possible only after a soft consonant and a back vowel only after a hard consonant. In more precise terms, the autonomous opposition between a front vowel and the corresponding back vowel was eliminated. For this to happen, only a small modification was needed in word-initial position. As a matter of fact, the following generalizations took place:

1. When a back vowel did not occur in word-initial position (prior to the unrounding of $\bar{u}$, a prothetic v had developed before initial $\breve{\bar{u}}$), the initial j was eliminated before the front-vowel correlate. Such was the case of the loss of j before initial i.

2. If a front vowel did not occur in word-initial position and the correlative back vowel preserved its rounding, then the initial v before the latter vowel was lost, since it was felt to be a prothetic consonant. Thus, the initial v before ǫn was lost—cf. ǫsъ, ǫtьlъ (cf. Fortunatov, *a* 254). There are no reliable examples of the loss of v before u that go back to ǫu, but, in any case, there are no examples in the Slavic languages of initial vu, coming from vǫu.

These generalizations were followed by one more: when a back vowel and its front vowel correlate could both occur initially, an initial j was generalized before the front-vowel correlate. Such was the case of the generalization of *j* before initial *e*.

These generalizations transformed the correlation of front and back vowels into a correlation of indissoluble, fixed groups of "(soft consonant + front vowel) ~ (hard consonant + back vowel)."[4] Neither the vowels nor the consonants of this correlation could be opposed to each other outside of the indicated groups. Replacement of one of the elements of a group by an element of the correlative group would inevitably lead to a parallel change in the other element of the group.

3.15 System of Palatal Consonants and Dialect Variations in Their Evolution

The consonants *j*, *č*, *ž*, *š*, k_1, g_1, x_1 all belonged to the category of unpaired softs in the period of the transformation of vocalic quantity into quality. The appearance of k_1, g_1, x_1 before vowels that normally could not be preceded by paired softs ultimately demarcated the *k*—k_1 relation from that of *t*—*t'*: k_1, g_1, x_1 took on the value of autonomous phonemes.

Consonants became palatalized before front vowels, but before *j*, and partly before other palatal consonants, the assimilation of dental consonants went farther and they were transformed into palatal consonants; this was a palatal mutation.

In sum, there were three categories of palatal consonants:

1. Products of the first velar palatalization

2. Products of the second velar palatalization

3. Reflexes of dentals before *j* and before other palatal consonants

(The reflexes of *t*, *d*, *s*, *z*, *r*, *l*, *n* before palatal consonants are notated as t_1, d_1, etc.)

In the phonological system of East Slavic, all of the nonsonorant consonants of the third category were assimilated to those of the first category ($t_1 > č$; d_1 and $z_1 > ž$; $s_1 > š$). In the systems of the South Slavic dialects, only the reflexes of dental fricatives were assimilated to the consonants of the first category, but the reflexes of dental stops are distinct. (Cf. Bulgarian *št*, *žd*, *k'*, *g'*, Serbian dorsal affricates, and Slovene *j*.) In both East and South Slavic, one sees a systemic tendency to preserve consonants of the second category as an independent group, distinct from the consonants of both the first and the third categories (consonants of the second category were transformed into the soft sibilants *c'*, *ʒ'*, *s'*). In West Slavic, consonants of the second and third categories came to coincide, yielding reflexes of sibilant affricates for both dental

stops and velar stops, and reflexes of hushing fricatives for both dental fricatives and the velar fricative. Thus, the fricatives of the three categories were
merged into a single series—that of soft hushers. The West Slavic evolution
in question, that of soft "unpaired" consonants, is determined by two tendencies that are realized consistently, but are unknown to the other Slavic dialects:
reflexes of dentals preceding *j* are merged with the products of the second velar
palatalization; and "unpaired" softs are not changed into "paired" softs. The
latter tendency explains why fricatives preceding *j* and the product of the
second palatalization of *x* are changed into hushers, rather than sibilants, as
one would have expected, given the evolution of the corresponding stop
consonants.

In the majority of Proto-Slavic dialects, $\overline{z}'$ changed to z', due to the instability of voiced affricates. (Cf. the Common Slavic change of $\overline{z}$ to $\check{z}$; see Broch
[Brok"], *b* 44.) In any case, this change is more recent than the change of x_1
to $\check{s}$ in West Slavic; and, in West Slavic, except for Slovak, it is more recent
than the change of *d* to $\overline{z}'$ when preceding *j*.

3.16   Dialect Differences in the System of Vowels in Sequences with Paired Softs and the Treatment of the Affricate $\overline{z}$

In these dialects [primarily East Slavic—RF], where we had $s' < x_1$ and $z' <$
$\overline{z}' < g_1$, or one of these sounds, the inventory of vowels united with paired soft
consonants was extended, yielding the following pairs:

s'ä—sa	z'ä—za
s'ü—su	z'ü—zu
s'ǫn'—sǫn	z'ǫn'—zǫn

(x_1, g_1, preceding ϱ in the diphthongs $\widehat{on}$ and $\widehat{ou}$, which later became *u*,
appeared as a result of grammatical analogy.) All of these new pairs were
added to the traditional pairs with the correlation "soft group ~ hard group."
The appearance of the combination "soft paired consonant + *ä*" was probably
linked to an essential innovation: the inherent tonality of the paired soft, which
hitherto had always adapted to that of the following vowel, could henceforth
exceed it; that is, the groups *s'ä, z'ä*, when opposed to *sa, za*, must have
had the approximate sound value of $s^e\ddot{a}$ (i.e., *s* with the palatalization level
equivalent to "*e*" + *ä*), $z^e\ddot{a}$ (cf. §3.11). This emancipation of the inherent consonant tonality was undoubtedly an essential premise for the ultimate dialect
realization of the autonomous correlation of "soft ~ hard consonant." The
combinations of *s'* and *z'* with *ä, ü, ǫn'* entered the phonological system of
East Slavic, while the combinations of *z'* with these vowels also entered the

phonological system of Czecho-Slovak and Sorbian. In the Proto-Lekhitic dialect, the correlation "soft group ~ hard group" was not enriched as a result of the evolution of the unpaired soft consonants because in this zone the reflexes of x_1, g_1 were $\check{s}$ and the affricate $\mathfrak{z}$, which was not subject to later changes. The Bulgarian evolution was unique. After $\bar{e}$ changed to $\bar{a}$ following a palatal consonant, $\bar{e}$ and $\bar{a}$ continued as combinatory variants of a single phoneme, since the two vowels did not occur in the same environment. Unpaired softs did not occur before $\bar{e}$ and the group "unpaired soft + $\bar{e}^{n}$'" was replaced by the group "unpaired soft + en'." When $\bar{e}$, in the process of diphthongizing, merged with the reflex of $\widehat{oi}$, it happened that paired soft consonants could appear before the diphthong $\widehat{ie}$, just like the unpaired softs c, $\mathfrak{z}$ (which came from k, g), by virtue of the metathesis of $\widehat{oi}$. This development was avoided in two ways.

1. Dialectally, $\widehat{cie}, \mathfrak{z}\widehat{ie} > c\ddot{a}, \mathfrak{z}\ddot{a}$. This change is attested by Middle Bulgarian texts. The change of $\widehat{cie}$ to $c\ddot{a}$ is equally attested by the Western Bulgarian dialects, where the reflexes of $\widehat{ie}$ and $\ddot{a}$ are distinct and where the sequence $\widehat{cie}$ goes to ca: for example, $cal, cana$ (Kul'bakin, a 49ff.; Ščepkin, a 189ff.; Seliščev, b 88ff.).

2. Dialectally, c', $\mathfrak{z}'$ were converted from unpaired softs to paired softs, becoming hard before vowels that did not combine with paired softs; the vowel following the hardened c, $\mathfrak{z}$ was then backed ($c'\ddot{a} > ca$). As a consequence, $c'\widehat{ie} : ca = t'\widehat{ie} : ta$ (cf. Ščepkin, c 5).

The two dialect developments led to the same result: $\widehat{ie}$ and $\ddot{a}$ became combinatory variants of the same phoneme.

The change of x_1 to s' would have created the inadmissible combination of "paired soft + $\ddot{a}$," but this combination was rejected. Old Church Slavonic texts already reflect two different dialect phenomena: while $s'\widehat{ie}$ ($< x_1\widehat{ie} < x\widehat{oi}$) is preserved, merging with older $s'\widehat{ie}$, the combination $s'\ddot{a}$ is eliminated, in certain dialects, by hardening the s': $s'\ddot{a} > sa$ (written in texts as $v\mathtt{ь}sa, v\mathtt{ь}sak$-), and, in others, by the change of $\ddot{a}$ to $\widehat{ie}$ following s'. Cf. Cyrillic texts, which distinguish $\check{e}$ (ѣ) and ja (ꙗ), v's$\check{e}$, v's$\check{e}k$-, as well as Modern Bulgarian dialect $seki = v\mathtt{ь}s\check{e}ki$. Bulgarian offers systemic proof of the resistance to increasing the number of vowels that were admissible with paired consonants. It not only abolished the "paired soft + $\ddot{a}$" combinations, but also eliminated "paired soft + $\ddot{u}$, $\ddot{o}$." The dialectal z', which came from $\mathfrak{z}$, is regularly hardened before these vowels (in Old Church Slavonic texts: $k\mathtt{ъ}n\underset{\mathrm{\,}}{e}za, k\mathtt{ъ}n\underset{\mathrm{\,}}{e}zu, pol\mathtt{ъ}z\underset{\mathrm{\,}}{o}$, etc.).

The generalization of j before the front vowel correlate of a threatened to break the line of demarcation between the two combinatory variants: in the environment following j, $\widehat{ie}$ appeared along with $\ddot{a}$. However, $j\widehat{ie} > j\ddot{a}$; that is, in the Bulgarian dialect of Proto-Slavic, the law of changing $\bar{e}$ (or its reflex) to $\ddot{a}$ after a palatal consonant continued to operate.

The fact that the Glagolitic alphabet has only one letter that corresponds to old Proto-Slavic $\widehat{ie}$ and $\ddot{a}$ speaks only in favor of the assumption that this was a single phoneme in Old Church Slavonic, not in favor of the assumption that there was also just a single sound; that is, it does not prove that $\widehat{ie}$ and $\ddot{a}$ had merged phonetically, as found in Eastern Bulgarian. It is most probable that the phoneme marked by this grapheme included both combinatory variants, one occurring in the environment after unpaired softs, and the other after paired softs.

A comparison of the phonological evolution of the various Slavic languages shows that the affricate ζ was preserved in those dialects that did not permit the evolution of unpaired soft consonants to extend the number of front vowels that could be combined with paired soft consonants. However, ζ ($< g_1$) was not maintained in other dialects. Thus, we can state that there was a Proto-Slavic tendency for the elimination of the affricate ζ in the period of the mutation of unpaired soft consonants. This tendency failed to be carried out only where it conflicted with the tendency to preserve the old system of vowels that combined with paired soft consonants, without additions.

3.17   Link between the Fate of $\check{e}$ and the Dialectal Treatment of the Sequence $\zeta'\ddot{a}$

A consideration of the fate of $\check{e}$ and nasal diphthongs in the various Slavic languages in the light of the aforementioned facts demonstrates that there is a regular connection between them.

The vowel $\ddot{a}$ is the front vowel correlate of a. However, $\check{e}$, although unpaired within the phonological system, tends to be juxtaposed to a. The following scenario would often take place in the subsequent history of the Slavic languages: when the diphthong $\check{e}$ is not coordinated with the system of simple vowels, the linguistic consciousness is inclined to treat it in terms of its separate components—to treat it not as a phoneme, but as a phonemic sequence. However, when $\check{e}$ tends to be an indivisible phoneme, it seeks a place within the phonological system and its role makes one think of a game where all the players form pairs, except for one that is unpaired and that attempts to form a pair, to the detriment of another, resulting in an entire series of displacements.

Within the dialects of Proto-Slavic, we distinguish two basic types of $\check{e}$ (*jat'*) evolution.

1. Wherever ʒ'ä does not change to z'ä (and, consequently, s'ä does not occur either), that is, wherever ä cannot be preceded by paired softs, ě is juxtaposed to the phoneme a and tends to merge with its correlate. These are languages with a range of ě reflexes from a to e. As noted earlier, in some Bulgarian dialects ě merges with ä into a single phoneme. In Proto-Lekhitic, only the low combinatory variant of ě (before a hard dental) is merged with ä; before other consonants, the high variant was the only possibility after a paired soft, so that after an unpaired soft it had a phonological doublet ä (the existence of doublets is indicated, although with a different interpretation, by Rozwadowski, a 176). Subsequently, the high variant of ě became completely emancipated from the pair ä—a; j was lost after consonants, and new groups of the type "paired soft + ä" (b'ä, etc.) were introduced into the language and took root. Second, as a result of the contraction of the sequence ija, dentals also were among the palatalized consonants that could combine with ä, just as labials could. However, the transformation of nasals caused by the ě- -ä attraction (cf. §3.18) had already occurred by this time.

2. Wherever one sees the reflex z'ä from ʒ'ä (i.e., the group "paired soft + ä"), ě loses all of its affinity for a and departs from the system of vowel phonemes, later rejoining the system and finding or creating another partner (cf., e.g., §§7.6ff.), merging with one of the existing phonemes, or, finally, remaining outside the system. This is the case in Serbian dialects with a diphthongal ě, which is reflected in two stylistic variants: a true diphthong i͡e and a disyllabic vowel sequence (cf. Belić 191ff.). This ability of the diphthong to separate into two syllables indicates that it was sensed not as a phoneme but as a sequence of phonemes. The languages that separated ě from a are characterized by a range of ě reflexes from e to i.

3.18   Dependency of Nasal Diphthong Evolution on the Treatment of ě (jať)

In the languages where ě oscillates between e and i, the pairs ö, ǫ and ę, ǫ̈ do not merge either with each other or with the pair ь, ъ. Vowels in nasal diphthongs have evolved toward ü, u and toward ä, a. This evolution went to its extreme in Russian, Czecho-Slovak, and Sorbian,[5] while Serbo-Slovene had a tendency (even before jer-fall) to eliminate the "soft group ~ hard group" correlation and vowels that were opposed exclusively as front vs. back were merged into a single vowel; thus, ь and ъ merged, and the change y > i is reflected in the oldest Serbian texts (cf. Kul'bakin, c 96ff.). Wherever the front vs. back vowel opposition had any sort of additional acoustic mark, this concomitant difference saved the opposition, but it then left the series of correlated pairs and became a disjunctive phonemic opposition. Such was the fate of the *e—o* pair. Some Serbian dialects have had a split of *ě* into two variants, depending on whether it was followed by a hard dental or any other consonant; this split occurred prior to the fusion of *ь* and *ъ*, and of *i* and *y* (cf. Meyer 70; Jakubinskij). In Russian, Czech, and Sorbian, the change of *ẽn* to *ä* posed no risk of disturbing the principle of opposing soft and hard groups. We have already noted that the group "palatalized consonant + *ä*" was opposed to the group "hard consonant + *ä*" within the system of parallel correlated pairs.

However, other tendencies predominated in Serbian, and the "soft group ~ hard group" correlation faced total elimination. The different oppositions that made up this correlation could only be saved if they succeeded in moving to the category of disjunctive phonemic oppositions. That is why the change of *ęn'* to *ä* was obstructed, even though the other conditions for such a change existed—but the parallel change of *ǫ^n* to *u* did go through. In Serbian, the presence of the tendency for the change of *ę* to *ä* is illustrated not only by the fact of the parallel change of *ǫ* to *u*, but also by the dialectal change of *ę* to *ä* after unpaired softs. The group "unpaired soft consonant + front vowel" did not have a hard correlative group, so there also were no impediments for the change of *ę* to a lower vowel. If *ęn'* changed to *e* even after unpaired softs in some Serbian dialects, this can be explained by a tendency to unify the phoneme. It would seem that the Slovene evolution of the *ęn* diphthong is similar, except for the fact that in this language, the delay in the change of *ę* also stopped the parallel change of *ǫ* to *u*.

In the languages with a range of *ě* from *a* to *e* (Bulgarian and Lekhitic), we see the three following pairs of vowels merge into a single one: *ǫ̈, ǫ—ę, ə—ь, ъ* (cf. §3.9 for *ə > ǫ*; for *ö̈ > ę*, Ščepkin, *c* 17; for the fusion with *ь, ъ*, Trubetzkoy, *f* 36–37). The Glagolitic alphabet reflects a dialect earlier than the fusion and renders the vowels of the diphthongs *ǫn, ęn* as *o, e*. It is only *ö̈* that has a special letter: *ǫ* was a *complementary correlative phoneme* (cf. §1.6) and did not need a sign of its own. Nor was a sign needed for *ę*, which, in dialects with *ə*, was also a complementary correlative phoneme, and, in those without *ə*, a simple combinatory extragrammatical variant of the phoneme *e*.

The fact that in Bulgarian and Lekhitic, *ě* (i.e., probably a diphthong of the type *eä*), rather than *ä*, corresponded to the Proto-Slavic phoneme *a* after a soft paired consonant, did not permit the diphthong *ən* to change in the direction of *ä*. One can speak of a Proto-Slavic tendency for nasal diphthongs to change to pure vowels with a lower inherent tonality, a tendency that changed direction in the case of a phonological system that was not suited to such a change.

3.19   Limitation of the Role of *j*

The change of the correlation "vowel frontness ~ vowel backness" to the correlation "soft group ~ hard group" eliminated the word-initial opposition "front vowel—same front vowel preceded by an initial *j*." This only served as a later limitation on the phonological role of *j*. This role was definitively reduced to the opposition "initial back vowel vs. correlative front vowel accompanied by *j*." (Various dialects have endeavored to eliminate even this opposition.) The "consonant + *j*" combinations were eliminated.

There is reason not to confuse the elimination of postconsonantal *j* with the processes of the reciprocal assimilation of the consonants and *j*. The latter processes preceded the former. For example, in East Slavic the original *tj* corresponds to *čj*; both *dj* and *zj* correspond to *žj*; *sj* corresponds to *šj*; and "labial + *j*" corresponds to "labial + palatal *l*." It was only later that *j* was lost following consonants, a process that took place throughout Slavic. The fact that this modification of dental consonants preceding *j* was not the result of a contraction of these consonants with *j* is attested by Old Church Slavonic evidence, such as *bež njego* 'without him', *pomyšljati* 'think', *bъždrjǫ* 'more cheerful, fem. sg.', *xyštrjǫ* 'more cunning, fem. sg.'. In the later Slavic languages, the traces of the change of dentals to palatals preceding palatal sonorants have largely been lost, due to grammatical analogy.

Annotations to Chapter 3, Remarks on the Evolution of the Phonological System of Proto-Slavic

3.1 First and Second Velar Palatalizations

This section begins a more technical analysis of Slavic phonology, starting with the reconstructed system of Proto-Slavic and its phonemic system. It is not intended as an introduction, since many Proto-Slavic processes (such as velar palatalizations) are mentioned without examples. It will be helpful to familiarize oneself with the basic facts of how Late Indo-European evolved into Proto-Slavic (see Townsend and Janda 1996, 21–119; Jakobson 1955). Moreover, Jakobson does not perform most of the reconstruction himself, but relies largely on the work of his Prague School colleague Trubetzkoy (1922) and, to a lesser extent, the Russian linguist Šaxmatov (1915/2002). Thus, Jakobson implicitly accepts Trubetzkoy's chronology of the velar palatalizations by placing the progressive palatalization (following *i*) after the first, and considering it as the second velar palatalization, leaving the second regressive as the third velar palatalization. In reality, proving which velar palatalization is actually second or third is a difficult chronological issue, since the Old Church Slavonic data are contradictory and can prove either order.

On a second major controversial point—the results of the Proto-Slavic merger of Late Indo-European *o* and *a*—Jakobson also accepts Trubetzkoy's view without discussion. Following Trubetzkoy, he reconstructs the original Proto-Slavic merged value as *o*, long and short, although a large body of data leads many scholars to reconstruct it as *a*. In Jakobson's later work, he often used an *a* combined with a small diacritic *o* to indicate the origin of Slavic *a* and *o* from both earlier sounds, but in this early work the original Proto-Slavic vowel system is reconstructed without *a*. A raised *o* vowel occurs as well, representing the first component of nasal and -*u* diphthongs. As Ivić (1965/2001, 76) notes, the raised *o* could be considered a positional variant of *o*, since it occurs only in prenasal and pre-*u* environments, but Jakobson does not mention this. His focus is strictly the question of whether the rounding feature is maintained when a rounded back vowel is fronted by a preceding palatal consonant, in the process of creating uniformly synharmonic syllables in Common Slavic. Note that Jakobson returns to the issue of the phonemic status of raised ϱ in section 3.18, where he refers to it as a "complementary correlative phoneme," similar to the palatalized velars of Russian, which he posited as "imaginary or supplementary phonemes" in section 1.6. The special nature of these quasi phonemes is that a binary feature functions as positional for them but as distinctive for other phonemes.

Jakobson contests and rejects some details of Trubetzkoy's reconstruction, but he uses many of the most important ones without discussion, other than a reference to Trubetzkoy, such as his article of 1922. Apparently, he does so because his main goal in this book is not to reconstruct the Slavic protolanguage, but to demonstrate how the phonemic system and its evolution should be represented. For this reason, I recommend using other materials to delve into the complex issues of Proto-Slavic reconstruction per se, using Jakobson's work to study the systemic properties of the Slavic phonological systems and how the various Slavic languages have evolved in different ways through time and space, on the basis of their particular phonological features.

Jakobson concludes this section by indicating that the first and progressive velar palatalizations created no new phonemes, since the original velars and the products of these two palatalizations were still in complementary distribution (i.e., they were concomitant extragrammatical variants, in Prague School terminology).

3.2 Influence of Palatal Consonants on Following Vowels

In this section, Jakobson introduces the important concept of syllabic synharmony. Proto-Slavic developed a system in which "soft" consonants (i.e., palatal and palatalized) caused the fronting of vowels within the same syllable, just as front vowels caused consonants to become "soft"—either palatalized labials and dentals, or palatals, in the case of velars that originally followed front vowels. Syllables with "hard" consonants followed by back vowels remained unchanged. The result was that all syllables became synharmonic—agreeing in "softness" or "hardness," so that a given syllable's consonants and vowels shared this tonality feature. In other words, a synharmonic syllable consisted of either "soft" consonants and front vowels or "hard" consonants and back vowels. In the later evolution of Slavic, the frontness/backness of vowels and the softness/hardness of consonants become emancipated; they no longer function in synharmony, and either the vowels or the consonants assume this tonality feature, depending on the language (a development Jakobson discusses in great detail later in the book). The question Jakobson raises here is whether rounded vowels keep their rounding or lose it when they are fronted after a palatal consonant, a process he calls "progressive softening." Jakobson takes issue with Trubetzkoy's claim that the retention of rounding is based on tenseness; instead, he explains it on the basis of paired and unpaired phonemes. As noted above, Ivić (1965/2001) states that Jakobson does not address the phonemic status of the raised *o*, both before and after fronting, even though it was positionally restricted to the prenasal and pre-*u* positions and could have been treated as a variant of /o/.

3.3   Reciprocal Influence of Vowels and Liquids inside Diphthongs

Here, Jakobson introduces a second type of "progressive softening" in a variety of diphthongs consisting of a liquid preceded by a front vowel, which causes the liquid to palatalize. Under certain phonological conditions, the opposite assimilation occurred: the preceding vowel changed from front to back, and the liquid did not palatalize, as in Russian *moloko* 'milk', as contrasted with Polish *mleko*. However, there are East Slavic exceptions, such as Russian *lebed'* 'swan' and *selezen'* 'drake', where the front vowel does not undergo backing and the liquid is palatalized. Jakobson explains these cases as being due to a front vowel in the syllable following the original liquid diphthong. He also makes reference to the hard and soft doublets *član* and *člen* 'member' of Czech and wonders if the front-vowel variant might be due to front-vowel case endings in the next syllable, which palatalized the consonant *n*. However, Trubetzkoy (Trubetzkoy and Jakobson 1975, 144) disputed this in his correspondence with Jakobson, for two reasons: at this early stage the locative case had not yet changed to the front-vowel *jat'*, and the front-vowel vocative was unlikely to be used with this and other inanimate nouns.

Note that these processes all belong to the broad category of the establishment of synharmonic syllables. Since the elements of the liquid diphthongs belonged to the same syllable, the rule of syllabic harmony caused them both to conform to one of the two synharmonic types. The sole exception was a diphthong consisting of a palatal consonant and a front vowel, which could be followed by a hard *l*, as Jakobson indicates, commenting that these cases of *öl* diphthongs were positional variants of *el'*.

3.4   Influence of Vowels on Preceding Consonants

In this section, after presenting instances of progressive palatalization in the development of synharmonic syllables, Jakobson introduces regressive palatalization, in which a front vowel causes the palatalization ("softening") of the preceding consonant. He posits two levels of palatalization, depending on whether the front vowel is high or mid. The higher level of palatalization, symbolized by the superscript i (e.g., $t^i i$), is caused by the high front vowel i, while the lower level of palatalization, symbolized by the superscript e (e.g., $t^e e$), is caused by the mid vowel e. Palatalized consonants before i and e often behave differently in certain Slavic languages, such as Czech, and Jakobson's assumption regarding the two levels of palatalization provides a convenient phonological explanation for the difference.

3.5   Unification of the Syllable

In this section, Jakobson establishes a general "law" of synharmony, according to which a vowel caused a consonant of the same syllable to assimilate to its own level of palatalization. However, where the consonant could not conform to this process, since it was already palatal, it instead caused the assimilation of the vowel from back to front.

3.6   Ultimate Fate of the Products of Velar Palatalizations

This section deals with the change of phonemic relationship between the products of the first velar palatalization (velars k, g, x, followed by original front vowels, generally reflected as $č$, $ž$, $š$) and the products of the progressive velar palatalization, called k_1, g_1, x_1 by Jakobson, and viewed by him as the second velar palatalization. After the fronting of vowels following "softs," the products of these two palatalizations could occur in the same environment and be opposed phonemically. Since either series could be treated as positional variants of the unpalatalized velar phonemes, the analyst faces the choice of whether to opt for the products of the first or second velar palatalization as the variants of the velars at this time. Jakobson reasons that the products of the first velar palatalization were emancipated as separate phonemes first, since (1) the products of the progressive palatalization were more frequently in grammatical alternation with the velars, and (2) the change of the velars to k_1, g_1, x_1 was still current, as seen in the results of the second regressive (or third velar) palatalization, which occurred when the oi diphthong metathesized to ie after velar consonants, in Jakobson's interpretation.

3.7   Diphthongs of Proto-Slavic

In this section, Jakobson treats the broad category of Slavic diphthongs and their evolution. He notes the important historical fact that Indo-European possessed both long and short diphthongs, that is, diphthongs in which the first vowel component could be long or short. Slavic leveled diphthongal quantity, the vowel and sonorant components each being equivalent to one mora, which gave all Common Slavic diphthongs the two-mora length of a long vowel. The earlier Indo-European distinction of long and short diphthongs was often maintained on the basis of Slavic prosodic differences of tone (acute/rising vs. circumflex/falling). Trubetzkoy assumed a difference in the quantity of the two moraic elements of diphthongs under different intonations, but this must have been a predictable, phonetic feature, since any two-mora sequence was still phonemically equivalent to a long vowel. Generally, the change of Common Slavic diphthongs to monophthongs is treated as a manifestation of the tendency toward the open syllable, or rising sonority, which was violated by having the second, consonantal components of diphthongs at the end of a syllable. In section 3.10, Jakobson makes the valid point that the quantity of a Common Slavic syllable could not exceed that of a long vowel; the first attempt to remove diphthongal consonants as syllabic carriers of accent and quantity proved insufficient, after which all closed syllables were eliminated.

Diphthongs are classified into three basic categories: homogeneous, nasal, and heterogeneous, the latter including $\widehat{oi}$ and the series of liquid diphthongs. The categories are based on the rules for diphthongal evolution and the ultimate elimination of the diphthongs. The homogeneous category can be dispensed with very quickly (see section 3.8), since the first component simply assimilates to the second component, yielding a reflex that is equivalent to a long version of the second component. The heterogeneous and nasal diphthongs underwent a much more complex development, and Jakobson goes into great detail about their evolution.

Liquid diphthongs are the major type of heterogeneous diphthong. It is instructive to compare Jakobson's treatment of these diphthongs here with his treatment of the same topic in Jakobson 1952. Here, he deals with the issue chronologically, setting up four periods (A to D) that cover the developments in the major Slavic zones; later, he simply enumerates the geographical dialect zones (areas I to V) and specifies the developments in each. Another difference relates to the symbol used for the product of the Common Slavic merger of Late Indo-European a and o. As noted above, here Jakobson accepts Trubetzkoy's thesis that Slavic first merged these vowels as long and short o, and only later changed long $\bar{o}$ to $\bar{a}$; this meant that the back-vowel liquid diphthongs were represented with the vowel o. In 1952, Jakobson uses the combined symbol $\mathring{a}$ (i.e., a with a small o above) to represent both front and back low vowels.

The essence of Jakobson's thesis on liquid diphthongs is that low and high liquid diphthongs each contained a stronger and a weaker component and that the more southerly South Slavic and Czecho-Slovak zones emphasized the stronger component (leading to the South Slavic reflexes *trāt and *tr̥t, with syllabic liquid but no *jer* reflex), while the more northerly Sorbian, Lekhitic (i.e., Polish and related dialects), and East Slavic zones emphasized the weaker components (e.g., East Slavic *torr̥t and *tъ̱rt, with a strong *jer* reflex). This is a brilliant theory, but it depends on the notion that the original Common Slavic vowel in the low back liquid diphthongs was *o*, rather than *a*. Recent work (see Andersen 1998, 431; Feldstein 2003, 268; Feldstein 2006, 206–209) has tended to favor the idea that *a* was the original Common Slavic vowel in these diphthongs. Since short ă changed to short ŏ in Late Common Slavic, the difference between southern *trat* and northwestern *trot* can be associated with the relative chronology of the change of ă to ŏ. In other words, if lengthening in the diphthong took place before the change, long ā resulted; but, if lengthening in the diphthong took place after the change, long ō resulted. It is also worth noting that Jakobson (and many others; see, e.g., Stieber 1962) took the *o* of Lekhitic *trot* to be a short vowel, even though the *o* has the usual Polish reflexes of long vowels in accentual positions that correspond to historical length (e.g., Polish *król*, which Stieber (1962, 23) felt was anomalous and which he could not explain).

3.8 Elimination of Homogeneous Diphthongs

As noted above, homogeneous diphthongs are the simplest type of all. When the diphthongal components differ only in vowel height and agree in frontness/backness and rounding, the first component simply assimilates to the second and the result is a new long monophthong.

3.9 Evolution of Nasal Diphthongs

Here, Jakobson introduces the topic of nasal diphthongs. Nasals could be preceded by front or back and rounded or unrounded mid vowels. Jakobson accepts Trubetzkoy's proposal that the rounded mid vowels before nasals were raised mid vowels, while the unrounded ones were lowered, symbolized as ǫn and ęn, respectively. Some evidence for this assumed raising and lowering can be seen in Modern Russian reflexes, where the reflex of the rounded nasal is high *u* (e.g., *put'* 'path'), but the reflex of the unrounded nasal is low *a* (e.g., *vjanut'* 'wilt'). Each of these diphthongs could also be preceded by palatals, such as *j*, after which the fronted combinations ö̧n' and en' are assumed, respectively. The more familiar diphthongs *ǫn, en', ön'* are reflected in Old Church Slavonic as *ǫ, ę, jǫ* (Cyrillic ᴀ, ѫ, ѭ). The less familiar *ən* is the reflex of the *-ont* ending, which has variable reflexes in Slavic. It appears in the nominative singular form of the present active participle and is normally reflected as *-y* in Old Church Slavonic, but as *-a* in Old East Slavic (e.g., *nesy, nesa* 'carrying', respectively). Jakobson notes that the Old Church Slavonic Zographensis and Marianus codices have special symbols for the *ən* ending (e.g., Cyrillic ᴀ), which justifies the assumption of the additional diphthong. The resulting pattern, which systemically opposes both front-back and rounded-unrounded, is a neat structural system, despite relying on limited data for one of its units.

Jakobson indicates the two major paths for the evolution of nasal diphthongs in the Slavic languages. The first path recalls the evolution of South and Central Slavic liquid diphthongs in Jakobson's interpretation, in which the syllabicity of the diphthongal sonorant passes to the diphthongal vowel, making it a long vowel. The mid rounded vowels *ǫ/ö* usually become high *u/ü*, while the mid unrounded vowels *ə/ę* lower to *a/ä*, reflexes that can be seen in East Slavic and other branches. The movement of the rounded vowels higher and of the unrounded ones lower could well have been Trubetzkoy's reason for referring to the protovowels as raised and lowered, respectively. The second path for nasal vowel evolution recalls the reflexes of Bulgarian, in which the nasal vowel reflexes coincide with the *jer* reflexes. In section 3.18, Jakobson discusses the interrelationship of *ě* (*jat'*) and nasal vowel reflexes, namely, that *jat'* and the front nasal vowel reflex cannot both be a low *a* or *ä*. Therefore, if *jat'* is reflected as a low nonnasal vowel, the nasal reflex is something other than a low nonnasal vowel, such as a nasal vowel, as in Lekhitic, or schwa, as in Bulgarian. Conversely, when the nasal reflex is a low nonnasal vowel, as in East Slavic, the *jat'* reflex is a mid or high vowel.

3.10   Fundamental Tendency of Diphthongal Evolution

In this section, Jakobson makes a very important statement, meant to serve as a corrective to the commonly held notion that Common Slavic developed into an open-syllable language and had a tendency to rising sonority. Jakobson attempts to make this more precise, in view of syllables that do not conform to the open-syllable rule, such as the **tъrt* < **turt* groups of East Slavic, which generally do not evolve into open syllables (e.g., Russian *gorlo* 'throat'). Jakobson's correction is that the syllable could not exceed a long vowel in quantity; thus, when a long vowel was followed by a consonant, such as in a nonhigh vowel diphthong (e.g., **tort*), the liquid could not remain in this position and underwent metathesis or other change to an open syllable. However, a sequence such as *tъrt, consisting of a *jer* vowel plus a liquid, did not exceed the quantity of a long vowel and could retain its closed syllable, as in East Slavic.

3.11 Qualitative Differentiation of Long and Short Vowels

Here, Jakobson introduces several important changes in the vowel system, mostly aimed at differentiating long vowels from short vowels by additional features (beyond vowel quantity), which may have started as redundant features but eventually became distinctive. The qualitative differentiation of long and short vowels is a common process in Slavic and elsewhere. It is prominent in the history of Polish, where it is known as *pochylenie*. One of its first manifestations is the loss of rounding in long vowels. Since Jakobson proceeds from the assumption of an original long and short o in Common Slavic, he views the eventual relationship of long $\bar{a}$ and short $\ddot{o}$ as an unrounding of $\bar{o}$. Linguists who assume an originally long and short a would view this in reverse, as the retention of long $\bar{a}$, but rounding of short $\ddot{a}$. In any case, we are left with the unrounded long vowels $\bar{y}$ and $\bar{a}$. Jakobson also includes the assumed unrounding of the long front nasal diphthongal component $\bar{\bar{\varrho}} > \bar{e}$.

The lowering of long $\bar{e}$ to $\bar{a}$ after palatals (e.g., Russian *slyšat'* 'hear', but *skripet'* 'squeak') was another major vowel change at this time. A very important systemic property permitted this change only after palatals, since (given the prevailing system of syllabic synharmony) tonality was shared by both consonants and vowels. The level of palatalization was lowest for consonants that preceded the low vowel $\bar{a}$, so the only consonants that could effect this change were those with independent palatal quality—that is, the palatals themselves. Palatalized labials and dentals preceding $\bar{e}$ could not maintain their distinction from nonpalatalized ones preceding $\bar{a}$, and $\bar{e}$ therefore merged with the $\widehat{ie}$ diphthong, which itself had come from the heterogeneous diphthong *$\widehat{oi}$, which later became known as *jat'* (transcribed as $\check{e}$), from the name of the Old Church Slavonic letter (ѣ).

The development of the *jers* is another important vowel change, also connected to the qualitative differentiation of long and short vowels. Note that long vowels tended to occupy the highest and lowest vowel positions, while short vowels tended toward mid vowel height. Thus, the original long and short $\bar{\imath}$, $\imath$ changed into $\bar{\imath}$, ь and the original long and short u, $\ddot{u}$ changed into $\bar{y}$, ъ, with qualitative differentiation.

3.12 Evolution of "Long Vowel + *n*" Diphthongs

Jakobson next takes up the evolution of the diphthongs *-ons/*-jens*, which occurred in certain Slavic declensional endings, such as the *ā*-stem nom./acc. pl. The back-vowel type gave *-y* throughout Slavic, but the front-vowel type had different reflexes in South Slavic (nasal *ę* reflexes) and in West and East Slavic, (*jat'* (*ě*) reflexes). For example, where Old Church Slavonic had acc. pl. *ryby/dušę*, Old Russian had *ryby/duše*.

Jakobson treats the *-ons/*-jens* evolution by first assuming that a new type of nasal diphthong developed, with a long first component, after the other nasal diphthongs had already developed into sequences of two short components. The back vowel variety underwent unrounding and raising, giving $*\bar{y}^n$, while the front type became $*\bar{e}^n$. On the basis of these constructs, Jakobson formulates a rule for the whole of Slavic: if a nasal diphthong with a short first component existed in the language at the time, then the *-ons/*-jens* diphthongs simply joined it; if not, then the second, nasal component was lost and the first, long-vowel component survived. In the case of $*\bar{y}^n$, there was no such short nasal diphthong, so the reflex was $*\bar{y}$ in all zones, South and North. In the case of $*\bar{e}^n$, Jakobson assumes that long $*\bar{e}$ had already diphthongized to $\widehat{ie}$ in West and East Slavic, but not South Slavic, presumably as part of the development of *jat'*. This meant that the new $*\widehat{ie}^n$ of North Slavic had no equivalent short diphthong, so the northern zones dropped the nasal component and merged the reflex with that of *jat'*. South Slavic, which had not developed an $*\widehat{ie}^n$ diphthong, only had $*\bar{e}^n$, which did have a short-vowel equivalent—namely, the diphthong that produced front nasal vowel reflexes. This explanation seems somewhat forced since Lekhitic possibly had a lower-vowel *jat'*, as reflected in Polish, and not the $\widehat{ie}$ diphthong that might more reliably be reconstructed for other zones of West and East Slavic. Nevertheless, it is an ingenious idea that offers an extremely economical explanation of a very complex phenomenon, which is characteristic of Jakobson's methodology throughout the book.

3.13 Restructuring of Quantitative Relations

In this section, Jakobson sums up the phonological meaning of the qualitative changes to long and short vowels and prefigures his groundbreaking paper on Slavic accentology (1963/1971). First, he observes that vowel quality replaced quantity as a phonemic feature, along with the loss of long- and short-vowel partners that previously were opposed only by quantity and the rise of new long vowels from homogeneous diphthongs, which did not have short partners. Since the new quality of long vowels was high or low vowel height and the new quality of short vowels was mid, the original quantity now served as a redundant feature of vowel height.

Since distinctive quantity was felt to be an essential feature for the maintenance of the pitch opposition, this loss of phonemic quantity threatened the continued existence of pitch as a distinctive feature. The language reacted by developing new quantitative oppositions, by shortening vowels under certain pitch conditions, but retaining their length in other cases. The various branches and dialect areas of Slavic experienced prosodic changes differently, leading to major accentological differences. (Jakobson later fully explored and developed this topic in detail in his 1963/1971 paper, which inspired a new generation of accentologists and stimulated renewed research into the field. It is remarkable that he prefigured the future issues of accentology so accurately in a publication of 1929.)

Jakobson ends by observing that the zone that preserved the pitch opposition (Serbo-Croatian-Slovene, which he sometimes refers to as "Serbo-Slovene") maintained the original circumflex length, while the zone that uniformly shortened circumflex length (West Slavic) lost its pitch oppositions.

3.14 Redistribution of Prothetic Consonants and Its Consequences

The background of this section is the relative phonemic weight of consonantal and vocalic tonality in the synharmonic syllable. There was a dual redundancy, where front vowels followed soft (palatal or palatalized) consonants and back vowels followed hard (nonpalatal and nonpalatalized consonants). For a time in Common Slavic, each redundant element could only cooccur with the other, and it was only later that the individual Slavic languages developed either phonemic consonant palatalization or the phonemic front/back vowel opposition. In this section, Jakobson demonstrates that the pure opposition between a front and back vowel word-initially, without a preceding consonant, was eliminated by means of developing prothetic consonants. It was sufficient to have a prothetic consonant preceding the back vowel (e.g., word-initial *vy-*, instead of **y-*), so the prothetic plus front vowel *ji-* could eliminate its prothetic and the opposition *vy-* vs. *i-* still was not a case of a pure back vs. a pure front vowel. In cases where there was no correlative front vowel, the back vowel could lose its prothetic. In other words, the function of the prothetic was to prevent instances of a pure initial front- vs. back-vowel opposition.

3.15 System of Palatal Consonants and Dialect Variations in Their Evolution

In this section, Jakobson explores the fact that there are potentially three separate series of dental and velar palatalizations in Slavic, but no branch keeps them all distinct and each zone has its own particular pattern of merging them. The three series are the products of the first velar palatalization, the products of the second velar palatalization (the progressive one, in Jakobson's interpretation, but also equal to the third), and the dental-plus-*jot* (*j*) palatalizations (**tj*, **dj*, etc.).

In East Slavic, obstruent dentals (*t, d, s, z*) plus *j* had the same reflexes as the first velar palatalization (*č, ž, š*). In South Slavic, this was true only of the dental fricatives plus *j*; the dental stops plus *j* did not merge with the reflexes of the velar palatalizations. In West Slavic, the reflexes of the second (and third) velar palatalizations merged with the dental-plus-*j* palatalizations (**tj* > *c*, etc.), while the fricative reflex *š* was the same for all three palatalizations. Jakobson views the West Slavic *š* reflex of $*x_l$, rather than *s*, as an avoidance of paired hard-soft status, which occurs in East Slavic, for example.

3.16 Dialect Differences in the System of Vowels in Sequences with Paired Softs and the Treatment of the Affricate ʒ

Sections 3.16–3.18 are all related, directly or indirectly, to the rise of the independently palatalized *s'* and *z'*, which were the products of the second and third velar palatalizations of *x* and *g*, symbolized by Jakobson as $*x_l$ and $*g_l$ since the reflexes in the Slavic languages are not uniform. Notably, not all zones developed *s'* and *z'* as reflexes; East Slavic is the best example of a zone that did. When these sounds did appear, they had the potential to create two important innovations:

1. The independent palatalization of *s'/z'*, where the level of palatalization could exceed that of the following vowel *ä*
2. The emergence of a new phonemic opposition: $\widehat{ie}$ (so-called *jat'*, from both **ē* and **oi*) vs. *ä*

First, the new *s'* and *z'* changed the relationship of paired and unpaired soft consonants that could occur before the vowels **ē* and **ä*. Prior to the advent of the new palatalized *s'* and *z'*, paired palatalized softs (e.g., *t', d', s', z'*) could occur before **ē*, while unpaired palatal softs occurred before **ä*, due to the previous sound change of **ē* to **ä* after a palatal. The progressive velar palatalization then conditioned the change of **ix-(a)/*ig-(a)* to **is'-(a)/*iz'-(a)*, which could be followed by a variety of desinences, such as *-a, -u, -ǫn*. Second, when this happened, the newly palatalized consonants caused fronting in the following vowels (to *-ä, -ü, -ön*), which now meant that paired softs could occur before both **ē* and **ä*, potentially creating a new phonemic opposition between two former positional variants. The *s', z'* in the new combinations *s'ä, z'ä*, and so on, also were a novel instance of independently palatalized consonants, whose level of palatalized tonality exceeded that of the following vowel, in contrast to the previous situation.

Jakobson describes how the various zones of Slavic reacted to these potential innovations. East Slavic not only accepted the new *s'ä* sequences but also extended them to new vowel positions, and its system accepted the new phonemic distinction of *ē* (which had merged with the reflex of the **oi* diphthong, *ie*, as *jat'*) and *ä*. In Czecho-Slovak and Sorbian, this applied only to the voiced *z'ä* sequence, since **x* had changed to palatal *š*, rather than palatalized *s'*, in West Slavic. Lekhitic did not participate in this development at all, as none of the reflexes of the second or third velar palatalization produced *s'* or *z'* in that zone. Bulgarian dialects attempted to resist these innovations in various ways, with the result that *ie* and *ä* remained positional variants and did not become independent phonemes, as evidenced by the single Glagolitic grapheme for both sounds. According to Jakobson, this did not mean that both sounds were identical; rather, it meant that they remained in complementary distribution. Notably, in Old Church Slavonic texts **g$_1$* appears as hard *z*, rather than palatalized *z'* (see Jakobson's citation of *kъnęza* 'prince, gen. sg.'), indicating a limitation on phonemic palatalization, in contrast to East Slavic (cf. Russian *knjazja*, phonetically [kn'äz'ə]).

As the above observations indicate, the Slavic phoneme *jat'*, with dual origins in **ē* and **oi*, and reconstructed by Jakobson as *ie*, had a complex phonemic history in the various Slavic zones, closely related to two other important developments: the fates of **x$_1$* and **g$_1$* and the nasal vowels, which Jakobson discusses in sections 3.17 and 3.18, respectively.

3.17   Link between the Fate of *ě* and the Dialectal Treatment of the Sequence ʒ'ä

As described in this section, the *ě* (*jat'*) reflexes of Slavic can be divided into those areas where the reflex varies between *a* and *e* (mainly Lekhitic and Bulgarian) and those where *jat'* is in the *i ~ e* range (e.g., Serbo-Croatian, Slovene, Czecho-Slovak, Sorbian, East Slavic). This difference is correlated with the development or lack of development of *z'ä* or *s'ä*: the development of these sequences rendered *jat'* a separate phoneme from *ä*, freeing it to become an independent mid-high or high vowel; their absence maintained the low-vowel status of *jat'* and allowed it to function as a front-vowel partner of *a*. The latter process was more complete in Bulgarian than in Lekhitic, where *jat'* was split into two variants, depending on its phonetic environment. When *jat'* was in the *i ~ e* range, it could vary between *i* and *e*, as well as assuming diphthongal status, and could assume various back vowels as paired phonemes.

Jakobson analogized the latter development to a game like musical chairs, in which partners are chosen but one person is left without a partner. In this case, *jat'* often sought a partner within the system, but could also end up as an isolated phoneme without a corresponding back vowel partner.

3.18   Dependency of Nasal Diphthong Evolution on the Treatment of ě (jat')

Jat' also has a relationship to the nasal reflexes of the various Slavic languages. Here, Jakobson tends to view the *jat'* reflex as primary and the nasal reflex as a function of the value of *jat'*. There are other interpretations, which posit a variable *jat'* that cannot assume a value already taken by the nasal reflex (see, e.g., Rigler 1986, 140). In any case, *a/ä*, possibly preceded by a palatalized consonant, was a frequent Slavic reflex of the front nasal vowel, seen in East Slavic, Czecho-Slovak, and Sorbian, and a low *jat'* does not occur in any of these zones, avoiding a merger with the nasal vowel reflex. The Serbo-Croatian and Slovene high-vowel status of *jat'* is not matched by a low-vowel nasal reflex with a preceding palatalized consonant, because independent consonantal palatalization did not develop in that zone and palatalized-consonant-plus-*ä* sequences were not admissible in that system. However, Jakobson observes that Serbo-Croatian dialects could maintain the low-vowel reflex of the front nasal vowel, if the preceding consonant was an unpaired palatal rather than a paired palatalized consonant, which the system could not tolerate. Jakobson further indicates that part of this development was the "Serbo-Slovene" loss of pure front-/back-vowel pairs, including the jers *ь/ъ*, which merged, and *i/y*, where *y > i*.

Jakobson also makes the interesting point that two separate nasal vowel reflexes (*a/ä* and *u/ü*) arose for the front and back nasals in the zones where *jat'* was higher, but that the nasal vowels and *jers* merged where *jat'* was a low vowel. In fact, the two nasal vowels of Polish do not reflect original front and back nasals; rather, they are the long and short reflexes of a merged nasal vowel. In Bulgarian, the nasal and *jer* reflexes are the same and, of course, the *jat'* reflexes of both Polish (as a representative of Lekhitic) and Bulgarian are in the *a ~ e* range.

3.19   Limitation of the Role of j

Here, Jakobson describes the diminishing role of *jot* (*j*) in the Slavic consonant system, particularly the elimination of initial *j* plus front vowel vs. initial front vowel (e.g., *ji-* vs. *i-*). This was due to the new model whereby the front/back synharmonic group was the basic phonemic unit, rather than independent and separate consonant and vowel tonalities. Jakobson notes that the change of consonant-plus-*j* groups was a different phenomenon (e.g., **sj > šj > š*), in which the *j* was not immediately eliminated after palatalizing the preceding consonant. As evidence, he cites examples like *pomyšljati* 'think', *bъždrjǫ* 'more cheerful', *xyštrjǫ* 'more cunning', where the obstruent-plus-liquid clusters *-sl-*, *-dr-*, *-tr-* are followed by *-j-* and experience the *jot* palatalization across the liquid to *-šlj-*, *-ždrj-*, *-štrj-*, respectively.

4 The Proto-East-Slavic Change of Initial *je-* to *o-* and Similar Developments in the Other Slavic Languages

4.1 Reason for the Change of Initial *je-* to *o-*

All linguists who have dealt with the question of the change of initial *je-* to *o-* in Common East Slavic agree that the loss of the initial *j-* was the necessary precondition for the change of *e-* to *o-*.[1]

However, the question of why the loss of *j-* led to the change of *e-* to *o-* has not received a satisfactory answer, as scholars admit: for example, "It is difficult to explain the physiological cause for this process" (Jagič 73; similarly Smal-Stockyj and Gartner 72), and "There was nothing in the environment that could have caused the labialization of *e*" (Durnovo, *j* 257). It is true that Durnovo does his best to derive the change of *e-* to *o-*, not from a labialization of *e* but from a displacement of the articulation toward the back, toward the mixed vertical series. However, as Il'inskij replies, this hypothesis is very improbable from a purely physiological standpoint.

However, if one considers the change of initial *e-* to *o-* within the scheme of Proto-East-Slavic phonology, this development appears to be totally natural and logical. In the phonological system of Proto-Slavic, *e* is opposed to *o* in the correlation "soft group ~ hard group." However, while *e* could not exist outside of a group containing a preceding soft consonant (cf. §3.14), *o* also functioned independently of a group containing a preceding hard. Thus, *o* was the fundamental variant of the *e/o* archiphoneme. Due to this, the loss of the soft consonant preceding *e* deprived the *e* of its reason for being and transformed it into *o* in the Proto-East-Slavic dialect, just as *ü* was changed into the *u* of Proto-East-Slavic as a result of the loss of a preceding *j* (cf. Šaxmatov, *c* 142).

Of course, this was the fate not only of *e* and *ü* in front of which *j* was lost, but of all cases of *e* and *ü* that appeared without a preceding soft consonant in Old East Slavic—that is, those at the beginning of the syllable and, in particular, at the beginning of the word. Such were the *e* and *ü* of borrowed words, mainly from Greek: for example, *oktenija* 'litany', *oksamitъ* 'samite', *Olena* 'alternate for the name Elena', *Ofremъ* 'alternate for the name Efrem'; *Vifleomъ* 'Bethlehem', *Geona* 'Gehenna'; *opanča* 'long mantle', *osaulъ* 'esaul, Cossack captain', etc.; *upatъ* 'hypatos, Byzantine court dignity', *upostasь* 'hypostasis', *na ussopъ* 'to the hyssop (plant)', etc.

4.2   Conditions for the Loss of *j*- When Preceding *e* in Word-Initial Position

Under what conditions was the word-initial *je*- group preserved without change in the Proto-East-Slavic dialect?

One condition is without question: the *j*- is preserved before an *e* that is followed by a hard consonant. Phonetic forms of the type *ètot* 'this' are an apparent exception to the law of preserving *j*- before an *e*- that is followed by a hard consonant and to the law of changing all cases of initial *e*- to *o*-. However, as already observed by Ekblom, Slavic *e*- is an interjective prefix, and emphatic elements of this sort manifest "a strong tendency to deviate from the ordinary laws that govern the phonetic evolution of the language" (*a* 16–17).

But *je*- does not change to *e*- before all soft consonants. Fortunatov (*a*) has hypothesized that an initial *j*- is lost before *e* only when the *e* is followed by one of the following:

1. A "half-soft consonant" (which, in my conception of the Proto-Slavic phonological system, corresponds to a "paired soft") + *e*

2. A syllable with *ę* (there are no examples of *je*- in the environment preceding the group "unpaired soft + *ę*")

3. Any consonant + *i*

The loss of *j*- in the first and second environments is considered a dialectal fact of Proto-Slavic, while its loss in the third case is a dialectal fact of Common East Slavic (Fortunatov, *a* 279ff.). This theory, which restricts the fall of *j*- to a set of conditions, at the same time does not allow for any linguistic interpretation of these conditions. The conditions assumed by Fortunatov to motivate the difference between Russian-Ukrainian *eževíka* 'blackberries' and Russian-Ukrainian *ožína* 'blackberries' are extremely artificial. Why did *e*, having lost *j*- before a palatal followed by *i*, preserve *j*- before a palatal followed by *e*, and lose it before a paired soft followed by *e*? Furthermore, Fortunatov's complicated formula fails to explain such vocalisms as *erepénit'sja* 'bristle', dialectal Russian *esen'jú* 'in the autumn', *esenjás'* 'last autumn', and dialectal Ukrainian *jasetr* 'sturgeon'. Durnovo, after accepting Fortunatov's hypothesis, was forced to come up with especially risky explanations for these words (*j* 251ff.).[2]

This series of facts receives its most appropriate explanation if one formulates the second condition in which *j-* is maintained, in the following terms: when *e* is followed by a consonant that is not contiguous to the accented vowel. In other words, *j-* is preserved before *e-* outside of the accented syllable and the syllable that precedes the accent. This thesis is supported by the following facts:

1. In all cases of the loss of initial *j-* before *e-* (and of the change of *e-* to *o-*), *j-* is found in the accented syllable or precedes the accent: *ózero* 'lake', *ósen'* 'autumn', *órjabok* 'hazel grouse', *orjábina* 'Jarabina, Slovak village', *ožína* 'blackberries', *ožíka* 'luzula (plant)', dialectal *ómex-oméž-oméšiki* 'blade of a plow', *olén'* 'deer' (Ukrainian *ólen'*), *ovín* 'drying barn', and Old East Slavic *ože* 'what, if', *ose* 'here is', *oliko* 'as much as', *olišьdy* 'when'.

2. In the case of initial *j-* preserved before an *e* that is followed by a soft consonant, *j-* is located in the penultimate syllable before the accent: *eževíka* 'blackberries' (but *ožína, ožíka*), *esenjás', esen'jú* (but *ósen'* 'autumn'; cf. Dolobko, *b* 689ff.), *erepénit'sja* 'bristle'.

3. Cases of dialectal variation between *e* and *o* are easily explained by the following generalization:

   a. In related forms, the dialects generalize either *je-* or *o-*, as in the dialectal *esetr* 'sturgeon, nom. sg.' (giving *jasetr*), under the influence of *esetrá* 'sturgeon, gen. sg.', *esetrý*, nom. pl., although the nom. sg. *osetr* in most Russian and Ukrainian dialects has driven out the *je-* of the other cases; thus, by analogy to forms with two or more syllables preceding the accent, such as *ediníca* 'unit', *edinák* 'equally', *edináčka* 'lone', *edinéc* 'only child', *edinákovyj* 'same', *edná* 'one, fem. nom. sg.' (< **jedinō*), *ednogó* 'one, masc.-neut gen. sg.', etc., *je-* has penetrated dialectally into forms that phonetically had *o-* (*edín*); and vice versa, in other dialects it is *o-* that has been more or less generalized. I leave aside those forms in *je-* that come from Church Slavonic.

   b. There are certain auxiliary words that are sometimes affected by a strong accent, and sometimes weakly accented or completely unaccented. In the latter words, their accented syllables are phonetically equivalent to normal unaccented syllables and meet the same fate; therefore, *j-* was either lost or preserved, depending on whether the accent fell or did not fall on the word *ešče* 'still'. Later, certain dialects generalized the phonetic form *ešče*, while others generalized the form *ošče*.

The vocalism of such words as *esm'* 'am', *esi* '(you) are, 2sg.', *est'* 'is, 3sg.', *ee* 'her, acc.-gen. sg.', *eju* 'her, instr. sg.' is probably due to the fact that these words are usually weakly accented; also, it is possible that these pronouns were influenced by the masculine forms (*ego* 'him, acc.-gen. sg.', etc.).

In all cases where Common Slavic *je-* corresponds to Russian *o-*, the *o-* either precedes a syllable with a rising accent (*olén', osétr, odín, ovín, orjábina, ožína*, etc.) or has a falling accent (*ózero, ósen', órjabok*). The presence of a falling accent is attested by the accent shift in Slovene (*jezêro* 'lake', *jesên* 'autumn', *jerêb* 'partridge'), by retraction of the accent to a preposition in Serbian (*nä jezero* 'to the lake', *dö jeseni* 'until autumn'), and by the absence of a prothetic *v* in Russian and the presence of a low-vowel *o* in the dialects of Russian that have preserved the difference between the reflexes of *o* under rising and falling accent (cf. §7.7).

Bearing these facts in mind, one could formulate the law of the loss of *j-* before *e* in word-initial position as follows: initial *j-* is lost before an *e* that is followed by a contiguous soft consonant that is not at the *peak* but at the *trough* of the tonal accent. In other words, the group of three sounds with the characteristic high tone "*j* + *e* + soft consonant" was eliminated by the loss of the first of its sounds, on the condition that the last sound of the group was in a strong position, which was apparently defined by its adjacency to the consonant at the trough of the tonal accent. Cf. the tendency of Slovene and Bulgarian to shift the falling accent to the final syllable, and the rising accent to the preceding syllable.

Is it necessary to suppose, along with Šaxmatov, that the loss of *j-* did not occur before an *e* that was followed by a syllable with a weak *jer*? In support of this proposal, one can only cite the forms *el'* 'fir tree', *ež* 'porcupine', Belarusian *evnja* 'drying barn', Ukrainian *jevnja* (with oblique case vocalism explained by analogy: *eli, eža*, etc.). However, the form *ež* (cf. genitive *ežá*) very probably had a rising accent; Štokavian *jêž, jêža*, as well as Čakavian *jēž, jěža*, are an accentual innovation. In this case, the attested Russian forms are the result of generalizing the original vocalism *éž', ožá*; a characteristic example of the generalization is Belarusian *ëž, ëžyk*, where *j-* (belonging to the group *je-*) and *o* are contaminated. We do not find forms parallel to the form *évnja* in the other Slavic languages; it is very probable that it is a dialectal Russian loan from *jáuja* of Lithuanian (cf. Karskij I 133, Larin 114), cf. the dialectal variants *ëvnja, ëvna*, Old Belarusian *ev'ja*. The form *el'* (**jedli*) is regular, if one assumes that the process of differentiating *je-* before a soft consonant and *je-* before a hard consonant occurred prior to the Proto-Slavic dialectal loss of *d* before *l* (see note 1 of chapter 5).

4.3   A Bulgarian Parallel

Similar processes have been indicated in the other Slavic languages. In Old Bulgarian, at least dialectally, forms with the same *je-* correspond to the Russian forms with initial *je-*: *jego* 'him, gen. sg.', *jemu* 'him, dat. sg.', *jeję* 'her, gen. sg.', etc., *jegda* 'when' (cf. Belarusian *egda*), *jedva* 'barely', *jestъ* 'eats', etc. However, in the environment where initial *je-* changes to *o-* in Russian, one can observe forms with initial *e-*: *ezero* 'lake', *elen'* 'deer', *ese*, *eterъ*, *eša*; we also find *e-* at the beginning of Greek words, and, corresponding to Russian, *e-* without a preceding *j* in the interjective prefix *e* (*eda, ei*, etc.). This dialect is reflected in the Codex Suprasliensis and in the orthography of an entire series of original texts in Russian Church Slavonic (see Durnovo, *j* 226 ff.). Sava's Book and Glagolitic orthography reflect another dialectal variant, which corresponds to the pronunciation of contemporary Bulgarian: initial *je-* is regularly changed to *e-* (cf. Mladenov, *a* 46ff.). The first dialectal type is more archaic and evidently serves as the basis for the second type, which simply represents a more recent stage of development. In my view, the evolution of initial *je-* in Bulgarian can be outlined as follows: *j-* before *e* is dropped in Proto-Bulgarian, in environments more or less equivalent to those for the loss of initial *j-* before *e* in Russian. The details are impossible to establish precisely, in view of the lack of documentation. However, in Bulgarian, contrary to Russian, the *e-* does not change to *o-*. As a result, the *e—o* opposition becomes detached from the correlation "soft group ~ hard group" and is changed into a variety of disjunctive phonemes. This occurred easily, since the *e—o* pair differed from other correlative vowel pairs by the fact that besides the difference "front—back," it had the supplementary distinction "unrounded—rounded." The result of this change was that *e* and *o* remained distinct archiphonemes and that, at the base of this correlation, *o* was conceived of as an unpaired back-vowel phoneme, with *e* as an unpaired front vowel. Thus, *e-* and *je-* were able to coexist as two combinatory variants of the same phoneme under these conditions, and one should interpret the Bulgarian loss of *j-* before any *e* as a natural process of phonemic unification.

It is precisely the change of *e* and *o* into different archiphonemes that explains the fact that Bulgarian does not experience the change of *e* to *o*. This change was also unknown to those Bulgarian dialects that had the correlation "soft ~ hard consonant," while in all the other Slavic languages that possess this correlation, *e* has changed to *o* to a greater or lesser degree (cf. §7.2), and, on the other hand, several Bulgarian dialects have seen the other front vowels change into the corresponding back vowels under certain conditions (cf. §7.9).

4.4 A Sorbian Parallel

Where *j*- is maintained before *e* in Russian, it is always maintained in Lower Sorbian: for example, *jabnuś* 'fuck', *jëbaś* (Russian *ebát'*), *jëdła* 'fir tree' (Russian *el'*, *elka*), *jo* 'is' (Russian *est'*).

However, in the environment where Russian has an initial *o*-, corresponding to Proto-Slavic *je*-, one finds alongside Lower Sorbian *je*-, in some cases, a dialectal variant *he*- < *e*- (see Fortunatov, *a* 279ff.): *heleń* 'deer' (alongside *jeleń*), *hereb* 'rowan', *herebina* (along with *jereb*, *jerebina*), *hešće* 'still' (along with *ješće*). But, when *e* is followed by a consonant that has hardened in Lower Sorbian, *j*- has been maintained and there are no doublets in *he*-: *jazor(o)* 'lake', *jesotr* 'sturgeon', *ježyk* 'small porcupine', *ježava* 'nightshade' (see Muka, *b*).

In the Proto-Slavic dialect that is the ancestor of Lower Sorbian, the same process occurred as in Bulgarian, but here, unlike in Bulgarian, the fate of the *e*—*o* unpaired opposition and the transformation of *e* and *o* into independent archiphonemes were avoided by the following process: initial *o*- was provided with a prothetic *v* and was envisaged as a combinatory variant of the *e/o* phoneme, conditioned by the position after a hard consonant. After a hard consonant, this phoneme was represented by *o*; otherwise, it was represented by *e* when it was followed by a soft consonant, and by *je* when it wasn't. This role still favored initial *je*- at the relatively late moment in the history of Lower Sorbian when the sibilants and hushers had become hard: initial *e*- changed to *je*- before these hardened consonants. The data at our disposal do not permit us to resolve the question of whether Lower Sorbian, like Russian, was also influenced by accentological factors or not.

The languages that have initial *e*- without *j* under certain conditions—that is, Bulgarian and Lower Sorbian—possess a common trait, in spite of the different phonological conclusions drawn from this innovation by each of these two languages. Specifically, the appearance of *e*- at the beginning of the word, which necessitated a revision of the phonological value of the relation *e*—*o*, has primarily acted to cause a blurring of the boundary that separated *e* and *o* in the linguistic consciousness, under identical phonetic conditions. This blurring, however fleeting and ephemeral it might have been, was able to leave traces. Notably, the following can be interpreted as vestiges of these fluctuations and displacements of the phonological boundary:

1. Lower Sorbian *votery* 'a certain one' (< *otery*), corresponding to Old Church Slavonic *eterъ*

2. Lower Sorbian *herel* 'eagle' and Bulgarian *elov* 'lead', which have initial *o*- as their cognate in all of the Slavic languages (with a falling accent on the

first syllable, as indicated by Serbian *ȍd olova* 'from the lead', Slovene *olǫ̑v* 'lead', Russian *ólovo* 'tin', and a second-syllable accent, as indicated by Russian *orël* 'eagle', Štokavian *òrao*)

The presence of the dialect form *jerel* 'eagle' in Lower Sorbian leads to the interpretation of Lower Sorbian dialect forms of the type *jeleń* 'deer', *jeřeb* 'rowan', as the result of a secondary generalization of initial *j-* (a phonemic unification in the direction opposite to Bulgarian). This also appears to be a secondary generalization of the same type as Lower Sorbian *je-* (given that in Lower Sorbian one finds a prothetic *v* before *o*). In other words, it is very possible that the change of *je-* to *e-* is a fact of Common Sorbian.

4.5   A Czecho–Slovak Parallel

A fact clearly parallel to the Russian split of word-initial *j-* into two reflexes is found in Slovak and the eastern dialects of Czech. Where Russian preserves *je*, Slovak retains this group without change: for example, *jebat'* 'fuck', *jedl'a* 'fir tree', *jest* 'eat', *jeho* 'him', *jej* 'her', *jež* 'porcupine'. Along with *je-*, a dialect variant *ja-* corresponds to Russian *o-*: for example, *jaseň* 'autumn', *jazero* 'lake', *jarab* 'rowan', *jarábok, jarabý, jarabina, jalito* 'blood sausage' (a parallel form is absent in Russian, but the phonetic conditions are such that one would surely expect initial *o-* in Russian), *jaleň* 'deer' in the Lach dialect (*Laština*) (see Kálal 215ff.; Gebauer, I 148).

Each of the enumerated forms has its own isogloss, but, generally speaking, the area of words with initial *ja-* < *je-* is just about the same as the area where the change of *ä* between softs to the diphthong *i͡e* has not occurred. Surely, the isoglosses of isolated words with *e* coming from *ä* between softs cross the border of the area where the phonological process in question (called *přehláska* 'Czech vowel shift') has occurred. One is justified in hypothesizing that *ä* coming from *e* between initial *j-* and a soft consonant is a fact of Common Czecho-Slovak, and that the *e* of Modern Czech or dialectal Slovak is secondary in this environment: it is the result of the change of any *ä* to *e* between softs. In other words, Proto-Slavic *jelito* 'intestine' > Czecho-Slovak *jälito* 'blood sausage' > Czech *jĕlito* (*přehláska*) > *jelito*. It is known that *i͡e* (*ĕ*) after *j* changed to *e* early on; also, the fourteenth-century texts that distinguish *ĕ* and *e* do not give any sufficiently reliable indications about the origin of *e* in Czech *jezero* 'lake', etc.: for example, the Wittenberg Psalter has *giezera* 'lake', *gielen* 'deer'.[3]

Bulgarian and Lower Sorbian *e-*, Russian *o-*, and Slovak *ja-* are the ultimate and disparate results of an originally single process; the change of *e-* to *ä-*, between initial *j*- and a soft consonant, is the elimination of a group of three sounds of high tonality, accomplished by means of another process. The East Slavic dialect chose to radically eliminate the opposition "back vowel—correlative front vowel preceded by *j*," and it thus eliminated not only the *a—ja* opposition, just like all of the Slavic languages with distinct *ä* and *ě* (i.e., all of them, with the sole exception of the Bulgarian dialects, especially the dialect that served as the basis for the Glagolitic alphabet), but also the *u—jü* opposition, preserved in all of the other Slavic languages (e.g., Russian *uxa* 'fish soup' and Serbian, Slovene *júha* 'soup', Czech *jícha*, Polish, Upper and Lower Sorbian *jucha* 'blood, muck'). This tendency of Proto-East-Slavic explains the choice of the process by which "groups of three high-tonality sounds" were eliminated in initial position. However, the replacement of front vowels at the beginning of the word by the correlative back vowels remained alien to Proto-Czecho-Slovak, Proto-Bulgarian, and Proto-Sorbian, and the processes of eliminating these groups were different.

4.6   Hypothetical Isogloss of the Elimination of the Group "Initial *j* + *e* + Soft Consonant" and Attempt at an Explanation

As to the elimination of these groups per se, it is a dialectal fact encompassing a vast area. It seems to have affected all the Slavic dialects, except for Lekhitic and the Serbo-Slovene group. These two groups are distinguished by a specific phonetic trait: at the moment when all the other Slavic dialects had the tendency for front vowels to split into two variants, depending on whether they were followed by a hard or a soft consonant (Russian, Bulgarian, Czech), there is no trace of this differentiation in Lekhitic and Serbo-Croatian. In these zones, if there is a split into two variants, influenced by the following consonant, the consonantal categories sort themselves differently: the hard dentals in one group, all the other consonants in the other. Cf. the Polish split of *e* into *o* and *e*, and of *jat'* into *a* and *e*, and also the Serbian dialectal split of *jat'* into *e* and *i*.

Annotations to Chapter 4, The Proto-East-Slavic Change of Initial *je-* to *o-* and Similar Developments in the Other Slavic Languages

4.1 Reason for the Change of Initial *je-* to *o-*

This section makes reference to one of the best-known distinguishing features of East Slavic, in contrast to the other Slavic zones: initial *o-* in many words that have an initial *je-* in the other Slavic branches (e.g., Russian *ozero* 'lake', in contrast to Czech and Serbo-Croatian *jezero* and Polish *jezioro*). Jakobson addresses the reason and conditions for this evolution, then indicates its parallels in Bulgarian, Sorbian, and Czecho-Slovak. He concludes by demonstrating that this development had some common features in several Slavic languages, despite the prevailing opinion that it only opposed East Slavic to South and West Slavic.

4.2 Conditions for the Loss of *j-* When Preceding *e* in Word-Initial Position

According to Jakobson, linguists at the time all agreed that the loss of initial *j-* was a necessary precondition for the change of *je-* to *o-* in East Slavic, but the question of why the loss of *j-* led to the change of *e-* to *o-* did not yet have a satisfactory answer. He attributes the change to the nature of the syllabic synharmonic group. Without an initial *j-*, the basic variant of the *e/o* archiphoneme had to take over, since the opposition "initial back vowel—paired initial front vowel" was impossible once there was no preceding *j-* consonant. Thus, either *je-* or *o-* was a possible initial, but *e-* was not. Regarding the Russian demonstrative *èto* 'this' and related forms, Jakobson notes that the initial *e-* element is derived from an interjection, which was not typical of the lexicon as a whole. The same thing applied to other instances of front and back paired vowels, such as *u/ü* and *a/ä*. Word-initial position of Greek loanwords was affected, and even syllable-initial position of Old East Slavic (e.g., *Olena* 'Elena', *Ofrem* 'Efrem', *Vifleon* 'Bethlehem', rather than *Elena, Efrem, Vifleen*).

The phonological conditions specified that *je-* had to be followed by a soft consonant for the *je-* > *o-* change to go through; *je-* remained as such when preceding a hard consonant (e.g., Russian *edva* 'barely', *est* 'eat, 3sg.', *ego* 'him, acc.-gen.', *emu* 'him, dat.', all with initial phonetic [*j*-]). Jakobson demonstrates that *je-* was also retained when the initial syllable was noncontiguous to the accent (e.g., Russian *esenjás'* 'last autumn', *eževíka* 'blackberries'). Further, Jakobson observes that the *je-* > *o-* change is realized when the accent is either falling (circumflex) on the first syllable (as in Russian *ozero* 'lake') or rising (acute) on the second (as in Russian *olen'* 'deer'). As just noted, accent on the third syllable blocks the change. After the description of the accentual environment, Jakobson draws the interesting conclusion that the *e* of the initial *je-* must be followed by a soft consonant that is contiguous to the trough of the accent, rather than the peak, in order for the change to occur. Thus, if there is an initial falling accent on *je-*, it ends precisely at the end of the initial syllable; correspondingly, if the second syllable is rising, the rise begins from its low point to the right of the initial *je-* syllable. In other words, initial *je-* is contiguous to the trough in both instances. When accent falls on the third syllable, the first is not contiguous to the trough and the change does not occur.

4.3–4.6 Parallels to East Slavic *e* > *o* in Other Slavic Zones

After specifying the phonological and accentological environments for the *je-* > *o-* change, Jakobson devotes sections 4.3–4.5 to East Slavic parallels within the Bulgarian, Sorbian, and Czecho-Slovak zones. In Bulgarian, initial *j-* is deleted, as in East Slavic, but the *e* > *o* change does not take place and initial *e-* results, as in Bulgarian *ezero* 'lake'. Jakobson explains that *e* and *o* were not in the same front/back paired relationship in Bulgarian as they were in East Slavic and that, consequently, initial *je-* and *e-* could coexist in Bulgarian, unlike in East Slavic. Somewhat similar to Bulgarian, Lower Sorbian dialects had an initial *je-* that could also lose *j-*, but they substituted prothetic *h-* before the *e*, as in *heleń* 'deer', from *jeleń*. In Slovak and Eastern Czech, the East Slavic *je-* > *o-* change was paralleled by the change *je-* > *jä-*.

Summarizing the meaning of all these changes in section 4.6, Jakobson concludes that since the change requires a following soft consonant, the *je-* plus-soft environment implies a sequence of three softs in a row and that the changes all lower the tonality of one or more high-tonality segments. In East Slavic, the two high-tonality segments *je-* are changed to the single low-tonality segment *o-*, a direction of change similar to those cited for the other Slavic zones. Jakobson also notes a series of similar changes in East Slavic, which all have the common denominator of avoiding the *j*-plus-front-vowel vs. *j*-plus-back-vowel opposition in the initial syllable; as a result, either front or back predominates. Thus, in addition to the loss of *je-* vs. *o-* oppositions, the initial oppositions *a-* vs. *jä-* and *u-* vs. *jü-* are eliminated by generalizing initial *jä-* and *u-* (cf. Russian *jabloko* 'apple', *uxa* 'fish soup', but northeastern Bulgarian dialect *abălka* 'apple', Polish *jucha* 'blood, muck').

Jakobson ends the section by pinpointing two zones—Lekhitic and Serbo-Croatian-Slovene—that do not reduce the initial front/back oppositions as described above. He connects this to the fact that all the other zones have a tendency to split front vowels into front and back variants, on the basis of whether hard or soft consonants follow them. While recognizing the well-known split of front vowels preceding hard dentals in Lekhitic, he classifies it as a different category of change.

5   Dialectal Facts about Proto-East-Slavic

5.1   Fusion of *c* and *č* in Northern Russian

From the phonological standpoint, the soft consonants of Proto-East-Slavic constituted two categories: paired and unpaired softs. From the standpoint of the physiology of sounds, they were subdivided into palatalized and palatal. All of the palatal consonants of Proto-East-Slavic were also unpaired softs, while all of the paired softs were palatalized consonants. It is natural that the linguistic consciousness interpreted the palatalization of consonants as the objective mark of paired softs, and the palatal feature as the objective mark of unpaired softs. After the change of z' to z', c' remained as the only palatalized unpaired soft. There are two processes for eliminating the exceptional status of c' as the only instance of a phoneme that was both unpaired and palatalized:

1. *c* gets transferred to the series of paired softs, becoming hard in environments where paired softs are inadmissible. This is how Czech *c* hardened under the same conditions as paired softs, for example, before hard dentals (cf. *vzácný* 'rare', alongside *žádný* 'none', *jasný* 'clear', but *ječný* 'barley (adj.)', *obtížný* 'difficult', etc.).

2. *c* is changed to a palatal consonant and then merges with *č* as a prepalatal consonant (the symbol c_j; in Broch *b* §47). This process (called *cokan'e*) is the one employed by the Northern Russian dialect, taking the Finnish pronunciation of Russian as its model (cf. Trubetzkoy, *d* 293; Černyšev). One can only understand this isolated phonetic Finnish loan from the point of view of the needs of the phonological system.

5.2   Treatment of the *sk* + *oi* Reflex in Northern Russian

In the West Slavic languages and in the Northern Russian dialects, the group s_1k_1 (coming from *sk*, preceding the reflex of *oi*) was changed into *šč*. Durnovo (*f* 220) explains West Slavic *šč* in terms of the change of s_1 into *š*, which then assimilates the *c*. In Northern Russian, conversely, the second element of the group first took on the hushing feature (cf. §5.1) and assimilated the first element. The group s_1k_1 becomes identical to the old group *šč*. Subsequent modifications of the affricate in the Northern Russian dialects usually do not affect the *č* of the group in question. Thus, one can state the following formula: s_1k_1 becomes *šč* only in those Slavic languages where one of the constituent phonemes of this group has changed to a husher.

5.3   Other Dialect Features; Disparate Nature of Isoglosses

Every East Slavic dialect event that preceded the fall of weak *jers* possesses *its own* isogloss, not motivated from the linguistic point of view. The division of the East Slavic of this period into dialects is purely arbitrary and not very productive.

The area of the *dl* > *gl* change is incomparably smaller than that of the fusion of *c* and *č*.[1]

As for the graphemes *žg* in Northern Russian texts, their phonetic value is obscure. It is not impossible that *g* represented the affricate *ǯ*. In this case, the Novgorod graphemes *žg* and the graphemes *žč* of Galicia would have had the same phonetic value. However, even if we do not admit this explanation and if we identify the *g* with the usual *g*, following Sobolevskij (*a* 35), or even if we view it as a fricative mediopalatal, along with Trubetzkoy (*d* 291), or as a *j*, along with Šaxmatov (*c* 321), or as a prepalatal *d*, along with Seliščev (*a* 38), we still do not know whether the cited grapheme refers to a living dialect pronunciation or whether, as Durnovo supposes (*k* 18), it refers to a local "pronunciation of Church Slavonic." There are no reliable vestiges in the current northern dialects, and if one feels that the *žg* of the texts is a dialect feature, one has no data permitting the conclusion that this feature expanded vastly and establishing a link between its area and that of the fusion of *c* and *č*.

Finally, there is the problem of knowing when the southern *cokan'e* isogloss merged with the northern isogloss of the loss of noncontinuant *g*. In other words, up to what point does one have the right to assume the existence of two Old East Slavic dialects: a northern one with noncontinuant *g* and the merger of *c* and *č*, and a southern one that had lost the noncontinuant *g* and preserved the phonemes *c* and *č* as distinct? First, the data do not permit us to consider the *c* vs. *č* distinction of many Northern Russian dialects as secondary facts, due to imitation, which replaced the original *cokan'e* (cf. Sobolevskij, *b* 33ff.; Durnovo, *k* 112ff.). Second, there are many dialects with *γ* and *cokan'e*, among which are the "Meščera" dialects (cf. Durnovo, *k* 141) and the Belarusian dialects to the north of Smolensk. One could not consider these dialects as the products of subsequent hybridization. As for the Belarusian dialects, on the contrary we know that the *cokan'e* area has gradually been shrinking over the course of the centuries. In Russian, under the influence of the Moscow dialect with its noncontinuant *g* and its distinct *c, č*, the isoglosses of fricative *γ* and the affricate merger have gradually retreated—the former, naturally, toward the South, and the latter toward the North. This is how we explain the rarity of present-day Russian dialects that possess both *cokan'e* and *γ*. For example, at present, *cokan'e* can be seen to be receding toward the north of the Moscow State, while this trait still could be found in the Moscow suburban area (cf. Kokorev) in the mid-nineteenth century. In an earlier period, in the south of this state, in the Serpuxov district, *cokan'e* still existed in dialects with *γ*, as it appears from evidence regarding the dialect of peasants of this district, who were relocated to the Voronež province: in 1849, they still had preserved *cokan'e* (see Zelenin 378). The sharpness of the distinctions between Northern Russian and Southern Russian can probably be interpreted as being the result of later differentiations and adjustments.

If one more closely observes those dialectal phonetic changes of Old East Slavic that preceded the loss of the weak *jers* and if one compares them to the changes in the following period, one can conclude that along with the lack of linguistic motivation for the isoglosses, there is another trait that the earlier period possesses: these are all changes of little significance from the phonological point of view. They are either purely "phonetic" changes (i.e., innovations in extragrammatical differences without distinctive value, and not phonological differences) or cases of the fusion of disjunctive phonemes. The change of *g* to *γ* belongs to the first category (i.e., it was only the later change, that of sonorants not followed by sonorants into voiceless consonants, that led to a dialect difference between these phonological units: the reflex of the voiced velar merged with historical *k* in one instance, but with *x* in the other). However, this was precisely the case of the change of the *žǯ* cluster, if one treats the graphic *žg* as the reflection of a dialectal trait. This was also the case of the differing variants that represent the phoneme *v* in various dialects. Examples of the not very significant fusion of disjunctive phonemes or phonemic groups include the fusion of affricates and the change of the northwestern *dl* group to *gl*, which would have made the Common East Slavic change of *dl* > *l* vacuous in these dialects.

Annotations to Chapter 5, Dialectal Facts about Proto-East-Slavic

5.1 Fusion of *c* and *č* in Northern Russian

In this chapter, Jakobson deals with several early East Slavic dialect features that predate *jer*-fall. In comparison with the changes brought about by *jer*-fall, they are not very interconnected or related to systemic factors. However, Jakobson attempts to show possible systemic causes of these changes and relates them to the system as a whole.

The first is known as *cokan'e*, which refers to a lack of opposition between *č* and *c*. These sounds are the products of the earlier and later palatalizations of velars. After these palatalizations, there were two classes of softs from the systemic point of view, paired and unpaired, and two classes from the articulatory standpoint, palatalized and palatal. There was one outstanding exception to the rule that paired softs were palatalized and unpaired were palatals: the sound *c'*, which came from $*k_1$, using Jakobson's symbol. Originally, $*g_1$ was palatalized to *ʒ'*, but *ʒ'* (*dz'*) was simplified to *z'*, after which *c'* remained as the only unpaired palatalized sound in the system. This anomaly led to the elimination of *c'* as an independent phoneme in certain dialects; it merged with *č'* and could be phonetically realized as either *č'*, *c'*, or an intermediate sound. The general process is known as *cokan'e* in Russian, although the term *čokan'e* is sometimes applied to dialects that have the specific realization *c*, instead of *č'* or *č*. The model for the dialectal loss of the opposition between /č/ and /c/ phonemes was the Finnish pronunciation of Russian.

5.2 Treatment of the *sk* + *oi* Reflex in Northern Russian

In this section, Jakobson deals with the Northern Russian dialect feature that resulted from the palatalization of *sk* before the original $\widehat{oi}$ diphthong, that is, the second regressive velar palatalization (or the third velar palatalization, in Jakobson's interpretation). The expected result would have been *sc*, since *k* normally would have resulted in *c* after the second regressive palatalization. However, certain Northern Russian dialects have the hushing reflex *šč* in this case, identical with the results of the first regressive palatalization. As Jakobson states, when one phoneme in this cluster is realized as a palatal husher, this feature applies to both phonemes.

5.3 Other Dialect Features; Disparate Nature of Isoglosses

Jakobson notes the sporadic and unmotivated nature of the pre-*jer*-fall isoglosses of East Slavic, and then lists others of this type. These include the minor change of *dl* to *gl*, which is said to have used Baltic languages as a model. In East Slavic dialects that did not experience *dl* > *gl*, *dl* was later simplified to *l*.

Another minor dialect feature is found in written manuscripts and is represented by the Cyrillic graphemes *žg* (*жг*). No one is completely sure whether it reflected a dialect pronunciation or simply a style of Church Slavonic pronunciation. Jakobson suggests that the phonetic value of orthographic *žg* was the same as that of the southern East Slavic graphemes *žč* (*жч*), namely, *žǯ*. Several years after this book was published, Jakobson wrote a specialized article on this topic (Jakobson 1936/1962).

Jakobson considers the geographical relationship between the northern *cokan'e* isogloss and the southern isogloss for the continuant pronunciation of original *g* as *γ*. Two basic dialects may have existed at an early point, but Moscow, in the central zone, later combined an absence of *cokan'e* with non-continuant *g*. The prestige of Moscow caused the *cokan'e* line to retreat northward and the continuant voiced velar line to move southward.

Jakobson ends the chapter by recapitulating the marginal nature of the isoglosses that preceded *jer*-fall. As he shows in the later chapters, the changes connected to the loss of *jers* were motivated systemically and were necessitated by other changes in the system.

6 Consequences of the Loss of Weak *Jers* for the Slavic Languages

6.1 Loss of Weak *Jers* as a Factor in the Breakup of Proto-Slavic

The loss of weak *jers* was profoundly revolutionary in its consequences. In all the Slavic languages, it caused a radical reorganization of the phonological system, to say nothing of the basic change in the principles of phonemic combination and a whole series of morphological innovations. At the time of *jer* loss, the geographical connection that had existed between the various Slavic languages had already become too tenuous for the ensuing reorganization of the phonological system to lead to a single standard for all the Slavic dialects. The loss of weak *jers* was the generalization of a type of "rapid speech" (cf. §2.2). The main support for this thesis can be found, first, in the example of other languages, where certain dialects have lost reduced vowels and where other, more conservative ones lose them only in rapid speech; second, it was the *allegro* words that lost their weak *jers*, as attested by Old Church Slavonic and Old East Slavic texts—prior to the general loss of weak *jers* (*kъgda* 'when', *tъkmo* 'only').[1]

It is not difficult for "rapid speech" to become generalized and for weak *jers* to be lost not only in pronunciation, but even at a deeper level of intention. It is all the easier since the loss in question directly destroys only a minimal number of meaningful distinctions. This process was able to spread through the entire Slavic territory. However, the rate of its expansion since that time was extremely slow; it lasted more than three centuries (from the tenth to the thirteenth). The complex phonological processes that arose as an immediate consequence of the loss of weak *jers* were the product of specific local conditions.

Let us imagine two Proto-Slavic dialects, A and B. The impulse leading to the loss of weak *jers* has come from dialect A and has reached dialect B. The loss of weak *jers* has caused a restructuring of the phonological system in dialect A. Dialect B needed time to be able to assimilate the subtle principles on which dialect A based its restructuring. However, there was not enough time; the loss of weak *jers* had upset the balance of the phonological system and the urgent necessity of reestablishing order required irrevocable changes.

In addition, at the moment of weak *jer* loss, a series of local phonological changes had already occurred in the various Slavic languages that prefigured the eventual course of the phonological development of these languages. The basic tendencies of evolution were very marked, and the great restructuring had to deal with them. Thus, for example, the opposition "soft group ~ hard group" had been eliminated even prior to the loss of weak *jers* in Proto-Serbian (cf. §3.18).

In some Slavic languages, the direction for the reorganization of the phonological system was determined by the influence of neighboring non-Slavic languages. This was the case in Czech, for example, where the higher social stratum (which is often the leader of linguistic change) was bilingual at an early date.

The loss of weak *jers* was a powerful force in the breakup of Common Slavic. It deepened the differences in the phonological structures of various dialects, which were thus transformed into separate languages. This is precisely why this was the last event of Common Slavic, according to Trubetzkoy's correct formulation (*h* 56).

6.2   Consequences of the Loss of Weak *Jers* for the Correlation "Voiced ~ Voiceless Consonant"

The phonological correlations of the Slavic languages were all affected, directly or indirectly, by the loss of weak *jers*. It affected the "voiced ~ voiceless" correlation by enlarging the number of phonological oppositions in these two types. Prior to the loss of weak *jers*, voiced and voiceless consonants were phonologically opposed only before unpaired voiced phonemes (i.e., before vowels and sonorants). In all other positions, their value was determined by the phonological environment. After the loss of weak *jers*, the "voiced— voiceless" opposition was extended to all environments. Since the assimilation of voiceless to the following paired voiced and of paired voiced to the following paired voiceless had already occurred, the phonological opposition of voiced and voiceless in word-final position remained as a new fact, in comparison to the period that had preceded the fall of weak *jers*. Curiously, in the majority of Slavic dialects, particularly in the majority of Russian dialects, this opposition has been eliminated and the former relationship has been reestablished: voiced and voiceless are phonologically opposed only before vowels and sonorant consonants.

6.3 Consequences of the Loss of Weak *Jers* for the Correlation "Soft Group ~ Hard Group" and Subsequently for Accent and Quantity

The "soft group ~ hard group" correlation underwent fundamental changes as a consequence of weak *jer* loss. An autonomous opposition "palatalized consonant—hard consonant" (*klad'*—*klad*) came into being for the first time. The emancipation of the "soft consonant—hard consonant" opposition within the phonological system caused the opposition of soft and hard groups to lose their phonological value when taken as a whole.

The two terms of the correlation "consonant + vowel" group were disassociated by the linguistic consciousness. The soft and hard consonants, reciprocally opposed, which had previously been combinatory correlative variants, became autonomous correlative variants. The opposition "front vowel—back vowel" became a concomitant extragrammatical difference. One element of the group indivisibly takes on the function of the term of the correlation and, by this very fact, the other is changed into a combinatory extragrammatical variant. The two combinatory extragrammatical variants of the phoneme naturally are subjected to the tendency to unify the phoneme.

None of the Slavic languages admits both pitch correlations ("pitch accent ~ unaccented vowels" and "one ~ another intonational structure") and the "soft ~ hard consonant" correlation. The tendency to avoid their coexistence is without exception in the Slavic languages.[2]

In the Slavic languages where, at the moment of weak *jer* loss, the correlation "soft ~ hard consonant" no longer existed, the correlations "pitch accent ~ unaccented vowels" and "one ~ another intonational structure" naturally survived (Serbo-Croatian, Slovene). Therefore, it is not by chance that the isoglosses for both pitch accent and the merger of ъ and ь are identical prior to the loss of weak *jers*.

In the dialects where the two aforementioned correlations clashed, pitch accent was excluded from the phonological system. The correlation "one ~ another intonational structure" disappeared and the correlation "pitch accent ~ unaccented vowels" was replaced by "intensity accent ~ unaccented." As a result, a new conflict inevitably ensued—between the correlations "intensity accent ~ unaccented" and "length ~ shortness of vowel." This conflict had two types of resolution:

1. Eastern solution: the "length ~ shortness of vowel" correlation was eliminated. Such was the case of Russian and Bulgarian.

2. Western solution: the "intensity accent ~ unaccented" correlation was rejected; in other words, accent stabilized on a specific word syllable, thus

losing any phonological role within the limits of the word. Such was the case of Czecho-Slovak, Old Polish, and Sorbian.[3]

As for the correlation "soft ~ hard consonant," it either emerges victorious in its duel with the "pitch accent ~ unaccented" correlation (Russian, Eastern Bulgarian, Polish, Sorbian), or there is no victor at all, and both adversaries perish. In a similar manner, when two homonyms clash, we see one or the other perish, or else, at times, both.[4]

6.4 Changes in Czech

A characteristic example of the elimination of two incompatible correlations is the history of Czecho-Slovak, where the conflict occasioned by the loss of weak *jers* has led to the elimination of the "pitch accent ~ unaccented" correlation and, at the same time, led to the impulse to lose the "soft ~ hard consonant" correlation. At first, the "soft group ~ hard group" correlation was reestablished, but eventually it was gradually eliminated.

I will now give a brief sketch of the evolution of the Czech vowel system, from the loss of weak *jers* up until the complete elimination of the correlation "soft group ~ hard group." I will take up the details of this evolution in a specialized study, in order to motivate and date the periodization, as well as to analyze the dialect variants. Let us first trace the Czech vocalic system after weak *jer* loss.[5] A comma is used to separate combinatory variants. Each represented vowel forms a part of two correlative classes: long and short vocalism.

$$
\begin{array}{ccc}
\text{i, y} & & \text{ü, u}^{6} \\[4pt]
\text{e, ə} & \widetilde{\text{ie}}\text{, o} & \\[4pt]
& \text{ä, a} &
\end{array}
$$

1. ə goes back to strong ъ.

2. Long ə goes back to the groups *oje, yje* (the two facts are linked to each other; the change of ъ to ə, which ends by merging with *e*, is found only in Slavic dialects that underwent the contraction of groups of the indicated type prior to the loss of weak *jers*).[7]

3. Long and short ə go back to *e* after paired softs and before hard dentals (during the change of *e* to ə, the preceding consonant hardens; compare nom. sg. *přietel* 'friend'—gen. pl. *prátel; dětel, -e* = 'clover'—*datel, -a* = 'woodpecker'; *patero* 'group of five', *desatero* 'group of ten', *devatero* 'group of nine'; *svacený* 'sanctified', *vazen* 'prisoner'; cf. Gebauer, I 93, 53, 109; III-2 151).

In the phonological system of Czech, the vowel $\widehat{ie}$, with its composite articulation, was the true correlate of *o*. Cf. the tendency to diphthongize *o* under different conditions, which is reflected in the orthography of old texts (not to be confused with the later diphthongization of any *ō*),[8] as well as in the later dialect change of *o* to $\widehat{ie}$ after palatal consonants, due to grammatical analogy (*oráčovi* > *oráčěvi*, etc.). A lower vowel was originally represented by two combinatory variants after a soft consonant—one was farther back and probably lower before a hard consonant (which I represent as *ȧ*); the other is farther front and most likely higher, found in other environments (strictly speaking, *ä*). The loss of weak *jers* failed to introduce the correlation "soft ~ hard consonant" into the Czech phonological system, but the language rejected "palatalization in the restricted sense of the term," as defined by Broch, that is, "the presence of consonantal nuances of a higher basic tone and in systemic opposition to consonantal nuances of a lower basic tone" (*b* §176). Attempting to maintain the correlation "soft group ~ hard group" at all costs and, in parallel fashion, "palatalization in the larger sense, that is, the adjustment of the consonant to the following front vowel" (loc. cit.), the language had to institute clear and uniform types of this assimilative palatalization. The assimilative softness of consonants before *ä* and *ȧ* was insufficiently clear; consequently, *sȧ* merged with *sa*, and before *ä* the degree of palatalization was standardized as "*e*", with a parallel change of the vowel *ä* to a vowel with composite articulation, $\widehat{eä}$, which finally assimilated to the traditional composite vowel $\widehat{ie}$ within the phonological system. As a consequence of the phonological duality of *ä* and *ȧ*, the hardening of paired softs before *ȧ*, and the subsequent merger of *ȧ* and *a*, the consonants that could occur before *a* were unpaired softs as well as hard consonants. The vowel *a* was the first unpaired back vowel in the Czech phonological system. The unpaired softs—palatal consonants that had not assimilated their basic tone to the following vowel—were henceforth treated more independently than were paired softs, and grammatical analogy was equally able to combine the unpaired softs with other back vowels, in cases where the back vowel was the basic variant of a phoneme (*oráčovi*, etc.). However, subsequently, at least in dialects, the groups "soft unpaired consonant + paired back vowel" were eliminated; the back vowel was replaced by its front-vowel correlate (*oráčěvi*, etc.).

In the next period of the evolution of the Czech phonological system, the two high front vowels merged, as did the mid front vowels. The vowel system of these heights was reduced to three phonemes: an unrounded front vowel, an unrounded back vowel, and a rounded back vowel. Within the high vowels, the innovation amounted to the change of *ü* to *i*, but the process was more complex for mid vowels. Consonants with two levels of palatalization were

used with front mid vowels. On the one hand, these included consonants with
the *e* level of palatalization, such as soft paired consonants before *e*. On the
other hand, they included consonants whose palatalization exceeded the *e*
level; these included paired softs before *ie͡* and unpaired softs before both *e*
and *ie͡*. After the simplification of the vowel system, there was also a simplification of the gradations of consonants with respect to the level of their basic
tone; only the maximum degree of softness was preserved, and consonants
with a lesser degree of palatalization hardened. The group "paired soft + *e*"
changed into "paired hard + *ə*." After the generalization of the maximally soft
consonants, in place of the older *e* and *ie͡*, there was a single vowel: the short
variant equal to *e* and the long variant equal to *ie͡*. As a parallel to this, the
quantitative variants *u͡o* and *o* came into being.

The short-vowel system takes on the following shape:

$$
\begin{array}{ccc}
\text{i, y} & & \text{u} \\
& \text{e, ə} \quad \text{o} & \\
& \text{a} &
\end{array}
$$

The next phase saw the merger of *y* and *i*, and of *ə* with *e*, in connection with
the standardization of the tonal height of consonants.

The transformation of the long vowel system is more complicated.

The long-vowel system was characterized by a clearer tendency to preserve
distinct phonemes of a single vowel height. When the inherent tonality of
consonants was standardized and a paired soft followed by a front vowel
had to be eliminated, the only way to maintain the phonological difference
between a front vowel and the corresponding unrounded back vowel was
to diphthongize one of them. The second component of a Czech diphthong
reproduces the height of the long vowel that the diphthong goes back to.
However, a descending diphthong was possible only if its first vowel component did not have a long correlate. The central Czech dialect on which the
literary language is based preserves the difference between unrounded mid
vowels and had to sacrifice the distinction between the corresponding high
vowels (*ī, ȳ*):

$$
\begin{array}{cc}
\bar{\imath} & \bar{u} \\
i͡e & u͡o \\
\bar{e} & \bar{a}
\end{array}
$$

Subsequently, *i͡e* > *ī* and *u͡o* > *ū*. In tabular form:

$$\bar{\imath} \quad \bar{u}$$
$$\bar{e} \quad \bar{a}$$

Unpaired $\widehat{ue}$ is outside the system of simple phonemes.

The other central Czech dialects preserved the distinction between the high unrounded vowels, while the distinction between the corresponding mid vowels was eliminated ($\widehat{\partial}$ merges with $\widehat{ie}$):

$$\bar{\imath} \qquad \widehat{\partial i} \quad \widehat{ou}$$
$$\widehat{ie} \qquad \widehat{uo}$$
$$\bar{a}$$

After the monophthongization of the descending diphthongs, the vowel system assumed the following shape:

$$\bar{\imath} \qquad\qquad \bar{u}$$
$$\widehat{ei} \quad \widehat{ou}$$
$$\bar{a}$$

The nature of the system can be seen by looking at the correlations that Czech, in the final analysis, either eliminated or retained. The eliminated oppositions were "pitch accent ~ unaccented" (also absent in German), "intensity accent ~ unaccented" (accent has stabilized in German, as in Czech, on the first syllable of the word; the difference is simply that in German a compound is treated not like a simple word but as a word group, while Czech does the opposite, following the Proto-Slavic tradition). The correlation "length ~ shortness of vowel" survives (as in German). In other words, in its selection of correlations Czech follows the German model. In cases of a phonological "crossroads," Czech has chosen as its alternative the path that had a parallel in German (cf. §6.1).

6.5   Changes in Western Bulgarian and the Confrontation of These Changes with Those of Czech

Western Bulgarian has neither pitch correlations nor phonological consonant softness. Palatalized consonants, other than those preceding a vowel, have hardened. There is a natural tendency that accompanies this: palatalized consonants, when admissible and if so, only as an extragrammatical category, must not have an inherent tonality which surpasses that of the vowels that follow them. Western Bulgarian, in contrast to Eastern Bulgarian, does not have a low vowel as its *ě* (*jat'*) reflex.

Between related dialects that have different correlations, transitional dialects very often arise that lack all the correlations that are absent from either one or the other of the two neighboring dialects. Thus, for example, the Eastern Slovak dialects and the extreme western branch of Ukrainian, known as Rusnak, are a transitional zone of this type between Slovak and Ukrainian. The Rusnak dialect tends to lose the correlations "soft ~ hard consonant" and "intensity accent ~ unaccented" (Opyt 70), and the Eastern Slovak dialect has lost the correlation of vowel quantity. In both zones, the accent is fixed and falls on the penultimate syllable, while in the Czech and Slovak dialects that have preserved vowel quantity, the accent falls on the first syllable. Thus, as I have already observed, the change of initial accent to penultimate, which basically reinforces the accent, is probably linked to the loss of quantitative distinctions (Jakobson, *c* 51). The position intermediate between the dialects just discussed is analogous to that of Macedonian and Western Bulgarian, which lie between Serbian and Eastern Bulgarian. Only the elaboration of a South Slavic linguistic geography will permit a characterization of the entire range of transitional dialects, but it is already apparent that the fixed accent of Macedonian dialects is a clear case of transitionality. These dialects do not possess a single correlation that is present in Eastern Bulgarian but absent in Serbian (e.g., "soft ~ hard consonant," "intensity accent ~ unaccented"), nor do they have any that are present in Serbian but absent in Eastern Bulgarian (pitch or quantitative correlations). More distant from Serbian, from both the territorial and structural perspectives, is the group of Western Bulgarian dialects that opposes, to the Serbian correlation "pitch accent ~ unaccented," the correlation "intensity accent ~ unaccented" (identical to the one in Eastern Bulgarian). Typically, Western Bulgarian accent is considerably weaker than that of Eastern Bulgarian (cf. Ščepkin, *c* 6). The tendency to limit the application of the "soft ~ hard consonant" correlation has also gained ground in certain Eastern Bulgarian dialects: final softs have hardened there, and the opposition is only in effect before *a*.

As far as the impetus leading to the elimination of the two concurrent correlations is concerned, for Western Bulgarian and Macedonian it would be difficult to reduce it merely to their intermediate position, and for Czech, merely to an imitation of the German model. Does a common impulse exist in both cases? The languages that lack both "soft ~ hard consonant" and pitch correlations are located between the Slavic zone that has preserved pitch correlations and lacks phonological softness, and the zone that possesses phonological softness but has lost pitch correlations. The Czecho-Slovak zone is situated between the Serbo-Slovene zone and the Lekhitic-Sorbian-Russian zone; Western Bulgarian is situated between Serbian and Eastern Bulgarian. The loss of weak *jers* spread from the Southwest of the Slavic world toward the Northeast (Trubetzkoy, *d* 308). This direction of movement is very clear within the boundaries of East Slavic (cf. §7.4). Texts clearly attest that the loss of weak *jers* was experienced by the South Slavic languages and Czech well before it penetrated into Russian. One can reasonably assume that the process was older in the Serbo-Slovene group than in Bulgarian and Czech. For Slovene, at least, there are indications in the documents. The Freising fragments testify that Slovene had already undergone changes that were not yet found either in Czech, as far as we can judge from the Kiev Missal, or in Bulgarian, judging by the oldest Old Church Slavonic texts of the Bulgarian recension. Within the Serbo-Slovene group, the loss of the "soft group ~ hard group" correlation preceded the loss of weak *jers* (cf. §3.18) and caused the vocalic system to lose its equilibrium, thus possibly stimulating the tendency toward elimination of the *jers*. The next zone, which comprised Czecho-Slovak and Western Bulgarian, reproduced the loss of weak *jers* and therefore found itself faced with the conflict between pitch correlations and the "soft ~ hard consonant" correlation as a result, which inevitably led to the suppression of the former (cf. §6.3). As for the latter, it is possible that one of the initial impulses toward its elimination was the Serbo-Slovene model. During the expansion of the fall of the weak *jers* to further Slavic regions, the "soft ~ hard consonant" correlation managed to become established in these zones and thus erected a geographical barrier to its elimination.[9]

6.6 Changes in Northern Kashubian and the Problem of the Accentological Periodization of West Slavic

Northern Kashubian originally followed the Polish-Sorbian type of evolution. In sum, the "pitch accent ~ unaccented" correlation was lost and the "soft ~ hard consonant" correlation was established, with the intensity accent becoming extragrammatical. The accent became fixed according the following law: "If the final syllable was long or high, and preceded by a single short syllable, the accent fell on the final syllable; if the final was long or high, and preceded by a single long syllable or more than one syllable, the accent fell on the penultimate syllable; if the final was a short and low vowel, the accent fell on the antepenultimate, or, by default, on the initial syllable" (Bubrix 99–100). The correlation "length ~ shortness of vowel" was maintained. Subsequently, "the differences of quantity changed into differences of quality" (Lorentz, *a* 23). An originally concomitant difference—the opposition "high—low vowel"[10]—changes into a correlation, while the original correlation "length ~ shortness of vowel" becomes a concomitant difference and length goes from an autonomous phonological element to being an accessory mark of the high vowel and its individual duration. The conditions for the stabilization of accent directly depended on the facts of quantity for Northern Kashubian; as the phonological differences of quantity were being lost, the law that governed this stabilization became petrified and changed into a traditional and unmotivated rule, and the stabilization of the intensity accent itself lost its original coercive force.

Bubrix claims that there was undoubtedly a past break in the way speakers perceived the facts of accentuation. "At the start, there was the sense that the accent was on the word-final, penultimate syllable, etc. However, next came the perception of the accent on the desinence, on the final root syllable, etc. The break in speakers' perception of the value of the accent must have been based on some objective factor" (102). Bubrix considers that "the first disturbances leading to the adjustment of accent, which occurred in order to mark the morphological element to which a syllable belonged," are sufficient to account for the genesis of this break, where the disturbance was caused by the complex nature of the phonetic law. While I agree with Bubrix's interpretation of the evolution of Northern Kashubian accent, I depart from his explanation of the causes for the change. The change from fixed accent to free accent, just like the opposite change, is an essential reform of the phonological system. Grammatical analogy is not sufficient in and of itself to cause a phonological correlation either to come into existence or to disappear (cf. Jakobson, *b* 815). If grammatical analogy was able to provoke accentual disturbances, this means that the law governing the stabilization of Northern Kashubian accent stopped functioning and that the accent was no longer perceived as fixed. These two facts could only have occurred during the time of the loss of the correlation "length ~ shortness of vowel," since the position of the fixed accent in Northern Kashubian, as shown by Bubrix, was bound to the distribution of long and short vowels within the word.

In Northern Kashubian, the quantitative differences between high vowels and the corresponding low vowels normally existed under accent. However, in unaccented syllables, these differences were more or less obliterated, due to the quantitative reduction of unaccented vowels; and here, the quantitative opposition between high vowels and the corresponding low vowels is more of a potential relationship that is only realized under special conditions (emphasis, etc.). Within a word, the concomitant difference can be described not as "length ~ shortness" but as "ability ~ inability to be lengthened." Northern Kashubian has another tendency and another concomitant difference between high and low vowels under accent: "falling intonation—falling-rising intonation (or simply rising?)" (see Lorentz, *b* 168ff., *a* §73; Bubrix 119). This new difference permits the linguistic consciousness to perceive the existing differences and their mutual interrelations in a new way, shown in tables 6.1 and 6.2.

In place of the old correlations of "intensity accent ~ unaccented" and "high ~ low vowel," the correlations "pitch accent ~ unaccented," "one ~ another intonational structure," and "length ~ shortness of vowel" were established. The natural result of this phonological restructuring was the loss of the incompatible correlation "soft ~ hard consonant"; thus, original *t'*, *d'*, *s'*, *z'*, *l'* were changed into hard *c*, *ʒ*, *s*, *z*, *l* (Lorentz, *a* §49). Unpaired softs—the hushers—also hardened (op. cit. §51); the soft labials developed a following soft unpaired consonant, to which they transmitted their soft character, for example, a *j* with various nuances or a *š* that later hardens (op. cit. §59). The difference between palatal *ň* and hard *n* is a relation of disjunctive phonemes.[11]

It is very probable that direct or indirect contact with the Germanic world was able to provide all the West Slavic languages of the time with a model for eliminating the correlation "intensity accent ~ unaccented." A study that is more attentive to the relations of quantity in the various West Slavic languages could possibly provide suggestive data for determining whether there existed a Common West Slavic standard for the stabilization of accent. There are reasons to believe that the modern Polish accent on the penultimate followed

Table 6.1

Old prosodic relationships

Phonological differences	Concomitant extragrammatical differences
Intensity accent, high vowel	Pitch accent, falling intonation, vowel length
Intensity accent, low vowel	Pitch accent, falling-rising intonation, vowel shortness
Unaccented, high vowel	Unaccented pitch, length = ability to be lengthened
Unaccented, low vowel	Unaccented pitch, shortness = inability to be lengthened

Table 6.2

New prosodic relationships

Phonological differences	Concomitant extragrammatical differences
Pitch accent, falling intonation, vowel length	Intensity accent, high vowel
Pitch accent, falling-rising intonation, vowel shortness	Intensity accent, low vowel
Unaccented pitch accent, length	Unaccented, high vowel
Unaccented pitch accent, shortness	Unaccented, low vowel

an accentological type analogous to that of Czech, that is, with accent on the first syllable (see Lehr-Spławiński 177ff.; Muka, *a* 148ff.). The confrontation of the Southern Kashubian accent on the first syllable with the history of Northern Kashubian accent tempts one to pose the question of whether the Southern Kashubian accent, and, similarly, the first-syllable accent of the other West Slavic languages, goes back to a more complex accentological type, where the stabilization of accent is found to be more tightly linked to the relations of quantity in the interior of the word.

The restoration of pitch correlations that is claimed for Northern Kashubian is an exceptional fact in the Slavic world. The curious thing is that, other than along the Baltic coast, pitch correlations exist only in Serbian and Slovene; however, the role that they play in these languages, which inherited them from Proto-Slavic, is considerably more limited than in the latter. However, the majority of languages on the Baltic have pitch correlations. Such is the case in the Baltic linguistic family—Lithuanian, Latvian, and Old Prussian (now extinct)—and it is the case in Northern Kashubian, Swedish, Norwegian, the Danish dialect of East Schleswig and neighboring islands (see Kock §69), some Baltic German dialects (see Leskien 11), and Estonian (see Polivanov 169ff.). It is characteristic that in all these Baltic coast languages, except for the Baltic family, the pitch correlations are an innovative formation. Thus, outside of the Baltic region, pitch correlations are foreign to the Germanic languages—and even to Icelandic and Faroese, very close relatives of Norwegian (Kock §60). They even tend to disappear in Western Norwegian (op. cit. §59); they do not exist in Southern Kashubian, nor in Polish, nor in the languages related to Estonian, the other Finnic languages. Thus, along with the Far East and Africa, one can assume a third "habitat" for these correlations, namely, the Baltic coast.

Annotations to Chapter 6, Consequences of the Loss of Weak *Jers* for the Slavic Languages

6.1 Loss of Weak *Jers* as a Factor in the Breakup of Proto-Slavic

In this chapter, Jakobson deals with *jer*-fall and the phonological consequences that were forced upon the various Slavic systems by this event. Let us briefly review some of the reasons why this was so important to the history of Slavic phonology. Prior to *jer*-fall, syllables were in a synharmonic relationship, in which syllables were generally open and each syllable contained elements of similar tonality—either a soft (palatal or palatalized) consonant plus a front vowel, or a hard (nonpalatal or nonpalatalized) consonant plus a back vowel. If we assume that one syllable contained a soft consonant plus a front *jer*, but another syllable contained a paired hard consonant plus a back *jer*, the phonemic difference between the two syllables would lie equally in the consonant and the vowel as a synharmonic unit. However, if the *jers* were to disappear in word-final position, for example, the language would be at a crossroads: either lose the phonemic distinction or initiate independent consonant palatalization without the participation of a vowel. To give an actual example, *danʼь* 'tax' vs. *danъ* 'given, past pass. part.' was set to change to *danʼ* vs. *dan* after *jer*-fall, unless something else intervened. (As an English example of phonological deletion of a reduced vowel, consider the word *police*: [pəlís] (explicit code) vs. [plís] (rapid-speech elliptical code). While this reduction would not upset the system of English phonology, it may give an idea of the change involved in Slavic *danʼь/danъ* > *danʼ/dan*.) Some Slavic zones (e.g., East Slavic) maintained this opposition by incorporating phonemic consonant palatalization into their systems, which entailed changing the relationship of a large number of consonants and vowels—that is, a restructuring of the whole system. Other Slavic zones (e.g., Serbo-Croatian and Slovene) prefigured this change by an intervening loss of palatalized consonants before front vowels, which meant that they never went on to develop phonemic consonant palatalization; on the other hand, they were able to maintain prosodic tonality (i.e., phonemic pitch), which was lost elsewhere. As adherents of Jakobsonian linguistics might say, there was a choice between phonemic consonant tonality and phonemic prosodic tonality.

The above example illustrates several of the main points Jakobson makes in this chapter. A seemingly small change, based on a style of rapid speech taking over as the norm, wound up causing major changes in the various Slavic systems. Since the loss of *jers* was so slow, lasting from the tenth to the thirteenth centuries as it moved across the Slavic map, each zone reacted to it in its own way and at a different time. More than anything else, the fall of the weak *jers* caused the breakup of Common Slavic into the separate Slavic languages and, for this reason, Trubetzkoy aptly considered it to be the last event of Common Slavic, as Jakobson mentions.

As Jakobson notes, a given dialect A might have been undergoing *jer*-fall for a long time and have had time to prepare for the phonological consequences, but a neighboring dialect B might have come into contact with the process in a more abrupt manner, without much time to restructure its system. In addition, one zone might have used a foreign model to resolve the phonological issues, in contrast to another zone. Simply put, each small zone of the vast Slavic-speaking world had the potential to deal with *jer*-fall in its own systemic way, and that has created many of the differences between the Slavic languages and dialects that have survived to the present day.

6.2 Consequences of the Loss of Weak *Jers* for the Correlation "Voiced ~ Voiceless Consonant"

Jakobson next examines the consequences of weak *jer*-fall for the features of consonant voicing, consonant palatalization, accent, and quantity, then considers certain specific issues in several Slavic zones. With respect to the voicing feature, Jakobson mentions that weak *jer*-fall brought in newly closed syllables, creating the potential for new oppositions of voiced vs. voiceless consonants. (Prior to *jer*-fall, the voiced/voiceless opposition was restricted to prevocalic and presonorant position.) The potential word-final opposition of voiced vs. voiceless was not realized in most Slavic zones, such as Russian, due to the later devoicing of obstruents in word-final position. However, some Slavic languages, such as Ukrainian and Standard (Štokavian) Serbo-Croatian, do have the word-final voicing opposition, which arose as a result of *jer*-fall.

6.3   Consequences of the Loss of Weak *Jers* for the Correlation "Soft Group ~ Hard Group" and Subsequently for Accent and Quantity

Jakobson devotes this section to discussing how *jer*-fall affected palatalized consonants, specifically, the opposition between nonpalatalized and palatalized. Due to the absence of the critical vowel component in final syllables from which a weak *jer* had been lost, each zone had to deal with the novel situation of an independent hard or soft consonant, without a redundantly back or front vowel following it. As Jakobson observes, hard and soft paired consonants went from being predictable, combinatory variants to being autonomous. If the opposition of consonant palatalization becomes autonomous in the independent word-final position, this leads to the phonemic weight being located within consonants even in nonfinal position, which, in turn, deprives the front-back vowel opposition of its independent status and makes the choice of a front or back vowel a function of the preceding soft or hard consonant. In other words, the language faced a choice of whether consonant or vowel tonality would prevail as the distinctive, autonomous feature.

Jakobson adds important comments on how this development related to the accentual system. He states that accentual tonality (i.e., the pitch opposition between two types of syllables under accent—rising and falling) was incompatible with phonemic consonant palatalization, since the former involved two types of vocalic tonality and the latter opposed two types of consonant tonality. The options for all the Slavic languages were (1) to lose the consonant tonality (palatalization) and retain the pitch opposition (e.g., Serbo-Croatian and Slovene); (2) to do the opposite, that is, lose pitch but develop phonemic consonant palatalization (e.g., East Slavic); or (3) to lose both features and have neither the pitch opposition nor phonemic consonant palatalization (e.g., Czech, Slovak, and Macedonian). Jakobson notes that the Serbo-Croatian-Slovene zone of southwest Slavic lost consonant palatalization prior to *jer*-fall, which ensured a smooth transition to a system with no phonemic palatalization but with phonemic pitch in the vowel system. Otherwise, the features of consonantal and vocalic tonality would have existed simultaneously, leading to systemic instability and the possibility of losing both features.

In later chapters, Jakobson refers to the potential conflict between the incompatible features of phonemic consonantal palatalization and phonemic pitch as *conflict A*. This situation is important insofar as it is often followed by a second, related conflict. Phonemic pitch was accompanied by phonemic vowel quantity in Common Slavic and in those languages that retained phonemic pitch (Serbo-Croatian and Slovene). However, if phonemic pitch lost the distinction between rising and falling accents and became a phonemic intensity accent, then a new systemic conflict (known as *conflict B*) arose between intensity accent and vowel quantity, which Jakobson also viewed as incompatible. A brief explanation of the incompatibility goes back to the notion that long vowels were considered to be two moras in length and the pitch distinction opposed first-mora accent to accent on the second mora of the same syllable. In other words, phonemic pitch allowed for an accent not just on any word syllable, but in fact on any word mora, which created the joint system of free quantity and phonemic pitch. If free quantity were to combine with intensity accent, then each two-mora syllable would have to accent the same mora. There would be no *intra*syllabic freedom of accent, yet any syllable could bear the accent, so there would be an *inter*syllabic freedom of accent. Thus, the mismatch between intersyllabic free accent and intrasyllabic fixed moraic accent led to a situation in which the combination of phonemic quantity and phonemic intensity accent was extremely rare in the Slavic languages and dialects, causing Jakobson to regard these features as incompatible.

At the end of the section, Jakobson summarizes the results of the two potential conflicts. Serbo-Croatian and Slovene eliminated consonant palatalization prior to *jer*-fall and retained both phonemic pitch and quantity. East Slavic eliminated phonemic pitch in favor of consonant palatalization and was potentially left with an incompatible system of phonemic intensity accent and phonemic quantity, after which it opted to eliminate phonemic quantity, leaving the system of phonemic consonant palatalization and intensity accent that now exists. However, there are many important zonal differences in the progression of this evolution in East Slavic, which Jakobson presents in great detail in the next chapter.

West Slavic, the other major zone that eliminated phonemic pitch, was also left with the incompatible features of phonemic intensity accent and phonemic quantity. However, in contrast to East Slavic, this zone opted for phonemic quantity and developed a fixed and predictable accent, rather than a phonemic accent. In most of West Slavic, the accent was fixed on the first syllable of the word, using the model of Common Slavic words with falling pitch. Thus, word accent per se was not eliminated, and when Jakobson speaks of incompatibility, he does not mean phonetic incompatibility, but phonemic incompatibility. A fixed, nonphonemic, and predictable initial accent could be combined with phonemic quantity. This system can still be seen in Czech and Slovak, although in Modern Polish, fixed accent is manifested as penultimate accent, rather than initial, and phonemic vowel quantity has been lost.

6.4   Changes in Czech

In sections 6.4 and 6.5, Jakobson deals with the reaction to *jer*-fall in Czech and Western Bulgarian, respectively. The significance of these sections can be best appreciated by reading the final paragraphs of section 6.5. The essence of the Czech and Western Bulgarian reactions to *jer*-fall is that these zones were geographically transitional between the initial *jer*-fall zone in the extreme Southwest (the Serbo-Croatian and Slovene zone) and the final *jer*-fall zone in the Northeast (the Lekhitic-Sorbian-East Slavic zone). One of Jakobson's major points is that the extreme Southwest was able to prepare its system for *jer*-fall by first losing consonant palatalization, paving the way for a smooth process and the retention of phonemic pitch, since no incompatibility existed with consonant tonality and palatalization was absent. The extreme Northeast, particularly Russian, was able to do the opposite: lose phonemic pitch and phonemic quantity prior to *jer*-fall and thus avoid a conflict with consonant palatalization as well, with phonemic consonant palatalization and intensity accent taking over as distinctive features. Figures 6.1 and 6.2 illustrate the direction of *jer*-fall and some of its consequences, as depicted by Jakobson.

Czech and Western Bulgarian had systemic conflicts and were not able to prepare their systems for *jer*-fall in advance. Therefore, neither zone was able to preserve either phonemic consonant palatalization or phonemic pitch.

As Jakobson shows in his detailed review of the history of its vowel system in this section, Czech underwent a number of changes to preserve phonemic oppositions that would have been lost if all consonant palatalization had simply been eliminated. In a sense, the Czech system cut its losses by preserving the phonemic distinction of palatalized consonants only preceding vowels of the highest degree of tonality, such as *i* and the $\widehat{ie}$ diphthong, but not *e*. Thus, the reflex of the front nasal ($ę > ä$) is complex in Czech. Before hard consonants, *ä* lost its ability to palatalize, the preceding consonant hardened, and *ä* backed to *a*. In other environments, *ä* joined the $\widehat{ie}$ diphthong, which allowed the preceding consonant to maintain softness. However, Czech palatalized consonants could not maintain their purely palatalized quality, which was a supplementary articulation overlaid on another, such as dental. Their softness could only be preserved by the change from palatalized to palatal, with a new single point of articulation (e.g., in the case of *t'* and *d'*, which became palatal stops, and *n'*, which changed from a palatalized dental nasal to a palatal nasal). Parenthetically, we can observe that Polish has also modified its palatalized dentals, having developed palatal affricates and a palatal

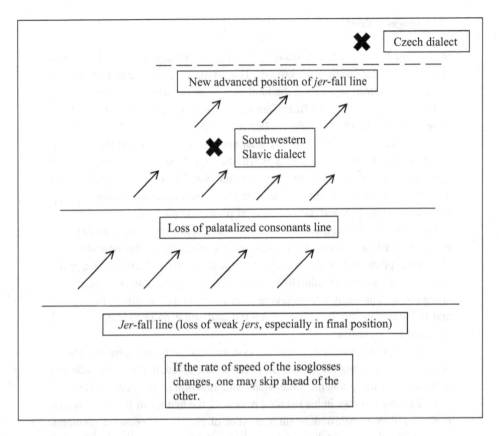

Figure 6.1
Depiction of how one isogloss (*jer*-fall) can move at a greater rate of speed and overtake another (loss of consonant palatalization), creating differences of rule order in different zones

nasal, but has retained purely palatalized labials in some dialects. However, this change considerably postdates *jer*-fall, after which the evidence supports the presence of true phonemic consonant palatalization in Polish, as described by Jakobson (see Stieber 1962, 61–64).

Jakobson also establishes some rules for the development of the falling diphthongs in the Czech literary language, as opposed to Czech dialects. The dialects could undergo the simple changes *ȳ > ej* and *u > ou*, but only the latter entered the vowel system of literary Czech as an unpaired entity. Jakobson's reason for this is quite interesting. He explains that a falling diphthong could only develop if its first component did not already exist as a long/short quantitative pair. In the case of *ej*, the first element *e* did exist and was retained by literary Czech as both long and short *e*, but the dialects with *ej* lost the long

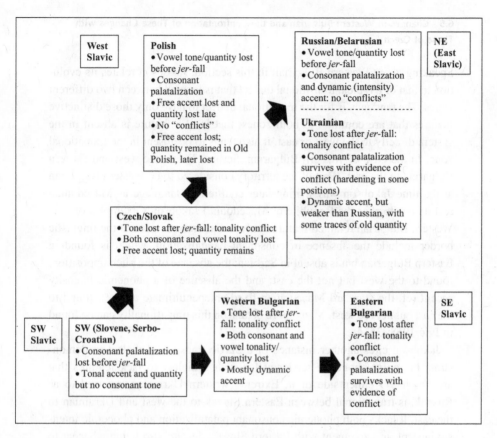

Figure 6.2
Depiction of *jer*-fall isogloss from southwest to northeast and southwest to southeast

ē and were able to integrate *ej* into their system. Literary Czech was able to develop *ou*, since long *ō* is not part of the vowel system, being found only in isolated loanwords.

Jakobson's detailed treatment of the Czech vowel system is somewhat off the main topic of the book. One of his most important points about Czech is that whenever there was a choice between two alternative phonological solutions, it opted for the one that matched the co-territorial German language system, which served as a model. This applied to the pitch opposition; the free intensity accent, which changed to a fixed first-syllable accent; and the survival of vowel quantity.

6.5   Changes in Western Bulgarian and the Confrontation of These Changes with Those of Czech

Speaking about Western Bulgarian in this section, Jakobson relates its evolution to that of a typical transitional dialect that is located between two different zones. The tendency is for the transitional dialect to have only those distinctive features that are common to both zones; that is, if a feature is absent in the system directly to the west or east, it also tends to be absent in the transitional zone. In the case of Western Bulgarian, Serbian lies to the west and Eastern Bulgarian to the east. (Part of the territory considered to be Western Bulgarian at the time Jakobson was writing later codified its language as Macedonian and its territory as the Republic of Macedonia.) Jakobson's examples of how Western Bulgarian retained features only found on both sides of the linguistic border include the absence of consonant palatalization, which is found in Eastern Bulgarian but is absent in Serbian; the absence of the pitch opposition, found to the west but not the east; and the absence of a phonemic intensity accent (cf. the standard Macedonian fixed antepenultimate accent), found to the east but not the west. Many more details on this transitionality can be found in Ivić 1958, 35–44.

Jakobson cites another instance of a Slavic transitional dialect to demonstrate his point about the tendency for such a dialect to lack features that are absent on either side of it. Extreme western Ukrainian, referred to as Rusnak, is transitional between Eastern Slovak to the west and Ukrainian to the east. It lacks both phonemic consonant palatalization and phonemic intensity accent, in agreement with Eastern Slovak, despite also being adjacent to Ukrainian.

6.6   Changes in Northern Kashubian and the Problem of the Accentological Periodization of West Slavic

Jakobson devotes this section to the Northern Kashubian dialect. I would suggest that he has two main purposes for this, in the context of his goals in this book. In the first place, Northern Kashubian had the most complex rules for establishing fixed accent of any Slavic zone. They were based on the quantity and the closed or open status of the final syllable, as well as on the nature of the penult. Jakobson suggests that this may be a key to how the accent once stabilized on either the initial or penultimate syllable in the other West Slavic zones. He also suggests that the Polish abandonment of phonemic quantity may be linked to a change from fixed initial accent to fixed penultimate accent.

A second issue relates to the fact that Northern Kashubian, like the rest of Lekhitic, eliminated the phonemic pitch opposition and established phonemic consonant palatalization, as a result of *jer*-fall. However, Northern Kashubian, like several other dialects of various languages along the Baltic Sea coast, developed a secondary phonemic pitch in its vowel system. For Jakobson, this was an excellent test of whether the new phonemic pitch would also be incompatible with the phonemic palatalization of consonants. As it turned out, phonemic palatalization was lost after the newly created pitch opposition was established, indicating latter-day systemic incompatibility of phonemic pitch and consonant palatalization, long past the time of *jer*-fall.

Jakobson ends the chapter by remarking that the Baltic Sea coast is one of the linguistic zones where phonemic pitch is found among several unrelated languages and dialects, on a par with the Far East and Africa.

7 The Establishment of the "Soft ~ Hard Consonant" Correlation in Russian and Other Slavic Languages, and Related Facts

7.1 Treatment of Palatal Sonorants

A comparison of the evolution of the Slavic languages in the period of weak *jer*-fall permits us to distinguish the facts that accompany the correlation "soft ~ hard consonant."

All of the Slavic languages that have established this correlation, as opposed to those that have not, have lost the distinction between the palatal sonorants (represented as *rj, lj, nj*) and the corresponding palatalized consonants (*r, l, n*, which were followed by a front vowel, at least before the loss of weak *jers*). This phonological difference could be maintained as long as the palatalized consonants were only *combinatory* correlative variants, but it disappeared when they became *autonomous* correlative variants. The palatal sonorants changed into palatalized consonants. Examples are Russian *niz* [n'is] 'bottom', *niva* [n'íva] 'field', *ne* [n'e] 'not', *k nemu* [kn'imú] 'toward him', *kljast'* [kl'äs't'] 'swear', *volja* [vól'ə] 'will', *den'* [d'ɛn'] 'day', *kon'* [kon'] 'horse' (the same in Belarusian); Ukrainian *nyz* [nyz], *nyva* [nyva], *ne* [ne], *k nemu* [knemu], *kljasty* [kl'asty] 'swear', *volja* [vol'a], *den'* [den'], *kin'* [k'in'];[1] Polish *nizki* [ńisk'i] 'low', *niwa* [ńiva], *nie* [ńe], *k niemu* [kńemu], *las* [las] 'forest', *wola* [vola] 'will', *dzień* [ʒeń] 'day', *koń* [koń] 'horse' (the same in Upper Sorbian); Eastern Bulgarian *niz* [nis], *niva* [niva], *ne* [ne], *k nemu* [knemu], *ljas* [l'as] 'forest', *volja* [vol'a], *den'* 'day', *kon'* 'horse' (= *deń, koń*)[2] [ʒ = voiced palatal affricate, ń = palatal nasal—RF].

Conversely, the languages that did not adopt the correlation "soft ~ hard consonant" have all maintained the difference in question to a greater or lesser extent. Compare Serbian *niz, njiva, ne, k njemu, lan* 'flax', *volja, dan* 'day', *konj*; Slovene *niz, njiva, ne, k njemu, lan, wǫlja, dan, konj*; Western Bulgarian *niz, njiva, ne, k njemu, volja, den, konj*; Czech *ne* [ne], *k němu* (= [kňemu]), *tah* 'move', *ňadra* 'bosom' [ň is the symbol for a palatal nasal in Czech orthography but when the palatal nasal precedes the vowel *e*, the *háček* is written over the vowel; *ń* is the Polish and Sorbian orthographic symbol for the same sound—RF].

7.2   Treatment of the Opposition of Front and Back Vowels

The languages that did not adopt the "soft ~ hard consonant" correlation display an absence of the oppositions of front and back vowels as such (cf. Meillet, *a* 18–19; e.g., the Serbian, Slovene, and Czech fusion of *y* with *i*, of ъ with ь; and, in Serbian and Slovene, that of *ü* with *u*);[3] the only oppositions that were preserved, as disjunctive phonemic differences, were those that also had an accessory mark, "rounded—unrounded," in addition to their basic mark, "front ~ back vowel" (*e—o*), just like the pairs that were changed into oppositions based on the absence or presence of rounding or on difference in vowel height (e.g., Czech *i—u* < *ü—u*, Western Bulgarian and dialect Slovak *e—o* < ь—ъ, Western Bulgarian *e—a* < *ě—a*).

  Given that the Slavic languages with the "soft ~ hard consonant" correlation changed the "front ~ back vowel" opposition into a concomitant extragrammatical difference, there was an evident tendency in these languages to unify vowel phonemes. Let us examine the particular results of this tendency.

1. It led to a decrease in the difference between fronted and backed variants of vocalic phonemes, since the opposition of these variants had lost all phonological value (cf. Broch, *b* 124ff.).[4]

2. Insofar as the reciprocal opposition of front and back vowels was an indispensable element in the correlation "soft group ~ hard group," having the same value as that of the soft and hard consonant opposition, any generalization of the basic variant of a vocalic phoneme after an unpaired consonant was impossible. The groups "soft unpaired consonant + front vowel" and "hard unpaired consonant + back vowel" were inseparable from the other groups that realized this correlation, since the vowels of these groups were paired vowels and were strictly associated with the vowels that were also paired and combined with similarly paired consonants. However, since these vowels had been changed to combinatory extragrammatical variants, there could be a tendency to unify phonemes, which was realized in most cases by generalizing the basic variant of a phoneme in the environment following a hard unpaired consonant.

  The basic variant of the phoneme *i/y* was *i*. After unpaired hards (i.e., after velars), *y* > *i*. The velars softened in parallel fashion; these soft consonants, just like the soft velars that had recently arisen in the Slavic languages, due to progressive assimilation (Russian dialect *van'k'a* 'Van'ka (first name, short for Ivan)', *čajk'u* 'seagull', *ver'x'* 'summit'; Bulgarian dialect *majk'a* 'mother', *jezik'* 'tongue'), are combinatory variants of velars, which remain unpaired hards from the phonological point of view. Together with the preservation of *y* after paired hards, we find *i* after velars in Russian, Belarusian, Polish, and Sorbian.

The extragrammatical mark that accompanies the correlation "soft ~ hard consonant" is the fronted or, respectively, backed quality of the following vowel; the accessory distinctive marks that characterize the various vowel pairs lose all of their meaning and, where the phonetic conditions are favorable, these marks are eliminated in the interest of phonemic unification. The *e* becomes rounded—changing to a nuance more or less farther front than *o*, if this change is not blocked by the quality of the sounds following *e*. In Polish, the change of *e* to *o* only goes through before a hard dental—a neutral category that does not cause any change in the preceding vowel (cf. Trubetzkoy, *i* 237). In Russian and Sorbian, the change of *e* to *o* was blocked when *e* preceded a soft; that is, the tonality of the vowel could not be decreased between two consonants that were on a high basic level. In particular, the *e* before a soft was a higher vowel; it was not of the same height as *o*, and, consequently, it could not be interpreted as its fronted partner. In Russian, the change in question was preceded by the fusion of the pair strong *ь*—strong *ъ* with *e—o*, while in the West Slavic languages it occurred before the merger of strong *ь* with *e*. A similar change did not occur in the Slavic languages that lacked the correlation "soft ~ hard consonant." These languages systemically maintain the opposition "unrounded front vowel—rounded back vowel of the same height," and its basic distinctive mark is precisely the presence or, respectively, the absence of rounding.

In this examination of the vowel system changes linked to the establishment of the "soft ~ hard consonant" correlation, it would be worthwhile to analyze, in turn, the evolution of Ukrainian and Eastern Bulgarian.

7.3 Details of the Establishment of the "Soft ~ Hard Consonant" Correlation in Ukrainian

In order to clarify the Ukrainian facts, one must rigorously distinguish two categories of soft consonants:

1. Consonants with an adjusted basic tonality that matches the front vowels that follow them, and

2. Consonants with an elevated tonality that is not adjusted to the following phonemes; a consonant in this category either is not followed by a vowel at all or is followed by a vowel whose basic tonality is lower than that of the consonant (cf. Šaxmatov, *b* 21).

What was the inventory of these two categories at the moment of weak *jer-*fall? It is clear that the final softs belonged to the second group. This group also included the palatal consonants (soft unpaired), independently of what followed them. As for paired consonants followed by a front vowel, there is reason to assume two degrees of palatalization: an *i*-degree before a high vowel and an *e*-degree before all other vowels. The consonants of the *i*-degree matched the high front unrounded vowel (*i*) in their basic tonality, but they had a higher tonality than the corresponding high rounded vowel (*ü*). The consonants of the *e*-degree matched the mid front vowel (*e*) in their basic tonality and had a higher tonality than the low front vowel (*ä*). Before the complex vowel ($\widehat{ie}$), the consonants were of the *i*-degree and their basic tonality was greater than that of the following vowel, since it was higher than that of one of the vowel's components. Thus, the consonants with an "adjusted" softness comprised paired softs before *i* and *e*, while the "autonomous" softs included the same paired softs before *ü*, *ä*, and $\widehat{ie}$, or anywhere other than before a vowel, as well as unpaired soft consonants in all positions. The "autonomous" soft was felt by the Ukrainian linguistic consciousness to be a phonologically autonomous category, opposed to hard consonants. The front vowels that followed the "autonomously soft" consonants came to be evaluated differently: they changed from *combinatory correlatives* to a series of *extra-grammatical combinatory* variants. This appears to have been the relationship between *ü* and *u*, *ä* and *a*, and $\widehat{ie}$ (from *ē* in newly closed syllables) and $\widehat{ou}$ (from *ō* in newly closed syllables).

The unpaired softs were included in the category of "autonomously soft" consonants, and, in like manner, the *e* and *i* that followed them were viewed as combinatory variants of the phonemes *e/o* and *i/y*. The tendency to unify phonemes was realized: before hard consonants, $\widehat{ie}$ changed to $\widehat{uo}$, and *e*, preceded by an unpaired soft, changed to *o* (*mjuod* 'honey', *žona* 'wife'). The fact that along with *sjuol* 'village, gen. pl.', one finds *siel* 'sat down' (i.e., *ě* did not share the fate of the Proto-East-Slavic *ē* reflex before a hard consonant) can only be explained by the hypothesis that the *ě* in question was not identified with Proto-East-Slavic $\widehat{ie}$ < *ē* before hard consonants. It is most probable that *ě* was a higher diphthong, equivalent to $\widehat{ie}$ (< Proto-East-Slavic *ē* before a soft consonant): *s'i$\widehat{e}$l* 'sat down' (< *sělъ*), *s'i$\widehat{e}$mъ* 'seven' (< *sem'*), *s'iel* 'village, gen. pl.' (< *selъ*) > *s'uol*.

In Ukrainian, one can observe a tendency that corresponds to the change of *e* after unpaired softs, namely, the tendency to replace *y* by *i* after unpaired hards in most Ukrainian dialects (i.e., *ky* > *k'i*, etc.). Only one Transcarpathian dialect area has preserved *y* after velars. The change of *ky* to *k'i* was in effect prior to the fusion of *i* and *y*, as attested by preserved texts (cf. Durnovo, *h* 169).

It is characteristic that in the Ukrainian dialects that underwent the change of *ky* to *k'i*, the softened velars originating in this way continued to be viewed as combinatory variants of hard consonants. This is due to the facts that in the southeastern Ukrainian dialects, where groups of soft velars with *i* from *ūo* (*k'in'* 'horse') arose, soft velars preceding *i* from *y*, in contrast to the former, have become hard (*k'i > kï*; cf. Durnovo, *k* 171), and that the soft velars have become a phonological category because, in one and the same environment, when preceding one and the same phoneme (see §7.6), both soft and hard velars could occur.

The fate of "autonomous" soft consonants in Ukrainian was identical to that of soft consonants in all the Slavic languages that have the correlation "soft ~ hard consonant"; it is also identical to the fate of the vowels that they precede. It was a different matter for "adjusted" softs. In the other East Slavic dialects, as well as in Polish and Sorbian, one sees the systemic opposition to hard consonants not only of "autonomous" softs, but also of "adjusted" softs, which have merged with the former in an indivisible category. (One of the consequences of this was the tendency to change a soft consonant into a nuance that surpassed the tone of the following vowel.) In Ukrainian, only autonomous softs were conceived of as soft sounds, while consonants with adjusted softness were viewed as hard and objectively realized as such.[5] The function of the phonological terms of the opposition "paired soft + *i* (or, respectively, *e*)—paired hard + *y* (or, respectively, *o*)" was taken over by the vowels. Thus, the same vowels (*i—y, e—o*) were the focal point of two contrary tendencies: the tendency to change combinatory correlative variants after paired consonants into autonomous archiphonemes, and the tendency to change the combinatory correlative variants after unpaired consonants into combinatory extragrammatical variants.

The two processes were undoubtedly simultaneous; they were both just a single bundle of phonic phenomena; they both had the same constellation of facts of the phonological system as their point of departure: the terms of the correlation "soft group ~ hard group" were dissociated. On the one hand, the language was heir to the old correlation "soft ~ hard consonant," but, on the other hand, a tendency was at work that eliminated this correlation by using the vocalic components of the originally dissociated correlation in the role of the terms of a phonological opposition. This tendency was derived and reflects yet another tendency—an attempt to preserve pitch correlations (or, respectively, the quantitative correlation)—whose struggle with the tendency to institute the correlation "soft ~ hard consonant" in the language ended with the triumph of the latter. However, the field of application of this correlation was reduced, in comparison with the old correlation "soft group ~ hard group": the oppositions "soft consonant + *e* (or, respectively, *i*)—hard consonant + *o* (or, respectively, *y*)" were replaced by differences of the disjunctive phonemes *e*—*o* and *i*—*y*. Pitch correlations became extinct. The correlation "accented vowel ~ unaccented" subsequently acquired a new principle of division: instead of tonal height, now intensity accent. In turn, this causes the correlation "length ~ shortness of vowel" to disappear. One can assume that the totality of these processes, following the loss of weak *jers*, up to the change of *e, ie* to *o, uo* (in the conditions described above) and the hardening of paired softs preceding *i* and *e*, all occurred within the space of a single generation. In this generation, which began with the adoption of the traditional correlation "soft group ~ hard group," the system of oppositions that was called upon to replace this dissociated correlation was not able to definitively crystallize. The latter, not as yet totally removed from the linguistic consciousness, must have continued to exist as a conservative intention, which already was crossing paths with certain revolutionary tendencies, just as pretonic *e* still lives in the intention (or at least, in the linguistic consciousness) of cultivated middle-aged Muscovites, although in actuality this generation already pronounces *i*.[6] It is precisely in this sense that one should understand the thesis of the simultaneity of the processes in question: if the change of *e* to *o* had preceded the hardening of consonants preceding *e*, the latter process would not have been triggered (*t'o* would not have become *te*); if the hardening of paired softs before *e* had preceded the change of *e* to *o*, and if the autonomous archiphonemes *e* and *o* had succeeded in stabilizing in the linguistic consciousness, the preconditions for the change of *e* to *o* after paired softs would not have been present.

7.4 Dialect Split of East Slavic Due to Weak *Jer*-Fall

The fall of weak *jers* spread within the Russian linguistic territory, moving from southwest to northeast. Ukrainian underwent this process several decades earlier than did Northern Russian (cf. Šaxmatov, *c* 203ff.; Trubetzkoy, *d* 294ff.; Falëv 121). The phonological events experienced by the various dialects of East Slavic in connection with the loss of weak *jers* are part of a well-ordered picture:

1. The Southern Ukrainian dialects resolved the problems of reestablishing phonological equilibrium caused by weak *jer*-fall in an autonomous manner, without a ready-made model. Here, the fall of weak *jers* created a veritable battle between the "soft ~ hard consonant" correlation and the pitch correlations (conflict A). The struggle ended with the elimination of the latter. The result was the collision between the "intensity accent ~ unaccented" and

"length ~ shortness of vowel" correlations (conflict B), which ended with the triumph of the former.

2. The Northern Ukrainian dialects experienced conflict A, in connection with the loss of weak *jers*; however, the solution to conflict B was borrowed, with these dialects having taken the prepared formula for eliminating it from the dialects of the South. The evidence for the peaceful elimination of the conflict is examined below (§9.6).

3. In the dialects of Southern Belarusian, conflict A, caused by the loss of weak *jers*, was made harmless by copying the Ukrainian model. That is why Belarusian did not manifest the contrary tendencies that characterized conflict A in Ukrainian. The "soft ~ hard consonant" correlation could be established in the phonological system without hindrance. Conflict B had the same outcome as in the Northern Ukrainian dialects.

4. Northern Belarusian and 5. the dialects of Russian avoided conflicts A and B by making the elimination of pitch and quantitative correlations precede the fall of weak *jers*. The southern solutions to the phonological problems were thus reproduced in advance—even before the problems themselves might have arisen. These preventive measures ensured that the fall of weak *jers* could occur without a shock to the system. The dialects that lost the pitch correlations after the loss of weak *jers* diphthongized *o* and *e* in the syllable that had preceded the fallen *jers*, while the dialects with the reverse order of events naturally did not develop diphthongs of this origin and could not adopt them (Trubetzkoy, *d* 300). Consequently, the isogloss of the diphthongs that derive from *ō* and *ē* is identical to that of the loss of weak *jers* before the loss of pitch correlations. The area of this ordering of events takes in all of the Ukrainian dialects and the Southern Belarusian dialects. One must assume that the progression of the loss of weak *jers* was arrested for a certain period at this boundary line. P. N. Savickij has drawn my attention to the fact that from the western boundary of Russian up to the Don River, this isogloss more or less coincides with a geographic isoline that is particularly essential for agriculture: the isoline for 110 days of snowy crust, that is, one of the isolines that refers to the gradual increase in the severity of the Russian winter (see map 7 of Tanfil'ev, as well as Durnovo, *k*, map III—the northern boundary of diphthongs, and map II—the linguistic boundary of Russian and Ukrainian). The coincidence of the isoglosses of Russian and the winter isotherms is a fact that deserves a follow-up study.[7]

   The loss of pitch correlations, as well as the loss of weak *jers*, took place in Northern Belarusian earlier than in the Russian dialects (cf. §8.2).

The pattern described above sheds light on the fact that the phonology of the East Slavic dialects of the twelfth and thirteenth centuries was conditioned by the pace of the spread of weak *jer* loss and the innovations connected to it, going from the southwest toward the northeast. In the case of innovations that operated within the boundaries of distinct dialects, a typical trait was the absence of an internal linguistic cause for the isoglosses: they were conditioned by dialect boundaries. In the twelfth and thirteenth centuries, East Slavic did not yet have distinct a priori dialects, did not yet have unmotivated isoglosses and, in particular, did not have equally unmotivated isogloss bundles. During this entire period, there was no stoppage of isogloss expansion due to external causes, nor were there internal barriers limiting this expansion; there were only lines that held it back and slowed it down (cf. §8.1). The most palpable of these was the Russian-Ukrainian borderline, while Belarusian dialects were just a simple series of transitional areas between Ukrainian and Russian.

7.5 Phonological Details of Belarusian

In the period in question, there is not a single feature that can distinguish all of the Belarusian dialects from both Russian and Ukrainian dialects. There is not a single Northern Belarusian change that did not also take place in Russian. (On changes that were active in Russian but did not penetrate into Belarusian, cf. §§8.2–8.3.) It would be fictitious to operate with the notion of a Common Belarusian for the period under consideration. Furthermore, to a certain extent this notion remains fictitious to this day, at least with regard to phonology. Buzuk's atlas is very instructive in this respect. Its descriptions were summarized perfectly by Tesnière (284–285): "As one can see from his maps, and as he also states, isoglosses of features considered to be proper to Belarusian are independent of each other. In other words, between Russian and Belarusian there is no bundle of isoglosses, but only certain parallel isoglosses that run from the northwest to the southeast. Thus, the border between Russian and Belarusian is not abrupt, but of a progressive type, which means that there is essentially no boundary between Russian and Belarusian."

One can distinguish two basic layers of phonological facts in Belarusian:

1. Innovations of the twelfth and thirteenth centuries, which, as noted earlier, indicate the intermediate position of Belarusian dialects in the history of the expansion of Russian phonological innovations;

2. Innovations that are reflected in texts of the fifteenth and sixteenth centuries. There is no reason to suppose that these data appeared in the language much earlier than in writing. The attempt by Šaxmatov to interpret them as a

Lekhitic element, incorporated into prehistoric western East Slavic dialects, loses ground after the critical analyses of Porzeziński and Rastorguev (*a*). Nevertheless, the connection of these data to Polish is obvious. A Pole who speaks Russian, but who hasn't assimilated Russian phonology, pronounces hard *r* in place of Russian *r'*, since the soft correlate is absent in Polish; *ʒ'*, *c'* in place of Russian *d'*, *t'*, since the soft correlates of *d*, *t* have become affricated in Polish; and soft hushers in place of Russian *s'*, *z'*. In the Polish pronunciation, hard *č* corresponds to Russian *č'*, and the *jc* sequence, to the Russian *c* with prolonged occlusion.

Thus, the Polish pronunciation of Russian consonants turns out to be equivalent to the consonantal system of Belarusian. These specific features of Belarusian decrease from west to east, and there is no textual indication about them earlier than the fifteenth and sixteenth centuries, that is, before the period of the political, social, and intellectual hegemony of Polish in western East Slavic. The *dzekan'e* of Belarusian [pronunciation of palatalized *d'* as the palatalized affricate [dz']—RF], the hardening of *r'* and *č*, $\overline{c} > jc$, and the dialectal change to husher consonants thus have a simple explanation: these traits arose in western East Slavic in imitation of Polish—that is, as an aristocratic pronunciation of East Slavic. This partial Polonization subsequently expanded from the upper social strata to the lower strata and created few ripples, geographically, in its penetration of dialects where there has been no direct Polish influence. At the eastern periphery of the area of hardened *r*, there are dialects that have only hardened the adjusted soft *r* (cf. §7.3), that is, preceding *e* and *i* (see Rastorguev, *b* 42ff.; Buzuk 33). Parallel to the spread of phonological Polonisms was the spread of lexical items.[8]

7.6 Diphthongs and the Role of Prothetic *v* in Ukrainian

A natural consequence of the change of the low variety of $\widehat{ie}$ to $\widehat{uo}$ was the fusion of the *jat'* (*ě*) reflex and that of "*ē* followed by a syllable with a weak *jer*." (Concerning the new extragrammatical differentiation of nuances of $\widehat{ie}$, cf. Hancov, *b* 126.) The preservation of the unity of the phoneme $\widehat{ie}/\widehat{uo}$ was only possible on the condition that $\widehat{ie}$ (coming from *ě*) would change to *uo* before a hard consonant. The Slavic changes of *e* to *o*, or $\widehat{ie}$ (< *ē*) to $\widehat{uo}$, of ь to ъ, of *ě* to *a*, of *y* to *i*, etc., encountered an additional factor in the case of grammatical alternations. The change of the *ě* reflex to $\widehat{uo}$ could not be supported by a grammatical alternation. The phoneme $\widehat{ie}/\widehat{uo}$ would have been isolated in the phonological structure of Ukrainian; after the split of the phoneme *e/o*, the phonological separation of rounded and unrounded vowels became systemic, and, in order to avoid such a heterogeneous formation, initial *uo* took a prothetic *v*; consequently, $\widehat{uo}$ lost any chance of serving as the fundamental variant of the phoneme $\widehat{ie}/\widehat{uo}$, and the tendency to reduce $\widehat{ie}$ to $\widehat{uo}$ lost its force. Under identical conditions, between a soft and a hard consonant, both $\widehat{uo}$ and $\widehat{ie}$ were equally possible; that is, they had become two different phonemes. In Ukrainian texts from the end of the twelfth century and from the thirteenth, the first phoneme was written as *ě*, the second, in the absence of a special grapheme, was written as *e* after a soft consonant and *o* after a hard. This phonological differentiation resulted in the fact that neither *ie* < *ě*, preceding a hard consonant, nor *ie* < *ē*, preceding a soft consonant that hardened after weak *jer*-fall, changed to $\widehat{uo}$. (Cf. the Ukrainian texts of the twelfth and thirteenth centuries: *bězd'na* 'abyss', *trepět'no* 'anxiously', *plačěvnoje* 'lamentable', etc.; see Šaxmatov, *c* §455.)

The vowel system of Ukrainian during the period under discussion was as follows:

$$
\begin{array}{ccc}
\text{i} & \text{y} & \text{u} \\
\widehat{\text{ie}} & & \widehat{\text{uo}} \\
\text{e} & \text{a} & \text{o}
\end{array}
$$

The subsequent evolution was due to

1. The empty slot in the mid vowel height, and

2. The tendency to symmetry of opposed phonemes.

The phoneme $\widehat{ie}$ was higher than the phoneme $\widehat{uo}$. The latter reached its greatest height in the more fronted variants, which occurred preceding or following soft consonants: *üö* (cf. Hancov, *b* 129). In this sense, one sees an evolution of fronting and raising also for the other variants of the phoneme $\widehat{uo}$, which thus tends toward a symmetry of position with the phoneme $\widehat{ie}$ (op. cit. 127ff.). In the Northern Ukrainian dialects, the evolution of the phoneme in question stops at the following point: its combinatory and stylistic variants (or, optional variants, in the terminology of Baudouin de Courtenay) oscillate between $\widehat{uo}$ and *üö*, and even *üe* (op. cit. 131). An essential simplification was achieved by Northern Ukrainian: *y* merged with *i*, and the repertoire of horizontal oppositions was reduced to the series "front unrounded—back rounded":

$$
\begin{array}{ccc}
\text{i} & & \text{u} \\
\widehat{\text{ie}} & & \widehat{\text{uo}} \\
\text{e} & \text{o} & \\
& \text{a} &
\end{array}
$$

The evolution of Southern Ukrainian was more complicated. The fronting of the phoneme $\overline{uo}$, tending to reduce the opposition "front vowel—back vowel" to the opposition "unrounded vowel—rounded vowel," destroyed the equilibrium of the system as soon as it was introduced. This system underwent a restructuring in order to reestablish its equilibrium. The principle of the triple series (front unrounded vowel—back unrounded vowel—back rounded vowel) was maintained during the course of this restructuring: high unrounded vowels after hard consonants (*i* after hard consonant and also *y*) merged into a high vowel of the mixed vertical series, and diphthongs merged into a high vowel of the front series. The system took on the following look:

i   ï   u

e   a   o

In the western dialects of Southern Ukrainian, both paired hards and paired softs could occur preceding a front vowel; the group "hard + *i*" derives from the earlier sequence "hard + *o*"; *a* > *e* after soft consonants; the sequences "paired soft + *e*" can also come from original "long soft + *e*," by means of a contraction of the consonant (orthographic *žytje* 'life') [phonetic [žyt'e]; standard Ukrainian *žyttja*, phonetic [žyt't'a]—RF].

In the eastern dialects of Southern Ukrainian, consonants became soft preceding any *i* that came from a diphthong. High central *ï* is naturally viewed as a combinatory extragrammatical variant of high front *i*, conditioned by the environment following a hard consonant; typically, and quite objectively, *ï* is closer to *i* in the eastern dialects than in the western dialects of Ukrainian (cf. Durnovo, *k* 167). In the eastern dialects, among paired consonants, only the hards can be followed by *e*; the long softs have not contracted (i.e., they remain as unpaired softs, and *a* preceded by a soft consonant has not changed to *e*). Thus, both soft and hard consonants can be followed by *a*. The vowel system of the dialects in question is as follows:

Hancov has convincingly shown that the dialects situated between the Northern and Southern Ukrainian dialect zones, which have merged the diphthongs deriving from *ō, ē* as *i*, and which shortened long unaccented vowels even before the diphthongization, are the result of a later hybridization (*a* 20). It is quite probable that at the very beginning, the northern isogloss of *i* < *ē*, ō coincided with the southern isogloss of the shortening of unaccented long vowels and that, subsequently, we are dealing with the northward advance of the first of these isoglosses. Consequently, the merger of the diphthongs, together with the monophthongization, would only have originally occurred in the dialects where the reflexes of accented and unaccented *ē* and *ō* were identical. The diphthongs are not preserved, except in dialects that have a different reflex for accented and unaccented *ē* and *ō*. This relationship is not mere coincidence. The accented syllable is the point of maximum phonemic differentiation and the phonological separation of unaccented *e* and *o*, in alternation with *i͡e* and "*u͡o*" in the Northern Ukrainian dialect, was an obstacle to the complete merger of the latter. This obstacle did not exist in the Southern Ukrainian dialect.

In the Transcarpathian dialects, the phonemes *y* and *i* did not merge, and *y* was preserved as a distinct and autonomous phoneme; *i͡e* > *i*; and, depending on the dialect, "*u͡o*" became *u*, *i*, or *ü*.

There is a great resemblance between the structure of the southwestern vowel system and that of the "*u* dialect." In the latter, during the monophthongization of diphthongs, a system of two heights and three series was established: a series of unrounded front vowels, a series of unrounded back vowels, and one of rounded back vowels. However, these series, based on the existing data, were formed differently: the rounded vowels of the two greatest heights merged as *u*, while the corresponding front vowels formed combinatory variants of a single phoneme: *i* more fronted and high following a soft consonant (< *i͡e*) and in word-initial position (< *i*), but farther back and lower after a hard consonant (< *i*). The vowel system was as follows:

i   y   u
e   a   o

The vowel system of the other Transcarpathian dialects is close to that of Northern Ukrainian. Here is the system of the "*i* dialect":

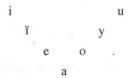

The sequence "hard consonant + *u͡o*" changes to the sequence "hard consonant + *i*"; in all other cases, the consonants preceding *i* are soft. Compared to *i*, the vowel *ï* is lower and approaches *e* under certain phonetic conditions (cf.

Durnovo, *b* 224). As for *y*, observers have remarked that it is intermediate between *u* and *o*, and that it is quite often more or less rounded (Durnovo, loc. cit.; cf. Broch, *d* 12–13 and others).

In the system of the "*ü* dialect," *ü* occupies the same relative position as the phoneme *ï* does in the *i* dialect, as the following vowel system indicates:

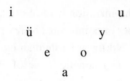

The composition of the *i* phoneme is the same here as in the *u* dialect; the articulation of *ü* is lowered (see Durnovo, *e* 159).

A characteristic tendency, possessed by the central core of Ukrainian dialects, is to simplify the vowel system (from six to five phonemes), while the vowel systems of the peripheral dialects each number seven phonemes (i.e., Northern Ukrainian dialects and the major part of the Transcarpathian dialects). This difference is due primarily to the conservative tendency that is typical of peripheral dialects, and secondarily to functional differences. It is not at all rare to observe that the tendency to simplify the phonological system grows as the geographical territory of the dialect increases, with the greatest variety of people speaking the generalized language. Linguistics has still not paid enough attention to the essential difference in structure and evolution that exists between dialects that gravitate toward the role of *koine*, or common language, and those of purely local usage. The Ukrainian dialects with seven vowel phonemes are typical local formations without any pretension to expand. Western Ukrainian, with six vowel phonemes and, especially, Eastern Ukrainian with five vowel phonemes are idioms that encompass a vast area (one need only glance at the map). The Transcarpathian dialect with six vowels is apparently a member of a linguistic alliance with a huge territory; geographically, it comes close to Eastern Slovak, where *ō* > *u*, and Polish, with its "*o* pochylone" sound. "It is difficult to say whether this reflex (of *u͡o*) was autonomously created on Ukrainian soil, whether it was in the proximity of neighboring dialects merely helping to maintain it, or whether its very creation was due to the influence of these dialects" (Kurylo, *c* 80).

7.7 Diphthongs and the Role of Prothetic *v* in Russian

The diphthongization of *ō* preceding fallen *jers* gave *jat'* (*ě*) a back partner in the phonological system. The southern diphthongal pair was able to serve as a model for the phonological system of Russian, a system that used different phonological material to create a corresponding pair *ie—u͡o* (*ie* coming only from accented *ě* and *uo* from *o*, under acute intonation) and that provided *u͡o* with a prothetic *v* (on the latter point see Trubetzkoy, *d* 313ff., Dolobko, *a*).[9] Trubetzkoy interprets "*o* with acute intonation" as a long *o* under a rising-falling intonation, with the rising portion longer and the falling portion shorter (op. cit. 302–303). I have no intention here of criticizing Trubetzkoy's Slavic accentology, where a number of points must be revised in light of the penetrating analysis of the state of Northern Kashubian by Bubrix. However, regardless of how one interprets the phonetic value of Proto-Slavic *o* under acute intonation, there is no reason to attribute the aforementioned characteristics, assumed by Trubetzkoy, to the Proto-East-Slavic ancestor of Russian *ô*. In the first place, there is no basis for deriving *ô* from a hypothetical Proto-Slavic long *o* under acute intonation, since even a recent *o*, in the Proto-East-Slavic *torot* < *tŏrt* sequence, goes to Russian *ô* (*morôz* 'frost', *korôva* 'cow'). The Ukrainian forms of the type *moroz*, in the context of the *i* < *o* of *narid* 'nation', attest that the recent *o* of Proto-East-Slavic *torot*, coming from *tort*, was short. It would be arbitrary to suppose that such an *o* lengthened in Russian under acute intonation. Second, there is no more basis for deriving *ô* from a rising-falling intonation with a longer rising portion and a shorter falling portion, given that in this case one would have no explanation for the *ô*, coming from recent Proto-East-Slavic *o*, in the sequence *torot* < *tŏrt*. The change of the *tort* sequence into a disyllabic group, according to Trubetzkoy's conception, was accompanied by the distribution of the old intonation across the two syllables. In the *tŏrt* type, this distribution is realized as in the following scheme:

(*a* 178). It would be arbitrary to suppose that the second half of this intonation changed to a new intonation with an initial long rising. It is simpler to interpret Proto-East-Slavic *o* under acute intonation > *ô* in Russian as an *o* under rising intonation. The change of *ő* (rising *o*) to a composite vowel with a higher onset is a manifestation of the tendency to substitute the inherent vowel tonality for the phonological role of pitch. O. Broch has claimed that if the vocal cords maintain the same tone from beginning to end while pronouncing *ô*, one has the impression of a rising tone, because the basic tonality proper to each portion of this composite vowel is higher than each preceding one (*c* 48). L. Vasil'ev prudently voices the hypothesis that in this case we may be dealing with the vestiges of an old rising accent (*a* 17). With this explanation, it becomes comprehensible that we do not have *ie* as the reflex of *e* under acute intonation, parallel to *u͡o* as the reflex of *o* under acute intonation. While *o* surpasses *u* in the height of its basic tonality, conversely, *i* is higher than *e*.

Thus, there was no possibility of changing the rising intonation of *e* into a sequence of one vowel with a basic low tonality plus another of higher tonality; falling diphthongs were foreign to the language.

Given that $\widehat{uo}$ could not appear after a soft consonant in Russian, the result of these facts was the formation of a phoneme $\widehat{ie}/\widehat{uo}$ with the equipollent variants of $\widehat{ie}$ after a soft consonant and $\widehat{uo}$ after a hard consonant. The absence of a basic variant of the phoneme, and of any grammatical alternation between $\widehat{ie}$ and $\widehat{uo}$, halted the tendency to unify the phoneme. Subsequently, the accented vowel system of Russian was dialectally restructured. The number of phonemes was maintained in the majority of dialects; prior to the restructuring they were *i, u, ($\widehat{ie}/\widehat{uo}$), (e/o), a*, and afterward *i, u, e, o, a*. In other words, two phonemes were merged and their extragrammatical variants were phonologically restricted. The front unrounded variant became one phoneme and the back rounded one became the other. In the western variety of Northern Russian dialects (cf. Opyt §22), the number of phonemes decreased: the phoneme $\widehat{ie}/\widehat{uo}$ was eliminated by means of raising the tone by one level ($\widehat{ie} > i, \widehat{uo} > o$); the phonemic system that was preserved is *i, u, (e/o), a*.

7.8 Diphthongs and the Role of Prothetic *v* in Northern Belarusian

Although the *jat'* (*ě*) of Russian received a partner and was maintained, by virtue of the diphthongization of *o* under acute intonation, the Northern Belarusian dialect was not able to create a diphthong either from *o* under acute intonation, since pitch correlations had been lost in this dialect, or from *o* in a syllable that preceded lost *jers* (cf. §7.4). The unpaired *ě* of Northern Belarusian merged with *e*. One finds confusions of *ě* and *e* in old texts of Northern Belarusian (cf. Karskij, II 234ff.; Šaxmatov, *c* 344). The dissimilative *akan'e* of Belarusian, contrary to certain types of *akan'e* in Southern Russian, also argues in favor of the identity of *ě* and *e* in Northern Belarusian, shortly after the fall of weak *jers* (cf. §9.3).

Northern Belarusian had its own reinterpretation of the Ukrainian and Russian pair, namely, as "one type of initial *o* with a prothetic *v*, as opposed to another type of initial *o*, without a prothetic" (cf. Buzuk 53). The relationships found in Russian are particularly favorable for this interpretation: in an accented syllable, there are two types of *o*, one of which has a prothetic *v*; but in an unaccented syllable, *o* never has a prothetic. If the prothesis preceding accented *o* had preceded the change of *ě* to *e*, one could then interpret these two facts as two stages in the realization of a single phonological tendency—the tendency to restrict *e* and *o*. Prior to the prothesis of *v*, *o* was the basic variant of the *e/o* phoneme; but, after this prothesis, the two variants were equipollent, and the tendency toward the unification of the accented *e/o* phoneme was halted. (On the fate of unaccented *e/o*, see chapter 9.) The fusion of accented *ě* and *e* changed *e* and *o* into autonomous phonemes. The prothesis of *v* occurred after the hardening of palatalized consonants preceding hard dentals (cf. Belarusian *sëdla* 'saddles', *cëmny* 'dark', *xrosny* 'godfather', etc.) and before that of palatal consonants (cf., on the one hand, Belarusian *adzeža* 'clothes', *dzešava* 'cheap', and, on the other, Russian *odëža* 'clothes', *dëševo* 'cheap', etc.).

The prothesis of *v* is the last change common to all East Slavic dialects, as stated by Trubetzkoy (*d* 316). Everywhere it occurred, this change contributed, to a greater or lesser degree, to the phonemic separation of unrounded vowels, which means that Trubetzkoy's (loc. cit.) assertion that in principle it introduced nothing new is inexact.

7.9 Evolution of Eastern Bulgarian Compared with Ukrainian

Eastern Bulgarian restructured the correlation "soft group ~ hard group" in conditions analogous to those of Ukrainian. It also incorporated the correlation "soft ~ hard consonant" into the system only as the result of a sharp conflict of incompatible correlations; here also, we see the effect of two contrary, conflicting tendencies, as in Ukrainian (cf. §7.3). This intersection of tendencies cannot be shown for the treatment of sequences of consonants with *e* and *o*, since Bulgarian had changed *e* and *o* to two distinct phonemes (cf. §4.3) prior to the loss of weak *jers*. On the contrary, one can demonstrate the change of *ь* to *ъ* after soft unpaired consonants, independent of the following consonants. This change affected not only the old *ь*, but the front-vowel reflex in nasal diphthongs as well. In this period, we must assume that *ъ* still maintained its rounding (examples taken from contemporary dialects: *šăv* 'seam', *šătam* 'walk', *žătva* 'harvest', *miličăk* 'dear', *jăzik* 'language'). Eleventh-century texts already contain an indication of the change of *ь* to *ъ* in the environment following a paired soft, at least when it was not part of a diphthong. Some of these texts still render weak *jers* more or less consistently in writing. If this means that the change of *ь* to *ъ* occurred prior to the fall of weak *jers*, with the correlation "soft group ~ hard group" in effect, the change in question would then be an absolutely unique fact in Slavic phonology. It is more probable to assume, following Kul'bakin (*b* §51), that the *jers* disappeared in word-final position earlier than in other positions. This is what would have caused the collapse of the correlation "soft group ~ hard group," making the correlation "soft ~ hard consonant" take over and making not only strong *ь*, but also weak *ь*, change to *ъ* after unpaired softs.

As in Ukrainian, only the soft autonomous sound was interpreted as a soft (softs in word-final position, softs preceding *ä* and *ü*, and unpaired softs in all environments); consonants with adjusted softness (i.e., paired softs preceding *e*, *ь*, *i*) were phonologically identified with hard consonants and even hardened in some dialects, while in others they continued to assimilate to the basic tonality height of the following high and mid front vowels, and they were felt to be combinatory variants of hard consonants (cf. Miletič, *a* 39). However, the languages that changed the correlation "soft group ~ hard group" following a prepared model (cf. §7.4) treated consonants with adjusted softness the same as consonants with autonomous softness, raising their degree of softness above the tonality of the following front vowels.

In Eastern Bulgarian, as in many Ukrainian dialects (cf. §7.6), it is the tripartite system of high vowels, *i*, *y*, *u*, that determined the structure of the entire system. This vowel height served as the model for grouping vowels of lower heights. It was necessary to have a front vowel (there were both *e* and strong *ь*, *ь* > *e*); an unrounded back vowel (*ъ* became unrounded and was maintained as an autonomous phoneme); and a rounded back vowel. We have the following pattern:

$$i \qquad y \qquad u$$
$$e \qquad ъ \qquad o$$
$$a$$

This system was simplified by merging *y* with *i*, or with *ъ* in some dialects:

$$i \qquad ъ^{10} \qquad u$$
$$e \qquad a \qquad o$$

The dialectal tendency to unite *u* and *i* in a single phoneme was probably linked to the change of *y* to *i*: initial *i* had a prothetic *j*, but when *i* was preceded by an unpaired soft, it sporadically changed into *u* (*žuv* 'alive', *šurok* 'wide', *jume* 'name'; cf. Ščepkin, *c* 10), while *u* changed to *i* when preceded by a paired soft (*klič* 'key', *libe* 'dear').

A particular structural resemblance to Ukrainian dialects can be seen in the vowel system of the Pavlikan dialect (see the description of Miletič, *b* 71ff.). Accented *e* and *o* were changed to *i* and *u* under unclear conditions. The entire picture of the change is confused: Miletič admits the possibility that its point of departure lay in the relations that closely resembled the conditions of diphthongization in Ukrainian (cf. *kun* 'horse (with *u* before lost *jer*)'—*konet* 'the horse (with *o* before vocalized *jer*)'). Unfortunately, the data presented by Miletič are not sufficient to make fully supported deductions, but it seems to me that one should rather seek the explanation for the qualitative differentiation in the old accentual conditions. The majority of examples of the change of old accented *o* to *u* imply an *o* under acute intonation. Let me cite parallel examples, taken from the Central Russian dialect, which has preserved the diphthongized reflex of *o* under acute intonation (see Šaxmatov, *e*): Bulgarian *kun* 'horse' (Russian *kôn'*), *dour* 'yard' (*dvôr*), *stuł* 'table' (*stôł*), *muj* 'my' (*môj*), *prúsăt* 'they request' (*prôs'ut*), *núsăt* 'they carry' (*nôsit*), *mujš, mújăt* 'is able' (*môžyt*), *uł* 'ox'. Exceptions: *gust* 'guest' (*gos't'*), *nušt* 'night' (*noc*), *sul* 'salt' (*sol'*). Old *i* and *y* merge in the Pavlikan dialect, resulting not in *i*, as in the other Bulgarian dialects, but in an *ï*-vowel, with a tonality, according to Miletič, that is quite similar to that of the Ukrainian *ï* (*b* 81). Just as in Ukrainian, consonants are hard when preceding *ï*, but the sequence "velar consonant + *y*" has changed to "soft consonant + *i*" (*k'i*, etc.) in the majority of Ukrainian dialects. However, in the majority of Bulgarian dialects, *y* after a velar has met the same fate as after other consonants. There is an indication of this in certain isolated Bulgarian dialects where *y* > *ă* (*kắtkắt'ä* = *kytkytě* 'bouquets', etc.; Miletič, *b* 170) and, similarly, in texts from the beginning of Middle Bulgarian, which systematically preserve *y*.

7.10 The Place of This Phonological Type on the Slavic Linguistic Map

The system of Slavic zones that formed as a result of the loss of weak *jers* is clearly delineated (cf. §§6.3, 6.5, and 7.4).[11] One can establish two opposite poles: that of Serbian (with a priori hegemony of pitch correlations) and that of Russian (with a priori elimination of pitch correlations and institution of the intensity correlation). The zone where the pitch correlations have triumphed has been judiciously separated from the zone where the "soft ~ hard consonant" correlation has been adopted by a third zone, where both of these correlations have been lost. The zone where the correlation "soft ~ hard consonant" has been adopted is divided into two domains: one with a priori elimination of pitch correlations and one with vestiges of the conflict between pitch correlations and the correlation "soft ~ hard consonant" (Ukrainian and Eastern Bulgarian). The second of these two domains is situated between the first zone and the zone where both correlations were lost.[12]

I have based my division of the Slavic linguistic territory on the results of processes, but if one takes the processes themselves as the point of departure as such, the classification will be somewhat modified. In this case, we distinguish the following zones:

1. The zone of the a priori hegemony of pitch correlations

2. The zone where pitch correlations conflict with the correlation "soft ~ hard consonant"

   a. Domain where the conflicting correlations are eliminated

   b. Domain where the correlation "soft ~ hard consonant" triumphed

3. The zone of the a priori elimination of pitch correlations

If one prefers a classification based on a compromise between the two preceding ones, the second zone can be divided in two, resulting in a four-zone system:

1. A priori hegemony of pitch correlations

2. Elimination of pitch correlations and of the correlation "soft ~ hard consonant"

3. Establishment of the correlation "soft ~ hard consonant," with traces of the conflict of this correlation with pitch correlations

4. A priori elimination of pitch correlations

Within the West Slavic area, the second zone is contiguous to the fourth, but an attentive study of the historical border of Czecho-Sorbian, the Czech Silesian dialect known as Laština, and Slovak dialects appears to permit the vestiges of the third zone to be discovered here as well. Thus, Bartoš describes a variety of the Laština dialect that is becoming extinct: the dialect of the northern area of Opava (97–139, especially 134ff.), where *e* changes to *o* after unpaired hard consonants (after *j*, *š*, *č*, *ř*, *c' < t'*, *ʒ' < d'*, after the palatals *l* and *n*), regardless of the following consonant (e.g., *joho* 'him', *jo = je* 'is', *šost* 'six', *vršok* 'hill', *žolezo* 'iron', *čolo* 'forehead', *křosny* 'christening', *plóćoš* 'you weave', *dźoň* 'day', *lon* 'flax', *ňosu* 'they are carrying'), but is maintained after paired softs (*s'*, *z'*, and labials), with simultaneous hardening of the consonants. The correlation "soft ~ hard consonant" exists (e.g., *oś* 'axle', *zaś* 'again', *kośba* 'mowing', *haluź* 'branch', *voź* 'transport by vehicle, impv.', *nośa* 'they carry', *śahać* 'touch', *źać* 'reap', *zavśu* 'village outskirts'; *s'*, *z'* preceding *e < ě*: *śeno* 'hay', *kože* 'goat, adj.'; *p'ata* 'heel', *v'az* 'bond').

Annotations to Chapter 7, The Establishment of the "Soft ~ Hard Consonant" Correlation in Russian and Other Slavic Languages, and Related Facts

7.1 Treatment of Palatal Sonorants

In this chapter, Jakobson deals with many of the specific details that were involved in the establishment of phonemic palatalization in East Slavic and the other zones—topics he treated in a more general way in previous chapters. Several sections deal with additional systemic changes implied either by the establishment of phonemic consonant palatalization or by the failure to establish it. So, for example, in this section Jakobson deals with the fact that there were three possible phonetic articulations of the basic sonorants *r, l*, and *n* in Common Slavic (nonpalatalized dental, palatalized dental, and palatal), yet no Slavic language could maintain more than two as phonemic units in the restructuring caused by *jer*-fall. In other words, two of the three merged in all of the Slavic languages, but the mergers were of two different types, represented by Jakobson's two lists of examples. The nonpalatalized dentals *r, l, n* were retained as phonemes in all Slavic zones. However, there were two possible fates for the palatalized type: either it merged with the palatal type (as in Russian, Ukrainian, Polish, and Eastern Bulgarian) or it merged with the nonpalatalized dental type (as in Slovene, Serbo-Croatian, Macedonian, Western Bulgarian, and Czech). The palatal and palatalized series can be described as follows:

1. Palatal sonorants came from original sequences of sonorants plus *j* and are conventionally represented as *rj, lj, nj* by many Slavicists (although they were actually single segments). That is, they are a single palatal flap/trill, a lateral, and a nasal, respectively.

2. Palatalized sonorants *r', l', n'* came from sonorants that preceded front vowels and regressively assimilated the high tonality of these vowels.

Prior to *jer*-fall, when consonant palatalization was not yet phonemic, the nonpalatalized dentals *r, l, n* and the palatalized dentals *r', l', n'* were predictable variants, depending on whether they preceded a front or a back vowel, but the palatal sonorants *rj, lj, nj* were separate phonemes. After the fall of *jers*, when *r', l', n'* could occur in word-final position (i.e., preceding a spot where a front *jer* had been dropped), with no front or back vowel following them, either they became phonemic, in opposition to hard *r, l, n*, as in East Slavic, or else phonemic consonant palatalization did not develop (as in Slovene and Serbo-Croatian) and they merged with hard *r, l, n*. However, when the new palatalized phonemes *r', l', n'* came into existence, as in East Slavic, the opposition between palatalized and palatal sonorants could not be maintained and the two "soft" series—palatal *rj, lj, nj* and palatalized *r', l', n'*—merged as phonetically palatalized, in opposition to hard and nonpalatalized *r, l, n*. However, some Slavic mergers of these two series resulted in palatals, rather than palatalized consonants, as in the case of Polish *ń*. The main structural point is that the potentially triple phonetic series always ended up as a double phonemic series, due to merger, but the specific result depended on whether phonemic consonant palatalization was established in the given language. Compare the following opposite cases:

1. Serbo-Croatian and Slovene: Phonemic consonant palatalization does not develop and "hard" nonpalatalized and "soft" palatalized consonants merge as hard; that is, *r', l', n'* > *r, l, n*. Palatal *rj, lj, nj* remain as separate phonemes, though *rj* > *r* in most areas. Examples are Serbo-Croatian /dan/ 'give, past pass. part.', /dan/ 'day', but /konj/ 'horse' < *danъ, *dьnь, *konjь*.

2. East Slavic: Phonemic consonant palatalization develops. After *jer*-fall, "hard" *r, l, n* become phonemically separate from "soft" palatalized *r', l', n'*, constituting two series of sonorants; however, the older series of palatal sonorants *rj, lj, nj* cannot be maintained as a third sonorant series and merges with *r', l', n'*. Examples are Russian /dan/, /dan'/, /kon'/ < *danъ, dan'ъ, konjь*.

7.2 Treatment of the Opposition of Front and Back Vowels

In this section, Jakobson presents another difference between languages with and without phonemic consonant palatalization. Vowels that differed only by the front/back feature, with no difference in height or rounding, were merged in zones that did not develop phonemic consonant palatalization, but were maintained phonetically—at least as automatic variants—in zones that did develop consonant palatalization. This applies to the vowel pairs *i/y, ü/u*, and the *jers* (ь, ъ). For example, *i* and *y* merge as *i* in Serbo-Croatian, but remain automatic variants in Russian. In fact, the front/back vowel feature is not phonemic itself in Russian; rather, it is a redundant feature of a preceding palatalized consonant. An even greater degree of frontness occurs between palatalized consonants, and minimal frontness occurs between hard nonpalatalized consonants; compare Russian *tjul'* [t'ül'] 'curtain lace' and *tut* [tut] 'here', which have the same phonemic vowel /u/, but have the phonetic vowels [ü] and [u], respectively. Jakobson also mentions the special case of Russian velars; there is no opposition of palatalized vs. nonpalatalized velars (*k, g, x*), except in rare loans from other languages and dialects. Jakobson considers the Russian velars to be hard unpaired consonants, since they are hard in isolated positions, such as word–final. However, when velars appear before vowels, the basic variant of each front/back vowel pair is selected, and the velar is automatically palatalized before front vowels: thus, *ky > k'i, gy > g'i, xy > x'i*. In a sense, the front/back vowel pairs can still function in a way reminiscent of their syllabic synharmonic past, especially when combined with unpaired hard velars in the same syllable. Curiously, a syllable such as Russian [k'i] (phonemically /ki/) basically consists of a hard unpaired velar preceding a high unrounded vowel; neither sound has distinctive palatalization or frontness, yet the phonetic syllable consists of a palatalized sound plus a front vowel.

Jakobson makes the point that during the period of the synharmonic syllable, any unification or merger of front and back vowels was impossible, since the front/back vocalic feature shared the phonemic weight with soft and hard consonants. However, in languages that developed phonemic consonant palatalization, after the phonemic weight of the syllable shifted to consonant tonality, the front/back vowel opposition was felt to be redundant and mergers of various sorts started to occur. In the case of the *e* vs. *o* opposition, the tendency to remove front/back redundancy was so strong that it even overrode the fact that these vowels were also opposed by rounding. Jakobson goes into detail about the change of *e* to *o* in several Slavic zones that established phonemic consonant palatalization. The change was restricted to environments where *e* and *o* were of the same vowel height, such as preceding hard consonants, since *e* was raised when preceding a soft consonant. The change eliminated redundancy; since paired consonants before *e* and *o* originally could only be soft and hard, respectively, the rise of new syllables consisting of a palatalized consonant plus *o* did not disturb any oppositions (e.g., *v'ésny > v'ósny* 'spring, nom. pl.'). In Russian, the /e/ vs. /o/ opposition regained its full force when *jat'* (*ě*) changed to *e*, but was not subject to the older *e > o* change, as in *les* 'forest' /l'es/, which would have changed its vowel to *o*, if it had contained an original *e*, rather than *jat'*.

Jakobson indicates that there was a chronological difference between the *e > o* changes in Russian and West Slavic (e.g., Polish). The fact that *jers* participated in the change in Russian, but not Polish, means that strong front *jers* must have changed to *e* prior to the *e* > *o* change in Russian, but only after it in Polish (cf. Russian *pĕs* /p'os/ 'dog', but Polish *pies* [p'es] < *pьsъ*).

7.3 Details of the Establishment of the "Soft ~ Hard Consonant" Correlation in Ukrainian

Jakobson next describes the unusual manner in which Ukrainian instituted phonemic palatalization. This section is significant because it makes plain that this process was not necessarily as clear in Ukrainian as it was in Serbo-Croatian-Slovene, where phonemic consonant palatalization did not develop, or in Russian, where it developed fully. In Ukrainian, the establishment of consonant palatalization depended strictly on the environment of the paired consonant in question. As Jakobson describes the process, the pre-*i* and pre-*e* environments caused "adjusted" palatalization in the consonant, which meant that its palatalization was a function of the following vowel and matched it. However, in all other word positions, such as word-final, pre-*ü*, pre-*ä*, and pre-*i͡e*, the consonant's palatalized tonality was felt to be autonomous and exceeded, rather than matched, that of the following segment. The result was that the "adjusted" softs lost their palatalization, while the "autonomous" softs kept it. Consequently, Ukrainian consonants lost their palatalization before the vowels *i* and *e*, but kept it otherwise, in contrast to Russian, where palatalization was retained in all of these positions.

In Ukrainian, the mergers and unifications of front vowels followed the pattern of the consonants that preceded them. In cases of adjusted soft consonants, which did not develop phonemic palatalization, the following vowels (e.g., *e*, *o*) did not merge or unify. However, in cases of autonomous soft consonants (either unpaired palatals or autonomously palatalized consonants), the front/back feature of the following vowel was redundant and mergers and unifications took place, such as the *e* > *o* change after palatal consonants (*žena* 'wife' > *žona*), but not after adjusted palatalized consonants (e.g., Ukrainian *temnyj* ([temnyj]) 'dark' vs. Russian *tĕmnyj* ([t'omnyj]). Jakobson makes the interesting point that this dual treatment of consonant palatalization is evidence of a systemic conflict and that the adjusted-softs-to-hard change and the front/back-vowel changes must have been simultaneous, since neither of the two possible rule orderings is adequate to explain the situation. On the one hand, if the *e* > *o* change had preceded the hardening of paired softs before *e*, the hardening in fact could not have taken place, since the environment needed for hardening (*t'e*) would not have existed; in its place would have been **t'o*. On the other hand, if the hardening of paired softs before *e* had preceded the *e* > *o* change, and if autonomous *e* and *o* phonemes had already been established, then there would have been no motivation for the $e > o$ change after unpaired palatals (see Feldstein 1980 for further discussion).

7.4   Dialect Split of East Slavic Due to Weak *Jer*-Fall

This section is one of the most interesting and important in Jakobson's book. In it, he explains the differentiation of East Slavic into separate zones on the basis of whether *jer*-fall occurred with or without a systemic conflict between incompatible linguistic features, the zones that he recognizes being Southern Ukrainian, Northern Ukrainian, Southern Belarusian, Northern Belarusian, and Russian (although for the purposes of this section, Jakobson treats Northern Belarusian and Russian as equivalent). For further details, see Feldstein 2000, from which some of the following comments are drawn.

This particular section was criticized by Trubetzkoy (Trubetzkoy and Jakobson 1975, 147) not only for its translated French rendering, but also for Jakobson's own formulations, which Trubetzkoy claims to have had great difficulty understanding:

V celom rjade otdel'nyx mest davaemye Vami formuly nejasny do zagadočnosti. Takovy napr. formuly, opredeljajuščie različija v protekanii konfliktov svjazannyx s padeniem gluxix v raznyx nevelikorusskix vostočnoslavjanskix govorax. ('In several places, the formulas you give are so unclear that they are puzzling. For example, this is true of the formulas that determine the differences in how the conflicts connected to the loss of *jers* occurred in the various non-Russian dialects of East Slavic.')

The first paragraph of the section highlights the main issues to be analyzed. In the first place, Jakobson speaks of a phonological situation that affected all Slavic zones: the loss of phonological equilibrium due to weak *jer*-fall and the phonological changes that occurred in reaction to it. Then, focusing on the specific dialect effects of *jer*-fall, Jakobson differentiates between two possible types of effects within the various East Slavic zones, stating that a given zone might undergo a systemic phonological "conflict," while a neighboring zone might then simply reproduce the first zone's model in order to *avoid* the conflict in question. After reviewing what the "conflicts" were and how Jakobson established the thesis that such conflicts exist in languages, I will examine how the concept of conflict applies to the various East Slavic zones and how this relates to the issue of relative chronology and rule ordering. In doing so, I will attempt to more precisely define what Jakobson meant by the somewhat vague notions of resolving a conflict "in an autonomous manner," as opposed to the opposite case of resolving it on the basis of a "preexisting model."

Let us review Jakobson's concept of phonological "conflicts" A and B. One of the most important characteristics of Jakobson's book, which clearly separates it from virtually all other descriptions of Slavic historical phonology, is that it attempts to deal with general and universal principles of historical linguistic evolution, rather than the specifics of the Common Slavic or East Slavic situation. Jakobson explains East Slavic linguistic history primarily on the basis of his concept of the compatibility and/or incompatibility of certain distinctive features (referred to as "phonological" features here, but called "distinctive" in Jakobson's later work). The full implications of the concept of feature incompatibility are not easy to infer directly from the paragraph about East Slavic dialect zones. In fact, many of Jakobson's implicit ideas on this topic are based either on other sections of this book, or on earlier works by Jakobson, Trubetzkoy, and others. Recall that in section 2.5, Jakobson attempts to establish various types of feature incompatibility. It is important to emphasize that Jakobson is dealing with the compatibility and incompatibility of *distinctive* features, rather than of phonetic features per se. These relations are said to be determined by "rigorous laws," which specify that certain pairs of distinctive features must cooccur, while other feature pairs cannot cooccur. Jakobson's law of feature cooccurrence (whose discovery he attributes to Trubetzkoy) states that "if distinctive feature *a* exists, then *b* also does." It is exemplified by phonemic pitch and phonemic quantity, said to imply each other. The next principle, which states the opposite relationship—two features that cannot cooccur ("If *a* exists, then *b* is absent")—is the one directly relevant to this section. Jakobson cites his own work (1923/1969, 24) as the source for this principle, which is exemplified by intensity accent and vowel quantity. In this section, he refers to another important manifestation of this principle: the notion that if phonemic palatalization exists, then phonemic pitch must be absent (stated as a Slavic rule that is not necessarily universal).

Thus, for Jakobson, for the purposes of analyzing the phonological evolution of East Slavic, two of the most significant pairs of incompatible, mutually exclusive features are as follows:

1. Consonant palatalization and the pitch opposition (inherent and prosodic tonality features, respectively)

2. Dynamic accent and quantity (both nontonal prosodic features)

Among the Slavic languages, phonemic pitch is never combined with phonemic palatalization. All Slavic languages seem to fall into three groups, in conformity with this principle:

1. Those that possess phonemic palatalization but lack phonemic pitch (e.g., all three East Slavic languages, Eastern Bulgarian, Polish)

2. Those that possess phonemic pitch but lack phonemic palatalization (e.g., Serbo-Croatian, Slovene)

3. Those that lack both phonemic palatalization and phonemic pitch (e.g., Czech, Slovak, Macedonian, Western Bulgarian)

Similarly, Slavic systems with both phonemic vowel quantity and intensity accent are also virtually nonexistent; as noted earlier, Jakobson regards these features as incompatible.

The catalyst for the appearance of the two sets of incompatible features A and B was *jer*-fall, which served as the first sound change in a chain reaction, insofar as it introduced a new instance of distinctive inherent consonantal tonality (phonemic consonant palatalization) into the system, which turned out to be incompatible with distinctive prosodic vocalic tonality (phonemic pitch), potentially producing "conflict A." The essence of a Jakobsonian phonological "conflict" is the existence of a period in which two incompatible features are at least temporarily thrown together in a type of phonemic collision that results not just in the expected total elimination of one feature, but in the total elimination of one feature *plus* the partial or complete curtailment of the other feature during the period of conflict. Jakobson (1931, 247–267) advances the intriguing hypothesis that conflicting phonological systems are more characteristic of emotive and artistic speech, while intellectual speech is less likely to contain the disparate phonological elements that constitute a "conflict." In the case of the incompatible tonality features of consonant palatalization and pitch, conflict A meant not only that pitch was eliminated by a rule that might have transformed all phonetic manifestations of falling into rising (or vice versa), but also that the victorious feature—phonemic palatalization—was itself partially lost. The latter process is seen in the loss of consonant palatalization before front vowels (such as consonants before the original front vowels *i, e* in Ukrainian), although this occurred only after *jer*-fall itself, since traces of palatalization remain in Ukrainian consonants that preceded weak front *jers* that were lost.

The ultimate loss of phonemic pitch, which resulted from the establishment of phonemic consonant palatalization, temporarily left the coexisting prosodic features of free accent placement and phonemic quantity, which, in turn, led to conflict B. As noted earlier, Jakobson also views these features as incompatible: their coexistence in East Slavic was resolved by the loss of distinctive quantity, while in West Slavic it was free accent that was changed into a predictable, fixed type, leaving only quantity as a distinctive prosodic feature. The East Slavic evidence that conflict B occurred can be seen in the reflexes of compensatory lengthening (i.e., lengthening of *e, o* to *ē, ō* in a syllable preceding a fallen *jer*) in the southernmost regions of the zone. Although Jakobson does not state why the coexistence of phonemic accent and quantity is problematic, I would suggest that the issue is that free accent implies possible accent on any syllable or mora, but if either mora of a long syllable can be accented, then the accent is tonal rather than dynamic; consequently, elimination of quantity (i.e., two-mora syllables) restores the possibility of a truly free dynamic accent.

Now, how might differential rule ordering provide the key to understanding the various types of conflicts in the East Slavic zones? Jakobson offers a somewhat cryptic explanation of how weak *jer*-fall was able to produce such dramatically different results, providing strong evidence of conflicts A and B in southern zones of East Slavic, but little or no evidence of such conflicts in more northern zones. Let us assume that the following three processes could occur in different orders in the various East Slavic zones:

1. *Jer*-fall

2. Loss of the phonemic pitch opposition in favor of nontonal intensity accent

3. Loss of vowel quantity

As Trubetzkoy mentions, Jakobson's statements are expessed in terms that are difficult to understand. The first historical East Slavic rule ordering involving *jer*-fall applies to Southern Ukrainian, since this was the first East Slavic territory to experience *jer*-fall. The ensuing conflicts A and B make it clear that *jer*-fall had to occur first in this zone, leading to the conflict of consonant palatalization and pitch, and then to pitch loss. Conflict B then ends with the third rule: the loss of quantity. Therefore, the earliest East Slavic rule order must have been (1) *jer*-fall, (2) pitch loss, and (3) quantity loss. Regarding the more northern zones, Jakobson speaks of such a zone as having its model "prepared" by a southern one, or as "reproducing" a more southern model, in order to avoid either of the two phonological conflicts, A or B. Since the Southern Ukrainian rule order served to maximize the two conflicts, Jakobson's notion that a southern model was used to avoid conflict is just another way of saying that the more northern zones applied the three basic rules in different orders. In terms of isoglosses that were advancing across the East Slavic territory, the process can best be viewed as a motion picture, rather than a series of stationary isogloss maps.

The Ukrainian ordering of *jer*-fall, pitch loss, and quantity loss eventually changed in Southern Belarusian, where pitch loss preceded *jer*-fall. Thus, pitch was lost before phonemic palatalization ever came into existence, so that no conflict between the two ever occurred. Therefore, Southern Belarusian never experienced conflict A and consequently did not harden consonants before front vowels. In terms of isoglosses, this implies that the second iso-gloss of Ukrainian, pitch loss, sped up so as to overtake *jer*-fall. The point at which pitch loss advanced ahead of the *jer*-fall line can be defined as the Ukrainian–Belarusian border, north of which there was no longer any conflict between consonantal and vocalic tonality. Jakobson describes the Southern Belarusian situation as follows: "[C]onflict A, caused by the loss of weak *jers*, was made harmless by copying the Ukrainian model."

This metaphorical language, which continues the extended analogy of pho-nological struggle and conflict by the use of the term "harmless," unfortunately makes Jakobson's extremely interesting thesis difficult to understand. Since there are manifestations of compensatory lengthening in Southern Belarusian, Jakobson assumes that conflict B did occur there, although conflict A did not. By the time the isogloss reached the next zone (i.e., Northern Belarusian), there were no manifestations of either conflict A or B, meaning that both the pitch loss and the quantity loss isoglosses must have overtaken the *jer* loss isogloss. The absence of conflict B must have meant that pitch and quantity were lost at approximately the same time. Trubetzkoy had already assumed that this had to be the case, since he felt that free accent and quantity could never cooccur. Jakobson states this point rather clearly in this section. The reason he offers for the change in rule ordering is that Northern Belarusian and Russian "copied" the southern solution to conflicts A and B without expe-riencing the conflicts themselves. I would suggest rephrasing this to state that the deceleration of the advance of the *jer*-fall isogloss accomplished this end, along with the continued advance of the isoglosses of pitch and quantity loss.

Conflicts A and B and their chronologies are summarized in tables 7.1 and 7.2.

Table 7.1
Conflicts A and B, both based on the principle that two distinctive features can be mutually exclusive, that is, "incompatible" ("If *a* exists, then *b* is absent")

Conflict A: Segmental consonantal tonality and prosodic vocalic tonality (= pitch) are incompatible.	
Chronological reason for conflict A	*Jer*-fall precedes loss of phonemic pitch
Linguistic evidence of conflict A	Loss of palatalization in certain environments (e.g., *t'e* > *te*); maintenance of front-back opposition without rounding
Conflict B: Phonemic dynamic accent and phonemic quantity are incompatible.	
Chronological reason for conflict B	Dynamic accent and quantity coexist after loss of phonemic pitch
Linguistic evidence of conflict B	Compensatory lengthening of *e, o*

Table 7.2

The East Slavic zones with respect to conflicts A and B (JF = *jer*-fall; PL = phonemic pitch loss; QL = phonemic quantity loss; *t'e > te* symbolizes the loss of palatalization before front vowels, as found in Standard Ukrainian)

	Conflict A	Conflict B	Chronology of JF/QF/QL	*t'e > te*	Compensatory lengthening
Southern Ukrainian	+	+	JF, PL, QL	+	Total
Northern Ukrainian	+	+	JF, PL, QL	+	Partial (under accent)
Southern Belarusian	−	+	PL, JF, QL	−	Partial (under accent)
Northern Belarusian/Russian	−	−	PL, QL, JF	−	−

In the final paragraph of this section, Jakobson makes the important observation that isoglosses were able to move from Ukrainian to Belarusian, and then on to Russian, without any particular impediments or barriers. Belarusian itself functioned as a transitional zone between Ukrainian and Russian. Thus, there is an important difference between, on the one hand, the well-defined borderline separating Ukrainian and Russian and, on the other hand, the Ukrainian-Belarusian and Belarusian-Russian lines, which are gradual.

7.5 Phonological Details of Belarusian

In this section, Jakobson continues his comments about the special nature of Belarusian phonology. There are two important aspects of this issue. First, Belarusian is felt to be a transitional zone between Ukrainian and Russian, as there is no one feature that defines the entirety of Belarusian from both Russian and Ukrainian during the period of East Slavic disintegration due to *jer*-fall. Therefore, Jakobson regards the notion of a common Belarusian at this time (twelfth and thirteenth centuries) as a fiction.

Second, starting with texts that date from the fifteenth and sixteenth centuries, there is evidence of a massive Polish language influence in both Belarusian phonology and vocabulary. Jakobson makes the point that the phonological changes reflect the way a Pole would pronounce the sounds of an East Slavic language. These include

• Nonpalatalized *r*, instead of palatalized *r'*, which Polish lacks

• Affricates *ʒ'* and *c'*, replacing *t'* and *d'*, a change that also reflects the affrication of *t'* and *d'* in Polish, although the Polish affricates are palatal rather than dental

• Palatal hushers *ś* and *ź*, as in Polish, instead of East Slavic dental palatalized *s'* and *z'*

• The hard alveolar affricate *č*, also reflecting Polish phonology, replacing the palatal *č'* of East Slavic

Since Poles dominated the cultural and intellectual life of Belarus at the time, the Belarusian aristocracy imitated the Polish pronunciation of East Slavic; this pronunciation first affected the language of the upper classes and then spread to others, although not all Belarusian dialects were affected, especially as one got closer to the border of the Russian language.

7.6 Diphthongs and the Role of Prothetic *v* in Ukrainian

The common thread in sections 7.6–7.8 is the development of diphthongs in the East Slavic vowel systems. Generally, all three East Slavic languages shared an early *ě* (*jat'*) of the type $\widehat{ie}$, but their back vowel partners (such as $\widehat{uo}$) and other details varied from zone to zone. Jakobson first addresses Ukrainian, in which both *jat'* and the long *ē* that came from compensatory lengthening (*e* before a syllable with a lost *jer*) changed to $\widehat{ie}$, and the back partner $\widehat{uo}$ came from the compensatory lengthening of *o*. If the $\widehat{ie}$ diphthong (from both *jat'* and *ē*) were to have alternated with $\widehat{uo}$ before hard consonants, on the pattern of *e* > *o*, the two diphthongs might have remained as variants of the same phoneme in the early period of Ukrainian. However, Jakobson indicates that *jat'* did not have alternations that favored such a change, so he assumes a phonemic separation of the two diphthongs. Thus, for the early period of Ukrainian, Jakobson assumes an *i* vs. *y* opposition, plus the opposition between the front and back diphthongs, as follows:

$$
\begin{array}{ccc}
i & y & u \\
\widehat{ie} & & \widehat{uo} \\
e & a & o
\end{array}
$$

This system was subject to change, and Jakobson cites the hole in the system of the central vowels as the main reason. We might also note that this was a very large vowel system, with eight phonemes. Ukrainian dialects evolved from this point in different ways. Northern dialects kept the diphthongs intact but merged *i* and *y* as *i*, leading to a seven-vowel system. Southern dialects (except for the Transcarpathian zone) changed both diphthongs to *i*, but the older *i* did not merge with the new *i* from the diphthongs, instead becoming the high central vowel *ï*. There was an important phonemic divergence between southwestern and southeastern dialects with respect to consonant behavior before the new *i* that came from diphthongs. In the Southwest, the difference between soft consonants (that previously preceded $\widehat{ie}$) and hard consonants (that previously preceded $\widehat{uo}$) remained as a phonemic opposition (e.g., /p'ič/ vs. /bik/), but the palatalized consonant was generalized before *i* in the Southeast (e.g., /p'ič/, /b'ik/). Thus, the high central vowel *ï*, which could only be preceded by hards, was in complementary distribution with *i* in the Southeast and was considered an allophonic variant of /i/ there. However, no such complementary distribution existed in the Southwest; there, /i/ and /ï/ were considered separate phonemes. It is for this reason that Jakobson sets up a six-vowel system for the Southwest but a five-vowel system for the Southeast, the main difference being the phonemic presence or absence of /ï/.

After adding several details about Transcarpathian vowel systems, Jakobson reviews the dialect geography of the larger and smaller systems, stating that the smaller (five-vowel) systems were more centrally located and were used by a wide range of speakers, in contrast to the larger (six- and seven-vowel) systems, which were located on the periphery and were primarily of local use, with no expectation of becoming the national norm. He also makes an interesting point about the Transcarpathian change of long *ō* to *u*, which he considers to be an areal feature since it also occurs in Eastern Slovak and Polish, where it is part of the general pattern called *pochylenie*. *Pochylenie* refers to the transcoding of vowel quantity to quality, where qualitative differences take over phonemic oppositions that had been based on vowel quantity. Diphthongization can be one manifestation of this.

Jakobson also indicates the status of prothetic vowels for diphthongs; in the case of Ukrainian, initial $\widehat{uo}$ developed a prothetic *v*. Since $\widehat{uo}$ evolved into *i* in Modern Ukrainian, initial $\widehat{uo}$- now takes the form *vi-* (e.g., *vivcjá* 'sheep, nom. sg.' vs. *ovéc'* 'sheep, gen. pl.'; cf. Russian *ovcá, ovéc*).

7.7 Diphthongs and the Role of Prothetic *v* in Russian

Next, Jakobson treats the similar issue of a back-vowel partner for *jat'* in Russian dialects. Since Russian did not develop compensatory lengthening, due to an early loss of quantity, this partner had a different source than in Ukrainian. The vowel in question was *o* under rising (acute) accent, which can appear in Russian dialects as $\widehat{uo}$ or raised *ô*, but is not reflected in Standard Russian. Like Ukrainian, Russian developed a prothetic *v* before the initial $\widehat{uo}$ diphthong (e.g., *vótčina* 'patrimonial estate'). Jakobson goes into detail about Trubetzkoy's phonological interpretation of the rising *o*, which he ultimately rejects, for two reasons. First, Trubetzkoy felt that the vowel had to be long, which Jakobson objects to on the basis of such dialect forms as *koruova*, where the *oruo* sequence goes back to a single long vowel, meaning that the second vowel was short, not long. Second, Trubetzkoy felt that the Russian dialect *uo* came from a vowel that had a longer rising portion, followed by a shorter falling portion, for which Jakobson sees no evidence. So, Jakobson concludes that it is best to simply say that the diphthong came from a rising *o*. Jakobson also adds that there was a type of prosodic-to-segmental transcoding of rising tonality, in that segmental *o* has a higher tonality than *u*, and therefore the diphthong *uo* had a rising tonality, despite the elimination of phonemic pitch in the Russian system. He also claims that the parallel diphthong *ie* did not develop from acute *e*, since this diphthong had a falling segmental tonality, with *i* higher than *e*, in contrast to the *uo* diphthong. Thus, the source of the front diphthong *ie* remained *jat'*.

Jakobson has an interesting interpretation of the history of the Russian vowel system. Originally, the pairs *ie/uo* and *e/o* constituted two phonemes, since each front/back pair was in complementary distribution, soft consonants preceding one member of each pair and hard consonants, the other. This implied the following system:

$$
\begin{array}{ccc}
\text{i} & & \text{u} \\
& \widehat{ie}/\widehat{uo} & \\
& \text{e}/\text{o} & \\
& \text{a} &
\end{array}
$$

After this stage, *jat'* (*ie*) changed to *e*, and *uo* to *o*, producing a real phonemic opposition of *e* and *o*. This greatly simplified the system, yielding the familiar five-vowel system:

$$
\begin{array}{ccc}
\text{i} & & \text{u} \\
\text{e} & & \text{o} \\
& \text{a} &
\end{array}
$$

7.8 Diphthongs and the Role of Prothetic *v* in Northern Belarusian

Here, Jakobson treats the similar issue of prothetic *v* and a diphthongal partner for *ie* in the North Belarusian zone. In his view, the development of a back–vowel diphthong was not possible on either the Ukrainian or the Russian model. Ukrainian developed it from an original quantity feature that was no longer found in Belarusian, while Russian developed it from an original pitch feature that also was absent in Belarusian. However, using the model of an original prothetic *v* that preceded an accented *o* in both Ukrainian and Russian, Belarusian developed the prothetic *v* before any initial *o*. Since *ie* (*jat'*) was in the process of changing to *e*, the previously allophonic relationship of *e* and *o* also changed, and the prothetic *v* was part of the effort to create distance between the /e/ and /o/ phonemes.

Jakobson suggests a relative chronology for the development of the prothetic *v*. It must have occurred after palatalized consonants became hard before hard dentals (e.g., *t'em'ъn-* > *t'em'n-* > *t'em'n-* > *t'omn-*), since *e* > *o* was still possible after this change, meaning that *e* and *o* were still variants. However, it had to occur before the hardening of hushers *š'*, *ž'* > *š*, *ž* (as evidenced by a lack of *e* > *o* in Belarusian *adzéža* 'clothes', *dzéšava* 'cheaply').

7.9 Evolution of Eastern Bulgarian Compared with Ukrainian

In this section, Jakobson treats the phonological developments of Eastern Bulgarian at the time of *jer*-fall. The most important point he makes here concerns the parallel between the Eastern Bulgarian and Ukrainian reactions. Like Ukrainian, Eastern Bulgarian maintained phonemic palatalization, along with losing phonemic vowel pitch and quantity and ultimately establishing an intensity accent. But, the parallel is even stronger, since both Eastern Bulgarian and Ukrainian lost palatalization in the originally "adjusted" soft positions, preceding the front vowels *i* and *e*, since it was unclear whether the consonant or the vowel tonality carried the phonemic weight in these cases. However, in the positions of "autonomous" consonant palatalization, such as word-final, pre-*ä*, and pre-*ü* positions, as well as all positions for unpaired soft palatals, consonant softness was preserved (see Feldstein 1980).

Jakobson draws a parallel between the vowel systems of Eastern Bulgarian and Ukrainian: namely, that the tripartite structure of high vowels was critical, opposing front unrounded (*i*), back unrounded (*y*), and back rounded (*u*). With the change of *y* to *i*, the Eastern Bulgarian system evolved to the following six-vowel system (note that the vowel Jakobson presents as ъ is roughly equivalent to schwa [ə]):

$$\text{i} \quad \text{ъ} \quad \text{u}$$
$$\text{e} \quad \text{a} \quad \text{o}$$

Jakobson presents a list of Bulgarian dialect forms in which *u* corresponds to Russian dialect forms with raised *ô*. However, in citing the Bulgarian dialect form *uł* 'ox', he apparently omits the Russian dialect correspondent; we can assume that it should have been given as *vôł*.

7.10 The Place of This Phonological Type on the Slavic Linguistic Map

In this final section of the chapter, Jakobson offers three possible classifications of the Slavic languages, primarily on the basis of how they treated phonemic pitch and consonant palatalization in the face of *jer*-fall. The first type of classification is based on the results of these processes (e.g., triumph of phonemic pitch or establishment of phonemic palatalization), the second principle of classification refers to the processes themselves (e.g., loss of a feature due to a clash of incompatible features), and the third is based on a compromise between the first two. There appears to be some overlap between the classification types. A summary of Jakobson's classifications follows.

Classification based on *results*:

1. Triumph of the phonemic pitch opposition (Serbo-Croatian-Slovene)

2. Adoption of phonemic consonant palatalization, with two subcategories:

    a. A priori loss of pitch and no phonemic struggle (Russian)

    b. Remnants of a phonemic struggle before establishment of phonemic consonant palatalization (Ukrainian, Eastern Bulgarian)

3. Loss of both phonemic pitch and phonemic consonant palatalization (Czecho-Slovak, Western Bulgarian)

Classification based on the *processes*:

1. Zone of the dominance of phonemic pitch

2. Zone of a clash between phonemic pitch and phonemic consonant palatalization

    a. With loss of both phonemic pitch and consonant palatalization

    b. With establishment of phonemic consonant palatalization

3. Zone of a priori elimination of phonemic pitch

Compromise classification, based on the above lists:

1. A priori dominance of phonemic pitch (Serbo-Croatian-Slovene)

2. Elimination of both phonemic pitch and phonemic consonant palatalization (Czecho-Slovak, Western Bulgarian)

3. Establishment of phonemic consonant palatalization, with traces of a struggle between this correlation and phonemic pitch (Ukrainian, Eastern Bulgarian)

4. A priori elimination of phonemic pitch (Russian)

Jakobson observes that if we take the final classification into four types, West Slavic appears to belong to the second type and is contiguous to the fourth, but at first glance the third type appears to be lacking. In other words, Czech and Slovak, with the loss of both pitch and consonant palatalization, are contiguous to Polish, with its full adoption of consonant palatalization, at least historically. However, Jakobson indicates that the Lach dialects (also referred to as Laština, located in the environs of Ostrava and Opava in the Czech Republic, and elsewhere), which are transitional between Czech and Polish, actually can be said to represent the third type, with phonemic consonant palatalization, but also evidence of a struggle related to its establishment. Like Ukrainian, Lach changed *e* to *o* after unpaired palatals, but retained *e* with the hardening of preceding paired soft consonants.

8 Features Common to Russian and Absent in Other East Slavic Dialects

8.1 Classification of Developments Linked to Weak *Jer*-Fall on the Basis of Their Degree of Spread

Trubetzkoy has convincingly demonstrated that the decisive factor in splitting the Proto-East-Slavic dialects was the slow rate of the progression of weak *jer* loss, that is, a certain delay in the spread of this development from the dialects that later became Ukrainian and Belarusian to those of Proto-Russian (*d* 317–318). The slow pace of this expansion had a variety of effects, among those directly or indirectly caused by the fall of weak *jers*:

1. Developments that could occur without any obstacle prior to *jer*-fall were able to spread slightly earlier than the loss of *jers*. Thus, the loss of phonological pitch was repeated by the ancestors of Russian and Northern Belarusian, since it prevented the rise of a conflict of the "soft ~ hard consonant" correlation with pitch correlations.

2. Developments that were unacceptable from the standpoint of the phonological system prior to *jer*-fall were passed on to the Proto-Russian dialects, parallel to the loss of weak *jers*. Such was the change of *y* to *i* after velars, and the change of *o* to *e* when preceded by a soft consonant and followed by a hard consonant.

3. Processes that no longer encountered their necessary conditions in the corresponding dialects stopped expanding. Thus, outside of Ukrainian, there were no favorable conditions for the hardening of palatalized consonants preceding *e*, *i*, since, at the moment of *jer*-fall, the ancestors of Belarusian and Russian had already eliminated the pitch opposition and could realize the correlation "soft ~ hard consonant" consistently and without obstacle. Northern Belarusian and Russian no longer had the necessary conditions for adopting diphthongization, which were developed by Ukrainian and Southern Belarusian from *ō* and *ē* in newly closed syllables, since, at the moment of *jer*-fall, quantitative differences had already been lost in these dialects.

However, the restructuring of the phonological system that was provoked by these changes was able to partially serve as a model that could compete in the restructuring of a system from another dialect, where the restructuring was realized with other data (cf. §§7.6–7.8, on the diphthongs of Ukrainian and Russian and on the expansion of prothetic *v* in the East Slavic languages).

8.2   Russian Innovations Listed by Trubetzkoy

The facts of Russian following the loss of weak *jers* in the southwestern dialects and the cycle of innovations that immediately resulted were not able to penetrate into the other East Slavic dialects since the innovations in question had caused the disappearance of the conditions necessary for their expansion. Such was the case in four situations clarified by Trubetzkoy:

1. The change of weak *jers* to strong *jers* in the groups *trъt, trьt, tlъt, tlьt*, functioning in Russian, could not penetrate the southwestern dialects, where the weak *jers* had already fallen.

2. The change of initial *ĭ* (weak reduced *i*) [equivalent to *jь-* —RF] to *i*, functioning in Russian, could not penetrate the aforementioned dialects for the same reason.

3. The change of the "strong" type of "reduced" *i* and *y* (appearing only before *j* [known as *tense jers*—RF]) to the strong *jers* ь and ъ, functioning in Russian, was not able to spread to the southwestern dialects, where there no longer were any *jers*.

4. The change of *o* under acute intonation to *ô* (cf. §7.7), functioning in Russian, was not able to reach the dialects in question, where there no longer were any phonological pitch distinctions.

8.3   Elimination of Russian Reduced *i, y*

Among the various features that differentiate the southwestern group (i.e., Ukrainian and Belarusian) from Russian, Trubetzkoy also lists the formation of long soft consonants, which came from the sequences "consonant + *j*" that developed as a consequence of the loss of *ĭ*. According to Trubetzkoy, there is no linguistic reason for the inability of this feature to spread throughout the Russian zone. He appeals to the fact that at the moment of this Ukrainian-Belarusian change, the sequences of "consonant + *j*" were absent in Russian, where weak *jers* still were present, but this would only explain a delay in the expansion of this feature. In this case, one would expect to see the change in question share the fate of the features I have listed under point 2 (§8.1), while, in reality, it shared the features listed under point 3. Consequently, one can presume that Russian underwent a phonetic change that preceded the loss of weak *jers* and that was opposed to the penetration of the contraction of the group "consonant + *j*" into the Russian dialects. We can assume that parallel to the change of reduced strong *i* and *y* [i.e., tense *jers*—RF], preceding *j*, to strong ь and ъ, Old Russian underwent a change of reduced weak *i, y*, preceding *j*, to weak ь, ъ (*ĭj, y̆j > ь̆i, ъ̆i*). The greater opening of ь (ь̆) and ъ (ъ̆), in comparison to *i* (*ĭ*) and *y* (*y̆*), would have led to a correspondingly greater opening of the following sound: *j* would have changed to *i̯*. Consonant + *ĭ* + *j* > consonant + ь̆ + *i̯* > consonant + *i̯*. This sequence, unlike the sequence "consonant + *j*," was not susceptible to contraction.[1] Thus, in addition to the above-mentioned processes of Russian, one can add the changes *ĭj, y̆j > ь̆i̯, ъ̆i̯*, which could not spread to the southern dialects, where the *jers* no longer existed. The change of *i* (*ĭ*) and of *y* (*y̆*) to ь (ь̆) and ъ (ъ̆) (cf. §8.2, point 3), as well as the change reported in §8.2, point 2, are particular manifestations of the same tendency: Old Russian eliminated reduced *i, y* in two ways; weak *i* and *y*, when preceding *j*, changed to strong and weak ь and ъ; however, in word-initial position, *ĭ* lost its vowel reduction.

This hypothesis makes it possible to understand the fact that the contraction of the sequence "consonant + *j*," which occurred in the other Slavic dialects, did not occur in Russian, where the sequence "consonant + *i̯*" appeared after the fall of weak *jers* and resisted contraction.

Annotations to Chapter 8, Features Common to Russian and Absent in Other East Slavic Dialects

Let us start with a short excursus on the so-called tense *jers*. In order to properly follow many of the points in chapter 8, it is necessary to understand the concept of "tense *jers*" in Slavic. *Jer* vowels that preceded the palatal glide [j] did not always behave the same as other *jers* in Slavic. The term "tense *jers*" has now become standard, but is not used by Jakobson, who instead refers to these vowels as "reduced" *i, u*. Since tense *jers* acted like other *jers*, they could be either "weak" and subject to deletion or "strong" and subject to strengthening (i.e., a change to a more sonorous vowel), depending on their position. Generally speaking, a *jer* followed by another *jer* was strong, but other *jers* were weak, although there are many exceptions to this rule (see Townsend and Janda 1996, 73–74; Lunt 2001, 34–40). Tense *jers* could also be either weak or strong, so Jakobson's text refers to both "weak reduced" and "strong reduced" *i, u*, which would be the same as saying "weak and strong *jers*," except for the fact that these *jers* were located right before *j*, giving them their own set of Slavic reflexes and causing us to call them "tense." The main point about tense *jers* is that Russian differs from all the other Slavic languages with respect to its reflexes of these sounds. In Russian, both weak and strong tense *jers* have the same reflexes as regular *jers*, while in all the other Slavic languages, strong tense *jers* merged with high *i, y* (< *u*), rather than developing the normal nonhigh strong-*jer* reflex (which was *e, o* in Russian; e.g., Russian *zloj* (from *zlъjь*, which also could be written *zlÿjь*) vs. Ukrainian *zlyj* 'evil').

This chapter is largely devoted to a discussion of Trubetzkoy 1925, especially with regard to two main types of East Slavic isoglosses during the period of *jer*-fall in that zone. Since *jer*-fall is assumed to have been an isogloss that moved slowly across the map from southwest to northeast, a number of other isoglosses were able to start out behind it in the Southwest, but then catch up and move ahead of it. These other isoglosses could have a very different effect in a system where *jers* had already fallen (e.g., Ukrainian) than in a system where *jers* still existed (e.g., Russian). Correspondingly, if innovative iso-glosses appeared in the Northeast (e.g., in Russian) and depended on a pho-nological system with *jers* still present, they would have lost their applicability and become vacuous as soon as they crossed the *jer*-fall isogloss in their progression toward the Southwest. In section 8.1, Jakobson lists changes of three types:

1. Changes that came from the Southwest, which had already experienced *jer*-fall, and that had a very different fate once they crossed the *jer*-fall line and reached the Northeast, where *jers* were present

2. Changes that came from the Southwest that were successfully passed on to the Northeast along with *jer*-fall

3. Changes from the Northeast that required *jers* to function and became vacuous in the Southwest, where *jers* were absent

Type 1 is exemplified by the loss of phonemic pitch, which occurred against the background of *jer*-fall in the Southwest, leading to to Jakobson's conflict A and curtailing some aspects of phonemic consonant palatalization. The isogloss for the loss of pitch moved toward the Northeast faster than the *jer*-fall isogloss, eventually reaching Belarusian and Russian areas where *jers* were still intact; this led to an a priori loss of phonemic pitch, which enabled pho-nemic consonant palatalization to become established without phonological clashes and conflicts in northeastern areas like Russian.

Type 2 represents isoglosses that must have moved in tandem with *jer*-fall, having a similar effect in both zones, such as the change of *y* to *i* after velars (*ky > k'i*) and the change of *e* to *o* between a preceding soft and a following hard consonant.

Type 3, as Jakobson shows in section 8.2, represents isoglosses that applied to Russian at a time before *jer*-fall reached it, but became vacuous and inap-plicable as soon as they crossed the line that represented *jer*-fall in the South-west. These changes are some of the most important features that differentiate Russian from the other East Slavic languages. They include the generalization of "strong" *jers* in the sequences *trъt, trьt, tlъt, tlьt*; the change of initial tense *ĭ-* (*jĭ-*) to full-vowel *i-*, rather than a weak *jer* that was later deleted, as in the Southwest (e.g., Ukrainian *hraty* 'play' vs. Russian *igrat'*); the change of strong tense *jers* (i.e., *jers* preceding *j*) to regular *jers* in the Northeast, with mid-vowel tense-*jer* reflexes vs. high-vowel reflexes in the Southwest (see the discussion of tense jers at the beginning of this annotation); and the Russian change of rising acute *o* to *u͡o*, which could only occur before the loss of pitch, which itself occurred after the advent of *jer*-fall in the Southwest.

While citing many points from Trubetzkoy's paper, in section 8.3 Jakobson takes issue with Trubetzkoy's interpretation of why original sequences of the type -*t'ĭj*- developed into soft double consonants (e.g., *t't'*, as in Ukrainian *žyttja* [žyt't'á] 'life') in the Southwest, but retained their *j* (e.g., *t'j*, as in Russian *žit'ë* [žyt'jó]) in the Northeast. In other words, *j* assimilated to the preceding consonant in the Southwest. Trubetzkoy simply felt that this assimilation was inactive by the time that weak tense *jers* fell in the Northeast, but Jakobson connects it with the general change of tense *jers* to regular *jers* in the Northeast, that is, in Russian. When speaking of the particular regular *jer* reflex for originally tense *jers* of Russian, one usually cites strong *jers*, where the Russian mid-vowel strong tense-*jer* reflex contrasts with the high strong tense-*jer* reflex elsewhere (e.g., Russian *zloj* 'evil' < *zlŭjь*). However, Jakobson goes one step further and assumes that Russian tense *jers* changed to regular *jers* in *both* strong and weak positions, and that the difference between Ukrainian *t't'* and Russian *t'j* can be attributed to the difference in *weak* tense *jer* reflexes. Specifically, Jakobson claims that the Russian weak tense-*jer* reflex of *ŏ/ŏ*, rather than *ĭ/ў̆*, caused the change of *j* to *i̯*, which was then not susceptible to the change of *t'j* to *t't'*.

9   Russian Dialect Changes of Unaccented Vowels

9.1   Critique of Hypotheses That Derive *Akan'e* from Old East Slavic Quantity

According to Šaxmatov's hypothesis on the origin of the dissimilative *akan'e* type, its occurrence depended on the remnants of old quantitative distinctions. The sequence of events was as follows:

1. *ā* shortened.

2. Short, unaccented vowels (*e, o, a*) were reduced, but paired shorts (high vowels, *ě*, and old acute accented *o*) lengthened under accent when they followed vowels that had been reduced.

3. All of the long vowels shortened, but the reduced vowels changed to *a* and lengthened when they preceded accented longs that had shortened (*c* 331ff.).

This hypothesis has several vulnerable points:

a. The loss of weak *jers* clearly preceded the reduction of unaccented *e, o,* and *a* (cf. Trubetzkoy, *d* 311, 312), and the dialects with dissimilative *akan'e* (Northern Belarusian and Southern Russian) only lost weak *jers* after the elimination of the "length ~ shortness of vowel" correlation (cf. §7.4).

b. The hypothesis of a prior shortening of *ā* was advanced just to make the rule work. This hypothesis, as Trubetzkoy has remarked, is very improbable theoretically; ordinarily, the high vowels are precisely the ones more likely to shorten, while the low vowels are the most resistant to shortening (op. cit. 312).

c. Šaxmatov's theory implies the following postulate, which has no basis in fact: that the reflex of unaccented *ě* was shortened, while the unaccented high vowels preserved their length in the same way as accented *ě* and the accented high vowels.

d. Quantitative reduction is expressed by the change of vowels to acoustically neighboring sounds, but of a lesser natural duration (mid vowels change to high vowels); however, *akan'e* is a typical reduction of unaccented vowels and is linked to a reinforcement of accented vowels. Meillet clearly describes this type of reduction as follows: unaccented vowels tend to simultaneously lose a portion of their length and much of their quality; they often become reduced to a more or less neutral quality (*b* 88).

e. It is improbable that Old East Slavic *o* was always short when it preceded the accent: cf. Czech *průlom* 'breakthrough', *důstojný* 'dignified', Čakavian *pṑròd* 'childbirth', *prōsèk* 'axe, cut', Štokavian *prórok* 'prophet'.

f. If we derive the Russian *ô*, which corresponds to the Proto-Slavic *o* under acute intonation, from Proto-East-Slavic *ō*, in like manner we can assume that Proto-East-Slavic *e* also had been a long vowel in that environment (cf. §7.7). Cf. Slovene *čę́šem* 'I comb', *stę́lem* 'I spread out', etc., alongside *kǫ́lem* 'I slaughter', *nǫ́sim* 'I carry' (Russian dialectal *kôs'iš* 'you mow', *kôl'ut* 'they jab'); in Czech, *péče* 'he/she bakes', alongside *kůže* 'skin' (Russian dialectal *kôža*).

g. One of the most widespread types of dissimilative *akan'e*, that of Žizdra, appears to be secondary and inorganic from the point of view of this hypothesis.

h. Even if one attributes a historical reality to the quantitative relations from which Šaxmatov deduces dissimilative *akan'e*, these quantitative relationships, according to Šaxmatov's own history of the Russian language, were long extinct, while dissimilative *akan'e*—at least in the dialects where reduced pretonic vowels did not merge with high vowels—is undoubtedly alive and is a phonetic process determined by current conditions.

Durnovo has proposed a hypothesis to modify Šaxmatov's on the third point: long vowels did not shorten; rather, accented shorts lengthened and, if there were longs under the accent, the length was transmitted to the reduced vowels of the preceding syllable, which changed to *a* as a consequence (*a*-2 57ff.). All of the listed objections are equally valid against this second hypothesis.

In Durnovo's view, his own hypothesis had the advantage over Šaxmatov's of eliminating the necessity to assume the shortening of the diphthongs *ô* (*uo*), *ě* (*ie*), whose length in the Southern Russian dialects has been attested by many observers (op. cit. 54ff.). However, the observers have correctly noted this length in comparison with *o*, *e*, which seemed shorter to them; but Durnovo's hypothesis, just like Šaxmatov's, involves a process that would have leveled the quantity of *ô* and *ě* with that of *o* and *e*. (Šaxmatov presupposes the shortening of the former, while Durnovo assumes the lengthening of the latter.)

Durnovo's hypothesis is also forced to assume a lengthening of paired shorts—that is, high vowels—in the environment following reduced vowels, simultaneous with the reduction of pretonic low vowels, and preceding the lengthening of unpaired shorts (low vowels). Otherwise, it would remain incomprehensible that the sound *a* occurred preceding high vowels that came from old longs and that had been short at the time of the breakup of Proto-Slavic, while a reduced sound or its reflexes occurred preceding low vowels; that is, we do not have a lengthening of high-vowel shorts parallel to that of low-vowel shorts.[1]

The hypotheses we have examined leave a number of facts without a linguistic explanation and, at the same time, they complicate the origin of *akan'e*, which they break down into a series of specific events that are conjectured on an ad hoc basis and are confirmed neither by the concrete facts of the history of the Russian language nor by a logical analysis of the evolution of the Russian phonological system.

9.2   Attempt to Derive *Akan'e* from Intensity Relations

I shall attempt to treat *akan'e* as a process derived from the change of the correlation "pitch accent ~ unaccented" to the correlation "intensity accent ~ unaccented." Given that the phonological mark of accent is the intensity of the accented vowel in relation to the unaccented vowels, the distinctive factor for the linguistic consciousness is the intensity relationship. In the interest of a clearer opposition between the accented and unaccented vowels, one sees a tendency to weaken the unaccented vowels, linked to the tendency to reinforce the accented vowels. Each vowel possesses its own individual intensity. The comparative analysis of vowels, and of Russian vowels in particular (cf. Zernov 50; Stumpf, *a* 254), demonstrates that the strongest vowel is *a* (represented schematically here as 1); next is the *o, e* category (schematically, 2);[2] then, at the boundary of the weak vowels, the category *ô, ě*, (3); and finally the category of weak vowels, *i, u* (4).

Category 3 requires some additional clarification. The majority of dialect descriptions of *ô* and *ě* characterize these vowels as high *o* and *e*; many observe that *ô* and *ě* are slightly longer than *o* and *e*; and, finally, in most cases the descriptions indicate that *ô* and *ě* are composite vowels, having a higher initial component that approaches *u*, in the case of *ô*, and *i*, in the case of *ě*. The description of Ukrainian diphthongs found in the excellent work of Hancov is definitely applicable to these vowels of composite articulation: "*indivisible vowel phonemes*, which are distinguished from other vowel phonemes by the fact that they do not possess a homogeneous and constant articulation from start to finish, and that they contain a series of successive elements, physiologically nonuniform, which consequently lead to varied acoustic images" (*b* 1921). Compare the declaration of Griškin, a peasant from Leka, Egor'evsk district, Rjazan' government, in a dialect where *ô* exists. As Šaxmatov writes, "Griškin first thought of writing this sound with the Church Slavonic letter ȣ, but eventually wrote it with the letter *o* and a 'u' subscript, refusing to write it as I suggested, as 'uo', since 'the false *o*' is a single sound and not two sounds" (*e* 177). Short low vowels are ordinarily stronger than high vowels, which are naturally longer (Stumpf, *a* 262ff.); thus, *o, e* are stronger than *ô, ě*. The composite articulation of the sounds *ô* and *ě* does not change anything in this respect. As Stumpf has shown, a sound is not phenomenologically equivalent to the sum of its parts, and its intensity is not the sum of their intensities; a sonorous whole (*Klangganzes*), as long as it is composed of intensity elements that are equal or different, is never stronger than the strongest of its components, taken in isolation (*a* 306ff.). Both *ě* and *ô* also constitute a sonorous whole, indivisible by the linguistic consciousness of speakers where these vowels are found, and the elements making up these sounds of composite articulation are all high, thus weaker than the low sounds *o* and *e*.

When singers run into difficulty because of a strong divergence between the progression of a melody and the distribution of individual high tones, they are often forced to modify the text in order to avoid the coincidence of high tones and vowels that are naturally low, and vice versa (see Stumpf, *a* 249–250). The same is true in a language where the linguistic consciousness is oriented toward relations of intensity; strong vowels located in a weak portion of the word are an internal contradiction, which often tends to be eliminated.

The analysis of *akan'e* dialects shows that in unaccented syllables, other than the first pretonic, there has been a tendency to eliminate strong vowels (numbers 1–3). While the weak high vowels (number 4) remain intact in these syllables, vowels 1–3 yield to a reduced sound, farther back and lower after hard consonants, and farther front and higher after soft consonants. This sound tends to merge with unaccented *i*. On the basis of their intensity, both variants belong to the category of weak vowels. In the syllable preceding the accent, the intensity relations are a bit more complex. In the dialects under consideration, this syllable is also too weak to preserve the individuality of strong vowels. Where the accented syllable contains a strong vowel, we see that the vowel in the previous strong syllable undergoes a reduction analogous to that of strong vowels in other unaccented syllables. On the other hand, where the accented syllable contains a weak vowel, the preceding syllable maintains a strong vowel, but the intensity level of this pretonic syllable is simplified, with strong vowels of this syllable—if they have not undergone reduction—changing to a single *a* phoneme, since the intensity resources of the pretonic are insufficient to maintain the individuality of every strong vowel.

Thus, the strong vowel of the pretonic syllable is treated as a function of the tonic vocalism, in conformity with the principle of an equilibrium of forces. The pretonic vowel system is simplified, the intermediate types 3 and 2 being eliminated and type 1 being generalized.

9.3 Types of Dissimilative *Akan'e*

From the viewpoint of the theory just presented, let us examine the types of dissimilative *akan'e* that dialectologists have recorded.[3] The *Don* type, where categories 1, 2, and 3 change to 4 in the pretonic syllable, when the accented syllable contains a 1, 2, or 3, and change to 1 when the accented syllable contains a 4, is the clearest of all, since the categories 1–3 are treated together, both in the accented and in the pretonic syllable. Thus, in the Don type a new weak vowel appears in the pretonic syllable whenever there is no weak vowel in the accented syllable. Conversely, in the *Žizdra* type, it is the opposite, where the syllable preceding the accent generalizes the strongest vowel whenever the accented syllable does not contain a vowel of this category; that is, it is only the strongest vowel in accented position, and not the intermediate categories, that conditions the reduction of strong vowels in the preceding syllable (1, 2, 3 > 4 in the pretonic when the accented syllable is 1; 1, 2, 3 > 1 when the accented syllable is 2, 3, or 4).

The Don type treats the intermediate categories in the accented syllable as a single unit, just like the strongest category, while the Žizdra type treats the intermediates like the weakest category. It is quite typical that these dialect varieties have merged the two intermediate categories into a single one. Accented *ě* has merged with *e*. In the *Obojan'* type, the two intermediate categories are treated differently: 2 is treated like 1, and 3 is treated like 4.

> In sum,   1, 2, and 3 > 4, when preceding 1 and 2 under accent.
> 1, 2, and 3 > 1, when preceding 3 and 4 under accent.

Broch's hypothesis on the origin of dissimilative *akan'e* explains the Žizdra type in a satisfying way, but it cannot explain the Obojan' type. Broch assumes that the mid and low vowels merged as the reduced sounds α and ε in the pretonic syllable, just as in other unaccented syllables, but that in the pretonic syllable, the reduced sound would have changed, due to the effect of a lengthening to *a* before naturally short vowels (*a* 57ff.). If the individual length of *a* effectively exceeded the individual length of *i* and *u*, while *o* and *e*, being shorter than *a*, were also longer than the high vowels, one cannot assume that the individual length of *ô* and *ĕ* was shorter than that of *o* and *e*. Under these conditions, the Obojan' type clearly contradicts Broch's hypothesis. Cf. also point d of the objections to Šaxmatov's theory stated above.[4]

After soft consonants, the reduced vowel of the pretonic syllable merged with unaccented *i* in the majority of dialects with dissimilative *akan'e*. In a minority of such dialects, this vowel is differentiated from *i*, and it is a variety of reduced *e* (*ε*). In some locations, there also has been a merger with the *i* of the reduced vowel at the beginning of the word (cf. Durnovo, *a*-1 33). After hard consonants, the reduced vowel of the pretonic syllable has preserved its identity (*α*) in some dialects; in a small number of dialects, it has merged with *y*. In this manner, the vocalism of the pretonic syllable in dialects with dissimilative *akan'e* is comprised of three distinct phonemes, *i*, *u*, and *a*, the phoneme *a* being represented in most dialects by the combinatory variants *a* and *α*, and, additionally, by the variant *ε* just in part of this area. The relations *a:α* (*vadý* 'water, gen. sg.':*vadá* 'water, nom. sg.') and *a:ε* (*sjastrý* [s'astrý] 'sister, gen. sg.':*sεstrá* [s'εstrá] 'sister, nom. sg.') are extragrammatical variations, but the relation *a:i* (*sjastrý* [s'astrý]:*sistrá* [s'istrá]) is a phonemic alternation. The tendency toward phonemic unification sometimes transforms dialects with vowel systems of the type *vadý*, *vadá*, *sjastrý* [s'astrý], *sistrá* [s'istrá] into dialects with dissimilative *jakan'e*, but without dissimilative *akan'e* in the strict sense of the word: *vadý*, *vadá*, *sjastrý* [s'astrý], *sistrá* [s'istrá] (cf. Durnovo, *k* 125, 146). The same tendency transforms some dialects with vowel systems of the type *vadý*, *vadá*, *sjastrý* [s'astrý], *sεstrá* [s'εstrá] into dialects with strong *jakan'e*: *vadý*, *vadá*, *sjastrý* [s'astrý], *sjastrá* [s'astrá]. The difference between the two latter types is purely extragrammatical; that is why the unprepared observer often confuses one with the other (*vadá*, *sεstrá* [s'εstrá] and *vadá*, *sjastrá* [s'astrá]).

9.4 *Akan'e* and Other Types of Change in the Unaccented Vowel System

It would be a methodological error to consider dissimilative *akan'e* apart from its links to neighboring facts, in both time and space. In the first place, dissimilative *akan'e* is only one variety of a more general phenomenon, which is conventionally called *akan'e* in Russian dialectology. Both the dialects with dissimilative *akan'e* and those with other types of *akan'e* have a common trait: the unaccented vowel system is reduced to the three phonemes *i*, *u*, and *a*. The differences among the dialects in question are based on the system of alternation of the phonemes *a* and *i* in the pretonic syllable, that is, the conditions under which the pretonic reflexes of mid and low vowels merge with *i*, along with the conditions under which the phoneme *a* is represented by a reduced combinatory variant. Both of these features appear in different ways, even in the diverse dialects with dissimilative *akan'e*. The typical feature of the great majority of *akan'e* dialects is the different phonetic treatment of the pretonic syllable and the other unaccented syllables. The greater value of the pretonic syllable, as opposed to the other unaccented syllables, is not an innovation. The history of quantity in the various Proto-Slavic dialects presents a number of cases where the pretonic syllable is afforded special treatment. It is worth noting that the isogloss of the reduction of *e, o,* and *a* to a single phoneme in the pretonic syllable does not coincide with the isogloss for the elimination of strong vowels in all the other unaccented syllables. Thus, north of the *akan'e* dialects there is a zone of dialects that Moscow dialectologists refer to as "Northern Russian with a degree of transitionality" (Durnovo, *k* 142). Some of these dialects preserve *o* and *a* as distinct phonemes in the pretonic syllable, but in other unaccented syllables they only distinguish the three phonemes *i, u,* and *a,* in the form of reduced sounds. Contrary to this, the southwestern isogloss of *akan'e* in the pretonic syllable has advanced farther than that of *akan'e* in the other unaccented syllables. Belarusian dialects of the Southwest have incomplete *akan'e* (op. cit. 147).

However, *akan'e* can be examined as part of a more general phenomenon, covering a much greater area. This is the tendency to simplify the unaccented vowel system, in comparison with the vowel system under accent. This tendency is present in all of the East Slavic dialects, with the exception of Southern Ukrainian (op. cit. 165). All of the dialects, except for the latter, have merged unaccented *ě* with other vowels, either *e* or *i*.

Most of the Russian *okan'e* dialects have reduced their unaccented vowel system to four phonemes:

$$\begin{array}{cc} i & u \\ a & o \end{array}$$

The difference between the two main dialect types of Northern Russian lies in the fact that in one group of dialects, the unaccented phoneme that we conventionally designate as *a* is realized by two combinatory variants: *a* after hard consonants, and *e* after soft consonants; or else, *a* after paired hards and *e* after all other consonants. In the other group of dialects, *e* is a combinatory variant of the phoneme whose basic variant is *o*; *e* occurs between soft consonants or preceding a soft and following a soft or an unpaired hard. For example, in dialects of the first type (e.g., the *Arkhangel'sk* group; cf. Opyt §18): *sëló* [s'oló] 'village' or *seló* [s'eló], *peták* [p'eták] 'five-kopeck coin', *petí* [p'et'í] 'five', *petúx* [p'etúx] 'rooster', *žaníx* [žan'íx] 'groom' (or *ženíx* [žen'íx]); in dialects of the second type (e.g., those of *Vladimir*; cf. Opyt §26): *sëló* [s'oló] 'village', *pjatá* [p'atá] 'heel', *pjatí* [p'at'í] 'five' or *petí* [p'et'í], *pëtúx* [p'otúx] 'rooster', *žoníx* [žon'íx] 'groom' (or *ženix* [žen'íx]). Consequently, as far as the phonological system is concerned, the vowel system of *akan'e* dialects differs from that of *okan'e* dialects only in its lack of an unaccented *o* phoneme. It is only on this point that the simplification of unaccented Proto-Slavic vocalism was affected more radically by the *akan'e* dialects than by the Russian *okan'e* dialects.

9.5   Types of Nondissimilative *Akan'e*

The basis of moderate *jakan'e* is the pretonic vowel system of the second type considered above, where *e* and *o* were variants of the same phoneme. This phoneme had to be eliminated; this was done by elevating the tonality of the two variants by one degree—$o > a$, $e > i$ (or, dialectally, *e* close to *i*; cf. Durnovo, *k* 128): *vadá* 'water', *sjaló* [s'aló] 'village', *pjatúx* [p'atúx] 'rooster', *viljú* [v'il'ú] 'I order'. Cf. an analogous method for eliminating the phoneme *ě/ô* in the dialects of the western group of Northern Russian (cf. §7.7). In locations where the process of eliminating the *e/o* phoneme in pretonic position was preceded by the change of pretonic *a* to *e* between softs (a change also known to many *okan'e* dialects adjacent to those of moderate *jakan'e*), this *e* derived from *a* naturally shared the fate of old *e*: *pití* [p'ití] 'five', etc. However, in locations where moderate *jakan'e* was instituted by dialects that maintained a pretonic *a* between softs, the elimination of *e/o* had no effect on this *a*. In fact, in a number of moderate *jakan'e* dialects that were adjacent to *okan'e* dialects, one notes the retention of old *a* between softs (Durnovo, *a*-2 84): *pjatí* [p'at'í] 'five', etc. However, this retention created an obstacle to the simplification that was being carried out in the pretonic vowel system by *akan'e* dialects, especially where $e > e^i$. The natural result was a reinterpretation of moderate *jakan'e*, as follows: *a* is impossible in a pretonic syllable between two softs. In this position, either *i* (phonemic alternation) or e^i (extragrammatical variation) becomes generalized.

   Corresponding to the historical phonemes *a*, *e*, *o*, moderate *jakan'e* generalizes *i* (or e^i) between softs, and *a* in all other positions; another type of *akan'e* generalizes either *i* (*ikan'e*) or e^i (*ekan'e*) after softs, and *a* in all other positions. Russian strong *jakan'e* goes further down the path of generalization, substituting *a* for all strong pretonics in all positions; and, finally, the southwestern Belarusian dialects carry the generalization to its greatest length, generally substituting *a* for all strong unaccented vowels.

Certain types of *jakan'e* are the result of a cross between dissimilative and moderate types. These are not only the moderate-dissimilative and dissimilative-moderate types, in which Durnovo already sees the contamination of two types (*a*-2 86), but also the *Sudža* and *Ščigry* types. The Sudža type follows the dissimilative type when there is a 1 or 4 vowel under accent, and the moderate type when a 2 or 3 vowel is accented. The Ščigry type follows the dissimilative type when a 1, 3, or 4 vowel is under accent and the moderate type when a 2 is accented. Concerning the Sudža type, Durnovo wonders if the differing fate of the strong vowel before a mid accented vowel is due to whether it occurs before a hard or soft consonant, given such cases as *vidjan'ë* [v'id'an'ó] 'vision', *bjal'ë* [b'al'ó] 'underwear' (op. cit. 41ff.). However, it is easy to account for these cases by noting that speakers conceived of alternations like *sjaló* [s'aló] 'village, nom. sg.'–*silá* [s'ilá] 'village, gen. sg.' as morphological. The vacillating nature of the dissimilative principle with respect to the intermediate categories of accented vowels, as well as the variety of resulting types of pretonic vowels preceding accented vowels of heights 2 and 3, and the dialect tendency to merge categories 2 and 3 constitute a favorable nexus within which the pretonic vowel system of words with accented mid vowels favored another type of phonetic treatment, rather than the dissimilative principle.

9.6 Conditions on the Rise of *Akan'e* and Its Southward Spread

The confrontation of *akan'e* isoglosses and its different types with those of other dialect facts allows us to deduce a number of conclusions regarding the conditions for the genesis and spread of *akan'e*.

The late and secondary nature of *akan'e* in the Belarusian dialects of the Southwest is obvious (cf. Šaxmatov, *c* §514; Durnovo, *h* §304). The most essential mark of *akan'e*, vowel reduction, is alien to these dialects; in accented syllables other than the pretonic, *akan'e* is absent in the majority of these dialects, as noted above. The greater value of the pretonic syllable, compared with the other unaccented syllables, causes a less radical phonetic leveling in *akan'e* dialects, while in the southwestern Belarusian dialects that imitate the *akan'e* of Northern Belarusian, this greater value of the pretonic has had the consequence that *akan'e* has only been perceived and reproduced preceding the accent.

Along the Belarusian borders, if we take the southern border of dissimilative *akan'e* to be the old southern isogloss of *akan'e* in general, we observe that this isogloss is very close to the northern isogloss of diphthongs that come from *ō* and *ē* in newly closed syllables (cf. Durnovo, *k* 147), and that farther to the east, it almost coincides with the boundary that separates Southern Russian from Ukrainian—that is, once again, with the northern isogloss of diphthongs from *ō* and *ē*. The link between these two isoglosses—that of *akan'e* and that of the diphthongs in question—can easily be explained. It proves that *akan'e* occurred only directly in those East Slavic dialects that had lost their quantitative differences prior to the loss of weak *jers* (cf. §7.4). Prior to this loss, reduced vowels had another function in the language, constituting particular phonemes, and the use of reduction as a concomitant mark of unaccented vowels was impossible. However, as soon as the old reduced vowels were eliminated from the East Slavic phonological system, the reduction of unaccented vowels could become one of the language's phonetic resources.

For vowel reduction to be applied in actuality, one more major condition was missing: a strong intensity accent at the moment of weak *jer* loss. This condition was not realized where *jer* loss caused a conflict between pitch correlations and the correlation "soft ~ hard consonants" and where, as a result of this conflict, the correlation "intensity accent ~ unaccented" came into being, in turn giving rise to a conflict with the quantitative correlation. However, in those dialects that did not experience the conflicts in question in an autonomous manner and that, on the contrary, reproduced a ready-made model, making it likely that they would easily lose their weak *jers* and introduce the correlation "intensity accent ~ unaccented," this correlation was much clearer and the accented syllable was differentiated more straightforwardly from the unaccented syllables. That is why, with respect to the relative force of the accent, Ukrainian and Southern Belarusian do not equal Russian and Northern Belarusian, although, on the other hand, their accent intensity exceeds that of the extragrammatical accent of Polish (cf. Kurylo, *c* 18–31, which offers a great deal of compelling data). It is characteristic of the Southern Ukrainian dialects, where the unaccented vowel system is identical to the accented system, that the accent is still weaker than in the Northern Ukrainian dialects (cf. loc. cit.). One can consider the Southern Ukrainian dialects to be the zone where all of the phonological disruptions linked to the loss of weak *jers* were felt to the greatest extent. They are precisely the dialects that served as a phonological model to the others; within the Northern Ukrainian dialects, phonological innovations were still transmitted in the same order in which they had occurred in the South, the difference being only that the southern dialects had given the northern ones a cue about a solution to the problem which was caused by the clash of intensity accent with the quantity correlation (cf. §7.4).

I have already described the vowel system of Southern Belarusian as the product of the expansion of *akan'e* toward the South. A factor mitigating this expansion was the northern isogloss of the hardening of consonants preceding *e*—that is, the split of the archiphoneme *o/e* into two distinct archiphonemes, *o* and *e*. Where weak *jer* loss brought about this split, unaccented *e*, *o*, and *a* tend to preserve their phonological individuality. The progression of *akan'e* into the Northern Ukrainian dialects adjacent to the region of Belarusian and Russian is relatively slow and weak.

9.7 Genetic Relations between Different *Akan'e* Types

What is the genetic connection among dissimilative *akan'e*, moderate *jakan'e*, and strong *jakan'e*? Perhaps these are three independent solutions to the same problem: reducing the unaccented vowel system to three phonemes—that is, the three basic vowels that are the clearest and most typical of their tonality, the three "peaks of the vowel triangle" (cf. Stumpf, *a* 255, 329). This problem could have created the same situation for the Russian dialects as the fall of the weak *jers* created for the various Slavic languages. They only assimilated the general principles of innovation, with the remainder being created locally (cf. §6.1). However, perhaps strong *jakan'e*, following the assumption stated above (cf. §9.3), is the final transformation of dissimilative *akan'e*. Or, finally, it is possible that dissimilative *akan'e* was a model that moderate *jakan'e* and strong *jakan'e* were trying to reproduce, of course reinterpreting the details in their own manner (cf. Jakobson, *a* 36–37). There is no essential difference among the cited hypotheses (cf. §10.2).

9.8 Northward Spread of *Akan'e*

One thing is beyond doubt: the expansion of *akan'e* toward the North did not encounter any insurmountable barrier, but it was and continues to be realized there very slowly. At the end of the thirteenth century, Trubetzkoy states, the essential sound changes no longer had the power to extend to all of the East Slavic territory (*d* 317). Thus, we see the beginning of a period of individual unmotivated isoglosses (the northern isogloss of *akan'e*, and later that of the softening of *k* after soft consonants, etc.).

It is interesting that *akan'e* continues progressing across its entire northern front; there are no zones where its progression has been stopped, and, importantly, Moscow assimilated *akan'e* after a long period, although the villages in its immediate vicinity have preserved *okan'e* until recently. Thus, the famous Russian dialect expert Dal' still could write in 1852 that all one had to do was climb up to the golden cupolas of Moscow to view the borders of the *okan'e* dialects (p. XLI).

There have been many attempts to explain Muscovite *akan'e*, elevated to a rule by the Russian literary language, with the aid of historical facts external to the language. Thus, Šaxmatov taught that initially, Russians from the North held the leading positions in Moscow, but these more cultured strata had to inevitably yield to the influence of the masses speaking *akan'e* dialects, masses that were less stable and sedentary than the Russians of the North and therefore the main contingent of the common people who had immigrated to the city (*d* 13–16).

However, we have no data that allow us to assume that the lower social strata of Moscow consisted more of people from the South than of those from the North. On the contrary, we know that peasants from the north of the Moscow district and the neighboring areas of the Vladimir district had been coming to Moscow for a long time in search of a livelihood. In particular, when the common language is reproduced in Muscovite literature of the eighteenth century and the beginning of the nineteenth, notable linguistic features are those of the North, especially the pronunciation of unaccented *o*, mainly after a soft consonant. One need not resort to the risky hypothesis of a numerical superiority of *akan'e* speakers among the Muscovite masses to account for the triumph of *akan'e*. It suffices to assume a free competition between *akan'e* and *okan'e*. The *akan'e* speakers were immunized against *okan'e*, since they were not able to reproduce the *okan'e* vowel system with the resources of their own phonological system. On the contrary, the *okan'e* speakers assimilated the *akan'e* vowel system in the form of lexical loans, without violating their own vowel system. Reproducing *akan'e* phonology required no adaptation of their system; it was simply that a phonological distinction remained unused in unaccented position. Thus, the success of *akan'e*, and in particular its adoption in the *koine* of Moscow, can be fully explained by internal linguistic factors. Furthermore, the *koine* is a language that is destined for expansion, and—given what has been shown here—*akan'e* is clearly more apt to spread than *okan'e*. Consequently, *akan'e* is not only something that can be explained; it is also a factor that conforms to the interests of the Russian *koine*, and, therefore, welcome.

Annotations to Chapter 9, Russian Dialect Changes of Unaccented Vowels

9.1 Critique of Hypotheses That Derive *Akan'e* from Old East Slavic Quantity

In this chapter, Jakobson discusses Russian vowel reduction in unaccented syllables. Here, "reduction" can refer either to the reduction in the inventory of phonemic vowels in unaccented position, compared with the inventory under accent, or to the fact that the vowels themselves are weaker and reduced in unaccented position. I have retained the Russian term *akan'e* (*аканье*) in translating this discussion. In its literal, narrow meaning, *akan'e* refers to the specific pronunciation of [a] in unaccented syllables, but in its wider meaning, it is often used to refer to Russian (or Belarusian) vowel reduction in general. The term *jakan'e* is generally used to indicate vowel reduction in the pretonic syllable after a soft consonant, in contrast to *akan'e*, which refers to vowel reduction in the pretonic syllable after a hard consonant. (See appendix C, "Major Jakan'e Types," for a review of the major types of vowel reduction in tabular form.)

Jakobson uses normal Cyrillic orthographic forms to cite the phonetic shape of words in various *akan'e* dialects, especially in sections 9.3–9.5. I have transliterated these forms and, where their phonetic values might be unclear, I have added phonetic transcriptions in square brackets. In particular, an orthographic consonant plus the letter *ja* (*я*) does not represent the consonant [j] at all. Rather, it represents a palatalization of the consonant—that is, for example, [t'a] and not *[tja].

Jakobson begins with a summary and detailed critique of Šaxmatov's famous hypothesis on the origin of *akan'e*. There are a large number of *akan'e* types, but the most ancient is generally felt to be the *archaic*, or the Obojan' type of dissimilative *akan'e* or *jakan'e*. In the dissimilative type, an originally nonhigh pretonic vowel takes on the height opposite to that of the accented vowel in the next syllable. Dialects differ in their vowel systems and the definition of what constitutes a vowel of the opposite height. In the case

of archaic *akan'e*, the vowel system is as follows, including the line that
separates the higher vowels, which condition a low vowel in the pretonic syllable (e.g., *a*), from the lower vowels, which condition a higher vowel (e.g.,
i, or sometimes *e*).

For example, if a word has an accented *u* (a high vowel), a pretonic nonhigh
vowel will have the opposite height; that is, it will be a low vowel *a* (e.g.,
orthographic *nesú* 'I am carrying' will be pronounced as [n'asú]). If the
accented vowel is low, then the pretonic vowel will be high (e.g., orthographic
nesjá 'while carrying' will be pronounced as [n'is'á]). The archaic nature of
this dialect can be seen in the fact that it differentiates between *ě* (*jat'*) and *e*,
and between *ô* and *o*, for the purposes of determining the height of the pretonic; in other words, these vowels had to exist at the time the rule arose.

  As Jakobson outlines in this section, Šaxmatov attempted to derive this
pattern by assuming that archaic *akan'e* arose in a Russian system that still
had vowel quantity. The essence of his derivation is that the higher vowels,
which condition a pretonic low vowel, were long, in contrast to the low vowels,
which were short; and this difference is intended to phonologically account
for the dissimilation. Jakobson rejects this hypothesis, pointing out eight distinct errors of analysis. Some of these are chronological inaccuracies, such as
the notion that vowel reduction was based on quantity, even though the Russian
loss of quantity preceded *jer*-fall, which in turn preceded vowel reduction.
Šaxmatov also assumed that long *ā* shortened to *ǎ*, primarily to make it behave
like a short vowel, along with original short vowels *e* and *o*, rather than for
independent reasons. Generally speaking, Šaxmatov's hypothesis was con-
structed mainly for the purpose of deriving the correct result. Jakobson also
notes that Durnovo attempted to amend Šaxmatov's hypothesis, but he merely
switched a vowel shortening to a vowel lengthening; this leads Jakobson to
conclude that Durnovo made the same basic error as Šaxmatov, deriving the

dissimilative *akan'e* system from a quantitative vowel system that no longer existed at the time the *akan'e* system originated.

9.2   Attempt to Derive *Akan'e* from Intensity Relations

Jakobson starts this section by outlining his ideas on the origin of Russian vowel reduction—namely, that it was part of the process of transforming the prosodic system of phonemic pitch to one of intensity accent. Clearly, Jakobson's conception is far ahead of his predecessors', in that it deals with the transformation of entire information systems, rather than a mechanical scheme to change one unit into another. Of course, this is the main thrust of the entire book, in comparison to previous historical linguistic treatments. The change from a phonemic pitch accent system to an intensity accent system required systemic adjustments; the system of dissimilative *akan'e* allowed for the maximum vowel height contrast between the pretonic and tonic (accented) vowels, which redundantly signaled the location of accent. Jakobson's view marks a revolutionary step forward in explaining the systemic meaning of this process.

The ideas Jakobson puts forth in this chapter prefigure many of his important later ideas and themes. Vowel height is in the realm of inherent sonority features, while intensity accent belongs to the prosodic sonority feature category. It is perfectly understandable that there would be a systemic interplay between the inherent and prosodic sonority features, and it is quite remarkable that this notion appeared in print as early as 1929. Jakobson assigns each vowel height (equivalent to the inherent sonority level) a different number, 1 being assigned to the highest sonority level (low vowel *a*); 2, to lower mid *e, o*; 3, to upper mid vowels (composite vowels, with a higher vowel onset, usually transcribed as *ô, ê* in modern Russian dialectology); and 4, to the high vowels *i, u* (which Jakobson calls weak, because of their low sonority level).

Vowels other than the first pretonic tend to generalize a weak sonority level, which sets them off against the accented syllable, which admits the full oppositional inventory of sonority levels (vowel heights). In dialects with dissimilative *akan'e*, the first pretonic admits two choices, a low and a high sonority level, coordinated with the accented syllable.

9.3   Types of Dissimilative *Akan'e*

Here, Jakobson reviews the various types of dissimilative *akan'e*. As noted above, the primary differences relate to which accented vowels condition a pretonic high vowel and which condition a pretonic low. In the dissimilative system, an accented high always conditions a pretonic low, and an accented low always conditions a pretonic high. The nuances lie in the pretonic heights that are conditioned by the upper mid and lower mid vowels: these can condition either a pretonic low or a pretonic high, depending on the dialect, as Jakobson outlines.

At the end of this section, Jakobson touches on certain phonemic implications of Russian vowel reduction. In some dialects, phonemes may alternate, while in others, what alternates are predictable variants of phonemes. Phonemic unification can change a more complex system of dissimilative *akan'e* into a system in which the pretonic does not admit dissimilative variation, such as the use of *a* for all nonhigh vowels in the pretonic (called strong *akan'e/ jakan'e*); note that the high vowels do not participate in Russian vowel reduction, already being at the minimum sonority level.

9.4 *Akan'e* and Other Types of Change in the Unaccented Vowel System

Jakobson next presents some general structural considerations about *akan'e* as a phenomenon larger than its specific dissimilative implementation. He notes that the general principle is the reduction of the pretonic to a three–vowel system, while accented position typically has an inventory of five vowels. He also addresses the fact that the first pretonic syllable, coming immediately before the accented syllable, is often treated differently than other unaccented syllables in Russian dialects, which indicates that there is a more general process going on. Virtually all East Slavic dialects except Southern Ukrainian reduce the unaccented vowel inventory, making it smaller than that of the accented vowels, and merge the reflex of unaccented *jat'* with either *e* or *i*, whether they distinguish unaccented *o* and *a* or not.

Jakobson shows that the two major dialect systems of unaccented vowels in Northern Russian differ from *akan'e* dialects only in the fact that the former do not exclude unaccented *o*. All zones of Russian still display a reduced vowel inventory in unaccented syllables, as the examples given at the end of this section demonstrate. The major difference between the two examples of Northern Russian dialects is that the first, represented by Arkhangel'sk, has a rule of alternation between unaccented *a* and *e*, specifying that *a* occurs after hard consonants and *e* after softs (cf. [žaníx], but [p'eták]; standard *ženíx* [žyníx] and *pjaták* [p'iták]); thus, these dialects exhibit unaccented alternations of both *a ~ e* and *e ~ o*. The second type, found near Vladimir, has the familiar *e > o* change before hard consonants in the pretonic, but pretonic *a* is preserved: [p'aták] 'five-kopeck coin', [p'otúx] 'rooster', [n'emú] 'him, dat.'. Of course, in Standard Russian the *e > o* change is only reflected under accent, since *o* cannot occur in unaccented position.

9.5 Types of Nondissimilative *Akan'e*

"Moderate" *jakan'e*, in which the choice of pretonic *a* or *i* is based on whether the consonant following the pretonic is hard or soft, respectively, at first seems to be totally unrelated to the *akan'e* systems that depend on factors other than consonants for their realizations. However, Jakobson demonstrates in this section that moderate *jakan'e* is derived from a northern system of the Vladimir type; the *e* > *o* change is reflected in the pretonic, and an additional change converts both *e* and *o* alternants to the extremes of high and low vowels, with *e* > *i* (occurring before softs) and *o* > *a* (occurring before hards). Standard *vodá* [vadá] 'water', *seló* [s'ilo] 'village', *pjaták* [p'iták] 'five-kopeck coin', *veljú* [v'il'ú] 'I order' are realized as [vadá], [s'aló], [p'aták], [v'il'ú].

Jakobson notes that moderate *jakan'e* generalizes pretonic *i* between softs and *a* otherwise. Other variations also occur, the ultimate generalization being that of "strong" *jakan'e*, which generalizes *a* in the pretonic for all nonhigh vowels, as in Standard Belarusian. Combinations of dissimilative and moderate *jakan'e* also occur, where the pretonic follows the moderate model if mid vowels are accented but the dissimilative model if low or high vowels are accented, as in Sudža. The Ščigry type is almost the same, but follows the moderate pattern only for lower mid vowels.

9.6 Conditions on the Rise of *Akan'e* and Its Southward Spread

In this section, Jakobson discusses some very interesting ideas about the origin and relative chronology of *akan'e*. It is no accident that the isogloss for compensatory lengthening just about coincides with the southern border of vowel reduction. This shows that if vowel quantity continued to exist into the period of *jer*-fall, vowel length could not be used as a redundant feature of a new intensity accent, but was still used to oppose long, short, and *jer* (reduced) vowel phonemes. Also, the chronological coexistence of vowel quantity and *jers*, as in Southern Ukrainian, caused the intensity accent to be weaker, with less of a differentiation between accented and unaccented syllables, a situation unfavorable for the development of vowel reduction. On the other hand, in the more northern zones, where quantity was lost prior to *jer*-fall, the loss of weak (i.e., reduced) *jers* allowed the feature of reduction to be redirected toward supporting the differentiation of accented and unaccented syllables.

9.7 Genetic Relations between Different *Akan'e* Types

Jakobson observes that the three major types of *akan'e*—dissimilative, moderate, and strong—all share the important structural attribute of reducing the inventory of unaccented vowels in the pretonic to three vowels (i, u, a), regardless of which vowel is chosen to represent a in the pretonic syllable. They all achieve the same systemic goal, and the moderate and strong types may well have been the result of local efforts to reproduce the dissimilative model.

9.8 Northward Spread of *Akan'e*

In this section, Jakobson brings up a puzzling question: why *akan'e* did not spread across the entire Russian territory. He notes that there is no linguistic barrier to the northward spread of *akan'e* and that the Moscow region underwent this change slowly and rather late. Scholars such as Šaxmatov had offered sociological reasons for the triumph of *akan'e* over *okan'e* in the Moscow region and in the literary language, but Jakobson gives the best possible explanation, based on the logic of strictly linguistic reasoning. Non-*akan'e* speakers, who had more than three unaccented vowel phonemes in the pretonic, including unaccented *o*, could easily convert to *akan'e* with the simple rule that unaccented *o* became unaccented *a*. However, it would be much more complicated for an *akan'e* speaker, with only three unaccented vowels in the pretonic, to go the other way; that person would need a separate rule for each lexical item, in order to know which unaccented *a* corresponded to *a* and which corresponded to *o* in the *okan'e* dialect. Therefore, the linguistic system itself favored the spread of *akan'e* to non-*akan'e* zones, rather than the other way around.

10 Some Conclusions

10.1 Impossibility of Separating a Single Linguistic Process from the System as a Whole

Works that have appeared during the past decades in the field of linguistic geography have contributed much to our understanding of the spread of lexical features. However, as soon as we go from the domain of vocabulary to that of grammar or phonology, we see that the concept of *system*, so clearly emphasized by Saussure and Fortunatov, claims its position as the cornerstone of linguistics. The establishment of isolated isoglosses is an important procedure, but this does not justify the attempt to raise it to the rank of an autonomous and self-sufficient theory of linguistics. It is just one preliminary step that must be followed by a confrontation of the diverse isoglosses with respect to the system in which they function. Often, a grammatical or phonological isogloss, considered separately, is actually just a fiction, since features that seem identical in isolation are really not the same—that is, when considered as forming an integral part of a system.

As early as Dauzat, we find a distinction between the spread of lexical and phonological features: "Until now, we have not been able to establish any topical link between phonetic zones [I would say phonological] and lexicological zones, whose formation and development do not seem to obey the same laws" (173). However, he does not get to the heart of the essential difference, that is, the *systemic* nature of phonological data.

Examining a feature that forms an integral part of a system, without relating it to its system, is a *contradiction in adjecto*—a contradiction in terms. In particular, any attempt by an investigator to confront one element of a given system with a fact from a heterogeneous system is sterile from the scientific point of view, if the analysis of the correspondence between these features does not have a confrontation of the systems they belong to as its point of departure. Let me develop this point further.

While lexical innovations are caused by phonological or grammatical changes, by stylistic factors, or, finally, by phenomena external to language, phonological changes primarily receive their impetus from other changes that are equally phonological, or from other factors that are also in the realm of phonology. However, discovering the immanent laws of phonological evolution, while allowing us to describe each given change in a system, does not allow us to account for

1. The speed of the change
2. The choice of the path the system takes when it comes to a phonological crossroads—that is, if there are many theoretically possible evolutionary paths.

The immanent laws of phonological evolution only give us an indeterminate equation, which leaves open the possibility of an (albeit limited) number of solutions, not necessarily a single one. The question of the particular choice of a given path can be resolved, partly by analyzing the correlation of the phonological pattern with the other patterns of the language system, and partly by analyzing the connections between the system of the given language and other related social and geographical systems. In their reciprocal relations, all of these systems in turn constitute a system that is characterized by its own specific structural laws. A heteronomous explanation of phonological evolution cannot replace an immanent explanation, but can only complement it.

10.2   Spread of Linguistic Innovations

I have already said that by considering phonological changes as isolated processes, the observer is not able to interpret them; one can only account for them as part of the evolution of the phonological system. But does this thesis apply only to independent innovations, or does it also extend to the spread of innovations?

Since Saussure excludes the notion of system from diachrony, one of the inevitable conclusions of that view is a profound antinomy between the synchronic and diachronic evaluation of a borrowing. In its synchronic aspect, language for Saussure is "a system that has its own arrangement"; consequently, "a loanword no longer counts as such, when it is studied within the system; it exists only in its relation with and opposition to" the other elements of the system, "just like any other original sign" (42–43). However, as soon as Saussure goes from the synchronic to the diachronic domain, he rigorously separates the "borrowing of a phoneme" from "phonetic changes," and he insists that one should scrupulously distinguish between "the centers of innovation, where a feature develops only on the axis of time," and "the affected zones," where "it is not a question of the modification of a traditional proto-type, but of the imitation of a neighboring dialect, without regard to this prototype" (283–288).

Not having accepted Saussure's point of departure (i.e., the thesis that there is no connection between diachrony and synchrony), we would naturally be unable to accept its consequences.

The relation of a diachronic law to a synchronic law (cf. Saussure 131) can be defined as the relation of the means to an obtained result. I say "to the result," not "to the goal," not because I deny the nature of tendency, the teleo-logical spirit of diachronic laws, but because the realization frequently does not coincide with the problem in question—in the same way that in the other spheres of human activity, especially collective ones, the goal is not always attained.

No innovation of the language system can be interpreted without regard for the system that undergoes the innovation, no matter whether it is an indepen-dent innovation or one copied and assimilated from outside. A reference to borrowing cannot be the complete explanation for a fact taking place in the life of a linguistic system.

Certainly, there are loans that are purely imitative (e.g., the *akan'e* of south-western Belarusian dialects; cf. §9.6). The borrowing language attempts to reproduce many features of the other language; it is a typical example of linguistic hybridization. Nevertheless, however varied the forms of hybridiza-tion might be, when the system of language *A* "imitates" the system of lan-guage *B*, the selection and functional reevaluation of the adopted elements always takes place from the point of view of system *A*, corresponding to the possibilities of evolution and the tendencies of system *A*. In the contrary case, we are dealing with a simple substitution of system *B* for system *A*, that is, the extinction of system *A*. Hybridization is a process of synthesis and not a mechanical act of soldering.

Contagion is possible without the predisposition for a convergent evolution, and convergence is possible without contagion, but this still does not give us the right to oppose contagion and convergence to each other. In the majority of cases, the spread of a phonological innovation cannot be reduced to simple imitation. Thus, Dauzat warns against hasty explanations of the spread of phonological features by means of imitation: "[T]here can be simple mental contagion, unconscious or subconscious, as in the case of semantic phenom-ena; but this contagion can also be facilitated or provoked by a set of vocal [I would say phonological] patterns, common to a more or less considerable group of people" (172).

This union of borrowing and convergence bears a strong resemblance to the concept of mimicry in modern biology: "[F]actors of resemblance have always existed for the imitator as well as the model, and only a certain impetus is needed for its manifestation" (Berg 224). The biologists' convincing theory that mimicry is a particular instance of convergence and that there is no basis for attributing an origin or particular significance to it (op. cit. 229) can be applied to linguistics. In the history of language, the distinct property of reproducing a model with a shape comes down to the absence of the hesitations and the trial and error that are almost inevitable when there is no model and that sometimes leave traces in a language (cf. the Ukrainian circumstance of weak *jer* loss; cf. §7.3). The presence of a set recipe for a cycle of changes permits the imitating dialect to adopt a modified and more rational order of innovations (cf. the northward spread of Ukrainian features cited above; cf. §7.4).

What is true about the expansion of one community's linguistic innovations across the entire country can also be applied to the generalization of individual innovations that appear in the realm of speech: the prehistory of certain linguistic changes consists of borrowings by the community from some of its individual members. In this case as well, the essential thing is not the fact of a borrowing itself, but its function from the point of view of the borrowing system; the essential point is precisely that there is a demand for the innovation in question and that this innovation is sanctioned by the system as responding to the possibilities and needs of its development. The role of individual initiators of a phenomenon consists only in "hastening the phylogenesis," to use a term from modern biology, where there is a similar process. In other words, in this case "in a certain sense, ontogeny anticipates phylogeny" (op. cit. 49ff.). However, even without this condition, an innovation can be realized by means of pure convergence.

In particular, the role of precursor can be played by one of the functional types ("styles") of the language, and then "the form exceeds the function" (cf. §2.2). The native feature of the "style" is communicated to the other "styles" (cf. what was stated in §6.1 about the conditions favorable to the loss of weak *jers*).

10.3   Breakup of a Common Language

In these conditions, the debates over the separation of a "speech community"—say, of Proto-Slavic or Proto-East-Slavic—lose their sharpness. The criterion of separation is the inability of certain dialects to undergo common changes. We are not always able to determine the essence of the notion "common," and to state whether we are dealing only with convergence or whether it is convergence supported by contagion. If convergences predominate over divergences, one can employ the concept of a common language.

There is no need to explain that this conventional historical conception of the unity of language cannot be transposed to synchrony without adding something. In synchrony, there is no objective internal criterion that allows us to determine whether we are dealing with one or many languages. The answer is determined by the attitude of the speech community. The criticism of this attitude must, in the end, account for the notion of conformity and not for the notion of historical phonology. Only a provincial science can resolve the question of the legitimacy of this or that sort of linguistic separatism in the light of purely genetic issues. In the social realm, the notion of class replaced that of caste a long time ago. In the national realm, individual freedom pushes the question of origin to the background; similarly, in current linguistic issues we are more concerned with function than with origin.

The analysis of the phonological evolution of East Slavic dialects during the twelfth and thirteenth centuries shows that the tendency toward a convergent development still was predominant. We do not observe phonological separatism, and in that period there is not a single *intentional* divergence in the history of Ukrainian, Belarusian, or Russian dialects. In other words, there are no developments that were undergone by one of the three dialects in question and *that could have been adopted and used* by the others, but were not accepted.[1] The geographical expansion of Russian naturally slowed the pace of the spread of novel developments, but it still did not create unbreachable barriers between the dialects that would reduce their advancement to zero.

10.4 Tendency toward Structural Linguistics in Contemporary Ideology

Clearly, the present work is only a fragmentary application of the theory of linguistic changes, as outlined above. Until now, the sorting and systematization of the pertinent data regarding the history of the Slavic languages have, for the most part, been carried out from another point of view. Reworking these data is a difficult task; at first, they inevitably slip into obsolete concepts that still survive.

I have attempted to lay some foundations for the comparative historical study of the phonology of the Slavic languages and to point out a number of issues that favor a revision of the raw data. Certain convergences are too compelling to be merely fortuitous coincidences. Certain working hypotheses that I have presented will probably be replaced by others as specific problems in the historical phonology of the various Slavic languages are addressed.

As Grammont stated, "An inexact theory leads to a correction, while the absence of a theory leads to nothing."

The Neogrammarian concept of language history is tantamount to the absence of a theory. The theory of a historical process is possible only on the condition that the entity undergoing changes is considered as a structure subject to internal laws, and not as an accidental conglomerate. Saussure's doctrine about language as a system established the necessary premises for a theory of language as a synchronic fact, but it continues to attribute an accidental origin to this synchronic system, and continues to view diachrony as a conglomeration of changes of accidental origin. A theory of linguistic diachrony is possible only if it deals with the problem of changes of structure and the structure of changes.

A mechanical heap, due to chance or heterogeneous factors—this is the favorite image of the European ideology, predominant in the second half of the nineteenth century. Contemporary ideology, in its various manifestations, genetically independent of each other, more and more clearly highlights a functional system instead of a mechanical addition, immanent structural laws instead of a bureaucratic return to an additional check box, and evolution toward a goal instead of blind chance.

Do we need examples?

Regarding everything that surrounds him, from his own house to the universe, man has modified his ideas. We need only point to the functionalism laid bare by Constructivist architecture, or contrast the concept of an infinite universe, viewed from the dual aspects of space and time in yesterday's cosmography (a mechanical sum), to the universal space of Einstein—a finite and closed structure. To the discontinuous and episodic quality of a Naturalist painting, we can compare a composition by Cézanne—an integral system of the relationship of shapes. Doesn't one try to replace sequences of mechanical associations and apperceptive masses with today's structural psychology?

According to Darwin, evolution is the sum of divergences that result from accidental variations undergone by individuals and that produce slow changes, perpetual and barely perceptible. There are a huge number of hereditary variations, going in all directions. Modern biology, particularly Russian biology, opposes this doctrine more and more with nomogenesis, saying that, to a large extent, evolution is convergent, due to internal laws that unite enormous numbers of people across a vast territory, by leaps, paroxysms, and sudden mutations. The number of hereditary variations is limited and they move in definite directions (see Berg 280–281).

The problem of a structure with its own internal law is also a lively issue in modern geography (especially Russian), with its notion of geographic individuality or "Landschaft." Here, researchers attempt to establish the intimate connection between different planes, while abandoning the search for directions of diverse causal relationships and individualizing causes and effects (cf. Savickij 29ff., 39).

The notion of system is the point of departure for contemporary economic science, and the discovery of structural laws is a current issue. We already see that the explanatory role of mechanical causality is giving way to the principle of immanent teleology (cf., e.g., Engländer). True, the methodological problem of the evolution of systems remains in the shadows, since the development of economic science is distorted in certain cases by an a priori dogmatism and hindered in others by inherited premises of the past century, such as the theory of perpetual progress, and a sort of egocentrism that raises the individual and temporary to the level of an absolute.[2]

These few examples suffice to demonstrate that the current issues of linguistics, particularly those of the history of language, placed on the agenda as a consequence of the internal development of this science and completely independent of the other domains of contemporary thought, nevertheless display an intimate agreement with them.

Written in Prague in 1927–28 and published in the *Travaux du Cercle Linguistique de Prague*, II (1929).

Annotations to Chapter 10, Some Conclusions

10.1 Impossibility of Separating a Single Linguistic Process from the System as a Whole

Jakobson starts his concluding chapter with the notion that lexical studies differ from the grammatical and phonological in the importance of the system. Any given phonological feature must be evaluated in terms of its relation to other parts of the same system. Furthermore, whereas lexical changes have many causes, including those that may even be external to the linguistic system, phonological change is influenced by other phonological features and oppositions. Nevertheless, phonological laws do not account for how fast sound changes occur and what a language does when it faces a choice between two paths. Therefore, external data can be used to shed additional light on linguistic choices, although this is not a replacement for systemic analysis, but a complement to it.

The original edition of *Remarks* dates from 1929, but a reprint was published in 1962, as part of volume I of Jakobson's *Selected Writings*. Generally, few changes were introduced in the reprint, but the last three sentences of the first paragraph of section 10.1 are an exception, in that they differ in the two editions. The main text above follows the later, 1962 edition. The three differing sentences from the 1929 edition are as follows:

The establishment and confrontation of isoglosses taken separately is an important procedure, but it does not justify an attempt to raise it to the rank of a linguistic theory with its own value. Moreover, the isogloss itself of a grammatical or phonological fact considered separately is often really fictitious, since the facts that appear identical to us in isolation are far from always being so, that is, when they are considered as forming an integral part of a system. However, in any case, attempts at a linguistic interpretation of grammatical and phonological isoglosses considered separately have been sterile.

10.2 Spread of Linguistic Innovations

Next, Jakobson returns to his critique of Saussure's separation of synchrony and diachrony. (The sections of the French edition of Saussure's *Course in General Linguistics* that Jakobson cites here (Saussure 1922, 42–43, 283–288) correspond to pages 22–23 and 207–211 in the English translation by Wade Baskin.)

Saussure set up a strict dichotomy between phonological changes that take place in a dialect with no outside influence and changes that result from the outside influence of other dialects, called "contagion." He states that when a change arises in a dialect through innovation, only the time axis is involved, but a change from outside the dialect involves both the time and space axes and is different. Jakobson counters this by saying that although some phonological loans are imitative, a synthesis and a systemic evaluation will result in the borrowing dialect; it is never the case that a phonological borrowing is simply "soldered" onto the dialect. He notes that most cases of the propagation of phonological features are not due to imitation, quoting Dauzat's opinion that hasty conclusions about imitation are often not warranted and that there may well be deeper reasons for the spread of certain features from one dialect to another.

Of course, this fits in with the main thrust of Jakobson's book. Each successive Slavic zone did not just take *jer*-fall and implement it; rather, each one systemically restructured its phonemic system in the direction of either vocalic or consonantal tonality. In other words, the process was far from a simple borrowing by one dialect from another. As Jakobson further notes, "contagion" from one dialect to another did not necessarily result in convergence, since two dialects can take a feature and develop it in entirely different structural directions, as indeed happened with *jer*-fall in the Slavic languages. Jakobson compares the presence or absence of biological mimicry to dialects that either use or do not use a specific model, since the absence of a model leads to hesitation and a trial and error approach. He gives the examples of Slavic languages that underwent *jer*-fall with no prior model and experienced clashes of incompatible features (e.g., Ukrainian), as opposed to those that made changes prior to *jer*-fall and avoided such clashes (e.g., Russian).

Jakobson makes another comparison between biology and linguistics, relating ontogeny and phylogeny (i.e., an individual's development in relation to that of the species) to a stylistic innovation—such as rapid speech that deletes weak *jers*—that ultimately becomes the norm and forces a major restructuring of the system. The most important thing, in Jakobson's teleological view, is that the system itself is trending toward a change of this type anyway; the individual speakers with the phonological innovation only "hasten" the evolution, rather than actually causing it.

10.3 Breakup of a Common Language

In this section, Jakobson addresses the concepts of convergence and separatism in the evolution of Slavic languages. Convergence would tend to maintain various dialect zones as part of the same language, while separatism would lead to their breakup into different languages. In reference to the three East Slavic languages, Jakobson observes that during the twelfth and thirteenth centuries, convergence predominated and that no changes were rejected that were able to be passed on system-wide.

10.4 Tendency toward Structural Linguistics in Contemporary Ideology

Finally, Jakobson compares his innovative work with the older nineteenth-century Neogrammarian model of blind change. He regards the latter not as an incorrect theory, but as the absence of a theory, in contrast to his own work, which opposes the idea of blind change and supports the relevance of systemic interrelationships in the evolution of languages.

Jakobson ends his book by comparing his systemic replacement for the inadequate Neogrammarian model with other new approaches from the early part of the twentieth century; these include Constructivist architecture, Einstein's universal space, structural psychology, and modern biology, which opposes Darwin's theory of accidental variations. One might explore Einstein's revolutionary concept of time with Jakobson's innovative concept of how languages evolve systemically over the course of time.

Appendix A: Author's Transcription

Vowels

Series:	Front	Central	Back
High	i—ü	ï—u̇	y—u
Mid	e—ö	ė—ȯ	ə—o
Low	ä	ȧ	a

I use a special symbol for *ȧ* only when there are two phonetic variants—central and back; in all other cases, I use the symbol *a* for both the central and the back vowels (cf. note 3 of chapter 7).

Raised (closed) vowels: ẹ—ọ

Lowered (open) vowels: ę—ǫ

$\widehat{\text{ie}}$: series of units equivalent to a single phoneme

Consonants

$ʒ = \widehat{dz}$, $ǯ = \widehat{dž}$

g, k, γ, x—velar consonants

d$_j$, t$_j$—palatal stops; z$_j$, s$_j$—corresponding back hushers; ʒ$_j$, c$_j$— corresponding affricates (cf. Broch, *b* §§21, 41, 47)

t' = soft t

t^e = t to the "e" degree of softness

o^n = reduced o+n

r̥ = syllabic r

Other phonetic signs are explained in the text.

Appendix B: On Cyrillic Transliteration

The French edition of *Remarks* left Cyrillic examples in their original form and did not provide French glosses for Slavic words. Here, I have transliterated all Cyrillic examples into the Latin alphabet and given English glosses for all Slavic examples. Where the French edition uses phonetic transcription that does not appear in Cyrillic, I have retained Jakobson's symbols, which he explains in appendix A.

What follows is some information that will help in understanding the system of transliteration I have employed. The Cyrillic alphabet is used for several different Slavic languages, past and current (Russian, Ukrainian, Belarusian, Bulgarian, Macedonian, Serbian, and Old and New Church Slavonic). Since literary Macedonian had not been codified at the time *Remarks* was first published, there are no examples in Macedonian as such, but Jakobson does discuss the closely related Western Bulgarian dialect. Jakobson cites Old Church Slavonic but does not discuss New Church Slavonic. Serbian can be written in an official alternative Latin alphabet, which Jakobson uses here instead of a system of transliteration. Major modifications were made in the Russian Cyrillic alphabet starting in 1918, so that pre-1918 and post-1918 Russian Cyrillic systems exist. Both can be found within the covers of this book, since Jakobson's reference list contains many publications printed before 1918, with titles in the old Russian orthography, as well as many post-1918 titles. Jakobson gives all Russian examples in the post-1918 system.

For languages with alphabets relevant to this book (post-1918 Russian, pre-1918 Russian, Ukrainian, Belarusian, Bulgarian, and Old Church Slavonic), I have used the scholarly system of transliteration, in preference to so-called popular systems. The reason behind the choice is that the scholarly system is designed to provide a 1:1 correspondence between Cyrillic and Latin symbols, permitting the user to convert back and forth between the two forms. The popular system uses some Latin symbols for more than one

Cyrillic letter, making it difficult or impossible for the reader to reconstruct the Cyrillic original without knowing the language. For example, a common popular system uses the letter *y* to represent the consonant *y* as well as the high back unrounded vowel of Russian. It is also important to note that while most of the transliterated symbols are shared by the five target languages listed above, each language has some additional Cyrillic letters and/ or presents differences of transliteration. Therefore, I have provided tables of correspondences for both post-1918 and pre-1918 Russian and I sketch the differences in the other four languages, roughly in their order of prominence in the book.

A   Russian

First, consider the transliteration tables 1 and 2 for post- and pre-1918 Russian. Note that the strict 1:1 correspondence mentioned above applies to post-1918 Russian, but does not apply to pre-1918 Russian in the case of *I i* and *F f*. Also, the pre-1918 orthography used the symbol ъ (") after word-final consonants that were not palatalized, meaning that numerous words once ended in this symbol but now omit it, as one can see from Jakobson's pre-1918 bibliographical references.

B   Ukrainian

Ukrainian orthography differs from that of modern Russian in three ways:

1. There are least three Cyrillic letters with a different transliteration and phonetic value in Ukrainian than in Russian: Г г, with the transliteration and value of *H h*; И и, with the transliteration *Y y*; and Е е, which do not indicate palatalization of preceding consonants and have only the value of [e] initially—not [je], as in Russian. Ukrainian transliterated *y* differs from Russian transliterated *y*. The Ukrainian letter symbolizes an unrounded high or high-mid central vowel, roughly similar to [ɨ] or [ï], but the Russian vowel is high, unrounded, and back, closer to [ɯ]. In closed position (finally and preconsonantally), the Ukrainian transliterated *v* can have the value of the glide [w].

2. Additional Ukrainian Cyrillic letters that do not exist in Russian are shown in table 3.

3. The Cyrillic letters Ё ё, Ы ы, Ъ ъ, and Э э, which are used in Russian, are not used in Ukrainian.

Table 1

Post-1918 Russian Cyrillic transliteration

Contemporary standard (post-1918) Russian Cyrillic	Latin transcription	Comments on phonetic value
А а	A a	
Б б	B b	
В в	V v	
Г г	G g	
Д д	D d	
Е е	E e	[je] initially, as in *yet*, or postvocalically; indicates a palatalized consonant plus [e] after a paired consonant; sometimes has the value of the letter *ë* when the optional diaresis is omitted
Ё ё	Ë ë	[jo] initially, as in *Yo(rk)*, or postvocalically; indicates a palatalized consonant plus [o] after a paired consonant; the diaresis is optional in writing and printing, in which case this letter appears as *e*
Ж ж	Ž ž	Voiced palatal fricative; "hard" due to retroflexion
З з	Z z	
И и	I i	Indicates a palatalized consonant plus [i] when following a paired consonant; normally [i] initially, sporadically [ji] initially in some words for some speakers
Й й	J j	Palatal glide [j] as in *York*
К к	K k	
Л л	L l	
М м	M m	
Н н	N n	
О о	O o	
П п	P p	
П р	R r	
С с	S s	
Т т	T t	
У у	U u	
Ф ф	F f	
Х х	X x	Voiceless velar fricative
Ц ц	C c	Affricate [ts]
Ч ч	Č č	Voiceless palatal affricate
Ш ш	Š š	Voiceless palatal fricative; "hard" due to retroflexion
Щ щ	Šč šč	Long "soft" [š'č'] or [š'š']; palatal and not retroflexed, occurs only long
Ъ ъ	"	"Hard sign"; symbolizes a nonpalatalized preceding consonant

Table 1 (continued)

Contemporary standard (post-1918) Russian Cyrillic	Latin t¦ranscription	Comments on phonetic value
Ы ы	Y y	Back unrounded vowel; phonemic partner to [i]; occurs only after a nonpalatalized consonant; belongs to /i/ phoneme
Ь ь	'	"Soft sign"; symbolizes a palatalized preceding consonant
Э э	È è	[e] without preceding [j]; normally occurs only in initial position
Ю ю	Ju ju	[ju] initially, as in English *you*; indicates a palatalized consonant plus [u] after a paired consonant
Я я	Ja ja	[ja] initially, as in English *ya(rd)*; indicates a palatalized consonant plus [a] after a paired consonant

Table 2

Pre-1918 Russian Cyrillic letters

Additional pre-1918 Russian letters	Latin transcription	Comments on phonetic value
I i	I i	Same value as Russian и
Ѣ ѣ	Ě ě	Called *jat'* (yat'); same value as Russian *e*, but can never have the value *ě* [yo]
Ѳ ѳ	F f	
V v	I i	

Table 3

Additional Ukrainian Cyrillic letters

Ґ ґ	G g
Є є	Je je
I i	I i
Ï ï	Ji ji

C Belarusian

1. The only Cyrillic letter with a different value and transliteration in Belarusian than in Russian is Г г, transliterated as *H h* instead of *G g*.

2. There are two Cyrillic letters that are used in Belarusian but not in Russian: І і, transliterated with the same Latin symbols *I i*; and Ў ў, transliterated as *Ŭ ŭ*. Note that Belarusian transliterated *ŭ* is not a short [u] but a [w] glide.

3. The Cyrillic letters И и, Щ щ, Ъ ъ, which are used in Russian, are not used in Belarusian.

D Bulgarian

1. There are four Cyrillic letters that have a different value and/or transliteration in Bulgarian than in Russian. Е е and И и have the same values [e] and [i], but do not palatalize preceding consonants and are not jotized as [je] or [ji] initially. Щ щ are transliterated as *Št št*, and Ъ ъ are transliterated as *Ă ă*. Note that the letter ъ is not a short *ă*; rather, it is phonetically equivalent to schwa [ə] and occurs both accented and unaccented. In Russian, this letter is a "hard sign" and has no phonetic value of its own.

2. There are also three Cyrillic letters that are used in Russian but not in Bulgarian: Ё ё, Ы ы, Э э, because in fact Bulgarian uses the soft sign (Ь ь) in words like актьор 'actor' and Кольо (name).

E Old Church Slavonic

1. Two Old Church Slavonic letters traditionally retain their Cyrillic form in transliteration: Ъ ъ, Ь ь.

In Old Church Slavonic, these were actual vowels known as *jers* (or *yers*), roughly equivalent to short *ŭ* and *ĭ*. In Russian, they are silent and mainly used to indicate the nonpalatalized or palatalized quality of a preceding consonant, although there are instances where the "hard" or "soft" quality of the preceding consonant does not agree phonetically with the hard or soft sign that follows, in which case the signs are used historically. As shown above, the Russian transliterations of the hard and soft signs are " and ', respectively.

2. There are many Cyrillic letters that are used in Old Church Slavonic but not in Russian; see table 4.

Note: the letter ѩ was not part of the original Old Church Slavonic alphabet.

3. The following current Russian letters are not used in Old Church Slavonic: Ё ё, Й й, Э э, Я я.

Table 4

Old Church Slavonic Cyrillic letters not used in Russian

Old Church Slavonic Cyrillic	Latin transcription
Є є	E e
Ѕ ѕ	Dz, dz
I i	I i
Ï ï	I i
Ћ ћ	Ǵ ǵ
ОУ оу	U u
Ѣ ѣ	Ě ě
Ѩ ѩ	Ja ja
Ѡ ѡ	Ô ô
Ѧ ѧ	Ę ę
Ѩ ѩ	Ję ję
Ѫ ѫ	Ǫ ǫ
Ѭ ѭ	Jǫ jǫ
Ѯ ѯ	Ks ks
Ѱ ѱ	Ps ps
Ѳ ѳ	Th th
Ѵ ѵ	Ü ü
Ѥ ѥ	Je je

Appendix C: Major *Jakan'e* Types

General definition of all *akan'e/jakan'e*: nonhigh vowels all merge in a single variant outside accent. Choice of the merged variant in pretonic position determines the specific subtype of *jakan'e*.

I Nondissimilative

A. Strong (*sil'noe*) *jakan'e*

Merged value is always [a].

B. *Ikan'e, ekan'e*, etc. (not strictly *jakan'e*)

Merged value is [i], [e], etc.

C. Moderate (*umerennoe*) *jakan'e*

Choice of merged value depends on consonant after pretonic vowel.

[a] before hard C; [i] before soft C'.

For example: [p'aták] 'five-kopeck coin', [n'asú] 'I carry'; but [gl'id'át] 'they look', [pr'id'óm] 'we will come'

II Dissimilative

In all these types, a high vowel under accent ([i, y, u]) conditions a low-vowel ([a]) pretonic merged value for a nonhigh vowel, while a low vowel under accent ([a]) conditions a high-vowel ([i]) pretonic merged value for a nonhigh vowel. Any combination of the four mid vowels *ê, ô, e, o* under accent (or the reflexes of *ê, ô*, where these vowels no longer exist as such) can act either as high (conditioning pretonic [a]) or as low (conditioning pretonic [i]). The following classifications of mid vowels define the subtypes of dissimilative *jakan'e*.

A. Žizdra (*Žizdrinskoe jakan'e*) or Belarusian *jakan'e*

All four mid vowels act like high vowels, conditioning pretonic [a].

For example: [p'iták, s'alóm, p'atnô, d'at'éj, gl'ad'êl, zv'ar'ók, n'asú, n'as'í];
see figure C.1.

   Note that the symbol *'o* refers to an accented [o] following a "soft" consonant, which originally came from an *e* in certain environments, such as preceding a hard consonant.

B. Sudža (*Sudžanskoe jakan'e*)

After hard consonants, mid vowels act like high vowels, but after soft consonants they act like low vowels.

For example: [p'iták] 'five-kopeck coin', [s'alóm] 'village, instr. sg.', [p'atnô]
'spot', [d'it'éj] 'of the children', [gl'id'êl] 'he looked', [zv'ir'ók] 'small
animal', [n'asú] 'I carry', [n'as'í] 'carry, impv.'; see figure C.2.

C. Mosal'sk (*Mosal'skoe jakan'e*) or Vitebsk (*Vitebskoe jakan'e*)

Rounded mid vowels act like high vowels; unrounded mid vowels act like low
vowels.

For example: [p'iták, s'alóm, p'atnô, d'it'éj, gl'id'êl, zv'ar'ók, n'asú, n'as'í];
see figure C.3.

D. Ščigry (*Ščigrovskoe jakan'e*)

In the mid vowels, only original *e* (including *'o < e*) acts like a low vowel.

For example: [p'iták, s'alóm, p'atnô, d'it'éj, gl'ad'êl, zv'ir'ók, n'asú, n'as'í];
see figure C.4.

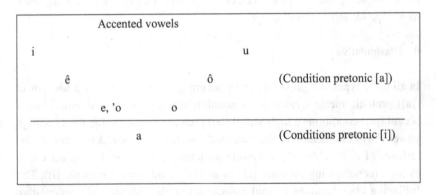

Figure C.1
Žizdra (*Žizdrinskoe jakan'e*) or Belarusian *jakan'e*

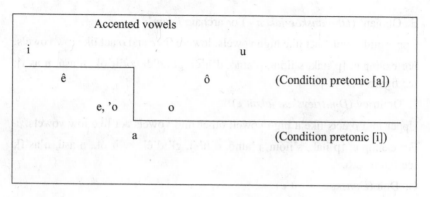

Figure C.2
Sudža (*Sudžanskoe jakan'e*)

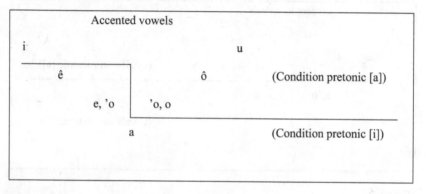

Figure C.3
Mosal'sk (*Mosal'skoe jakan'e*) or Vitebsk (*Vitebskoe jakan'e*)

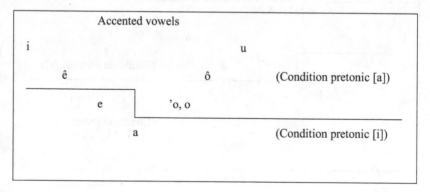

Figure C.4
Ščigry (*Ščigrovskoe jakan'e*)

E. Obojan' (*Obojanskoe jakan'e*) or archaic *jakan'e*

Upper mid *ê* and *ô* act like high vowels; lower mid *e* and *o* act like low vowels.

For example: [p'iták, s'ilóm, p'atnô, d'it'éj, gl'ad'êl, zv'ir'ók, n'asú, n'as'í]; see figure C.5.

F. Dmitriev (*Dmitrievskoe jakan'e*)

Upper mid *ô* acts like a high vowel; other mid vowels act like low vowels.

For example: [p'iták, s'ilóm, p'atnô, d'it'éj, gl'id'êl, zv'ir'ók, n'asú, n'as'í]; see figure C.6.

G. Don (*Donskoe jakan'e*)

All mid vowels act like low vowels.

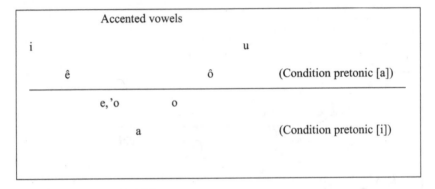

Figure C.5
Obojan' (*Obojanskoe jakan'e*) or archaic *jakan'e*

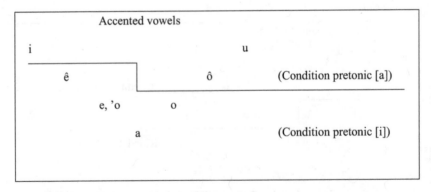

Figure C.6
Dmitriev (*Dmitrievskoe jakan'e*)

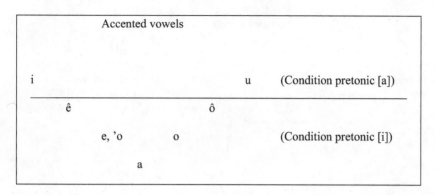

Figure C.7
Don (*Donskoe jakan'e*)

For example, [p'iták, s'ilóm, p'itnô, d'it'éj, gl'id'êl, zv'ir'ók, n'asú, n'as'í];
see figure C.7.

III Assimilative-Dissimilative

Accented "extreme" vowels, both high and low, condition pretonic [a]—which
means assimilation in the case of accented *a*, but dissimilation in the case of
the high vowels. Mid vowels, however, condition pretonic [i] or [a], and their
behavior defines the subtypes.

A. Kidusovo (*Kidusovskoe jakan'e*) (= Sudža plus assimilation to *a*)

Only mid vowels after soft consonants condition pretonic [i].

For example: [p'aták, s'alóm, p'atnô, d'it'éj, gl'id'êl, zv'ir'ók, n'asú, n'as'í];
see figure C.8.

B. Kultukovo (*Kultukovskoe jakan'e*) (= Mosal'sk plus assimilation to *a*)

Only unrounded mid vowels condition pretonic [i].

For example: [p'aták, s'alóm, p'atnô, d'it'éj, gl'id'êl, zv'ar'ók, n'asú, n'as'í];
see figure C.9.

C. Novosëlki (*Novoselkovskoe jakan'e*) (= Ščigry plus assimilation to *a*)

For example: [p'aták, s'alóm, p'atnô, d'it'éj, gl'ad'êl, zv'ir'ók, n'asú, n'as'í];
see figure C.10.

D. Orexovo (*Orexovskoe jakan'e*)

Only accented *e* conditions pretonic [i].

For example: [p'aták, s'alóm, p'atnô, d'it'éj, gl'ad'êl, zv'ar'ók, n'asú, n'as'í];
see figure C.11.

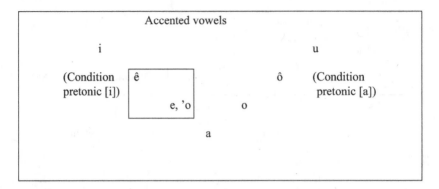

Figure C.8
Kidusovo (*Kidusovskoe jakan'e*) (= Sudža plus assimilation to *a*)

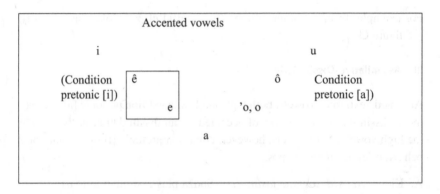

Figure C.9
Kultukovo (*Kultukovskoe jakan'e*) (= Mosal'sk plus assimilation to *a*)

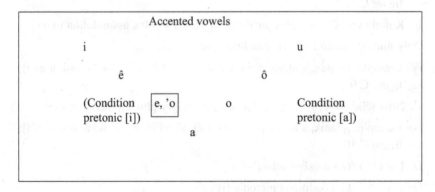

Figure C.10
Novosëlki (*Novoselkovskoe jakan'e*) (= Ščigry plus assimilation to *a*)

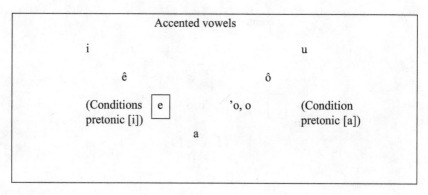

Figure C.11
Orexovo (*Orexovskoe jakan'e*)

IV Moderate-Dissimilative

This type combines moderate *jakan'e* before hard consonants (pretonic [a]) with various types of dissimilative *jakan'e* before soft consonants.

V Dissimilative-Moderate

This type combines moderate *jakan'e* before soft consonants (pretonic [i]) with various types of dissimilative *jakan'e* before hard consonants.

VI Assimilative

Low vowels condition pretonic [a] and high vowels condition pretonic [i], while mid vowels can act as either low or high. (This type is much less common than the previous ones.)

For example: [p'aták, s'ilóm, p'itnô, d'it'éj, gl'id'êl, zv'ir'ók, n'isú, n'is'í]; see figure C.12.

VII Moderate-Assimilative

This type is like the moderate type before hard consonants (pretonic is [a]), but before soft consonants it follows the assimilative *jakan'e* type above.

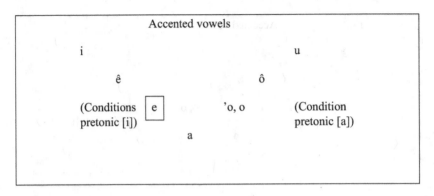

Figure C.12
Assimilative *jakan'e*

Author's References

Bartoš, Fr. *Dialektologie moravská*, 1 (Brno, 1886).

Belić, A. "Der stokavische Dialekt von Milan Rešetar." *Rocznik slawistyczny* 1 (1908), 184–202.

Berg, L. S. *Nomogenez, ili èvoljucija na osnove zakonomernostej* (Pb., 1922).

Boduèn de Kurtenè, I. A. *Ob otnošenii russkago pis'ma k russkomu jazyku* (Spb., 1912).

Brok", O. a) *Govory k" zapadu ot" Mosal'ska* (P., 1916).

   b) *Očerk" fiziologii slavjanskoj rěči* (Spb., 1910).

   c) *Opisanie odnogo govora iz" jugozapadnoj časti Totemskago uězda* (Sb. II. Otd. I. A. N., LXXXIII, 1907).

   d) *Ugrorusskoe narěčie sela Ubli (Zemplinskago komitata)* (Spb., 1899).

Brøndal, V. *Les parties du discours* (Copenhague, 1928).

Bubrix", D. "Sěverno-kašubskaja sistema udarenija." *Izv. II. Otd. R. A. N.*, XXV (1922), 1–194.

Černyšev", V. "Kak" proizošla měna c i č v" russkix" govorax"." *Rus. fil. věstn.*, XLVII (1902), 117–118.

Buzuk, P. *Sproba lingvistyčnae heohrafii Belarusi*, I-1 (Mensk, 1928).

Conev", B. "Dialektni studii." *Sbornik" za nar. umotvoren., nauka i knižn.*, XX.

Dal', V. *Tolkovyj slovar' živago velikorusskago jazyka*, I (1880$_2$).

Dauzat, Alb. *La géographie linguistique* (Paris, 1922).

Dolobko, M. a) "Der sekundäre *v*-Vorschlag im Russischen." *Zeitschr. f. slav. Phil.*, III (1926), 87–144.

   b) "Nóč'-nočés', ósen'-osenés', zimá-zimús', léto-létos'." *Slavia*, V (1927), 678–717.

Durnovo, N. a) *Dialektologičeskija razyskanija v" oblasti velikorusskix" govorov"*, I-1, 2 (M., 1917).

   b) "Dyjalektolëhičnaja paezdka ŭ Padkarpackuju Rus' ŭ letku 1925 hodu." *Zapiski Addzelu humanitarnyx navuk*, 2. Pracy kljasy filëlëhii, I (1928), 220–229.

   c) "K istorii zvukov russkago jazyka, I." *Slavia*, I (1922), 22–26.

   d) "K istorii zvukov russkogo jazyka, II." *Slavia*, II (1923), 599–612.

e) "K ukrainskoj dialektologii." *Slavia*, IV (1925), 149–160.

f) "Le traitement de *sk* dans les langues slaves." *Revue d. ét. slaves*, VI (1926), 216–223.

g) "Obščee i slavjanskoe jazykovedenie v Rossii s 1914 po 1925 god." *Južnoslovenski filolog*, V (1925–1926), 240–297.

h) *Očerk istorii russkogo jazyka* (M.-L., 1924).

i) "Russkie rukopisi XI i XII vv. kak pamjatniki staroslovjanskogo jazyka, V." *Južnoslovenski filolog*, V (1925–1926), 95–117.

j) "Spornye voprosy o.-sl. fonetiki." *Slavia*, III (1924), 225–263.

k) *Vvedenie v istoriju russkogo jazyka*, I (Brno, 1927).

Ekblom, R. a) *Der Wechsel (j)e ~ o im Slavischen* (Uppsala-Leipzig, 1925).

b) "Eine gemeinslavische Umwandlung des Partizipium Präsentis Aktivi." *Le monde oriental*, X.

Engländer, O. "Die Volkswirtschaft unter dem Einfluss der Beförderungskosten." *Hochschulwissen*, Heft 9 (1926).

Falëv, I. "O reducirovannyx glasnyx v drevne-russkom jazyke." *Jazyk i literatura*, II, 1 (1927), 111–122.

Fortunatov", F. a) *Lekcii po fonetikě staroslavjanskago (cerkovnoslavjanskago) jazyka* (P., 1919).

b) "Sostav" Ostromirova evangelija." (Spb., 1908). (Excerpted from *Sbornik" statej v" čest' V. I. Lamanskago*.)

Gebauer, J. *Historická mluvnice jazyka ceského* (Praha, I, 1894; III-2, 1909).

Gilliéron, J. *Pathologie et thérapeutique verbales* (Paris, 1921).

De Groot, A. W. *Summary of the Communication to be made at the First International Congress of Linguists in The Hague, April 1928.*

Hála, V. *Základy spisovné výslovnosti slovenské a srovnání s výslovností českou* (Praha, 1929).

Hancov, V. a) *Dijalektolohična klasyfikacija ukrajins'kyx hovoriv* (Kyjiv, 1923).

b) "Xarakterystyka polis'kyx diftonhiv i šljaxy jix fonetyčnoho rozvytku." *Vseukr. A. N., Zapiski Ist.-Fil. Vidd.* II–III (1920–1922), 116–144.

Hujer, O. "Evangelium sv. Matouse s homiliemi." *Věda česká*, I (1914), 87–93.

Il'inskij, G. a) "Ešče raz o praslavjanskix dubletax tipa *jelen':olen'*." *Slavia*, IV (1925), 387–394.

b) "K" voprosu o čeredovanii glasnyx" rjada *o, e* v" načalě slov" v" slavjanskix" jazykax"." *Slavia*, II, 232–276.

Jagič", I. *Lekcii po istoričeskoj grammatikě russkago jazyka* (Spb., 1883/4, Litogr.).

Jakobson, R. a) *Fonetika odnogo severnovelikorusskogo govora s namečajuščejsja perexodnost'ju* (Praga, 1927, Litogr.).

b) "F. Trávníček. *Příspěvky k nauce o českém přízvuku*." *Slavia*, IV (1926), 805–816.

c) *O češskom stixe preimuščestvenno v sopostavlenii s russkim* (Berlin, 1923).

Jakovlev, N. a) "Matematičeskaja formula postroenija alfavita." *Kul'tura i pis'mennost' Vostoka*, I (M., 1928), 41–64.

b) *Tablicy fonetiki kabardinskogo jazyka* (M., 1923).

Jakubinskij, L. "Die Vertretung des urslav. ě im Čakavischen." *Zeitschr f. slav. Phil.*, I (1925), 381–396.

Jones, D. "Das System der Association Phonétique Internationale." *Lautzeichen und ihre Anwendung in verschiedenen Sprachgebieten* (1928), 18–27.

Kálal, M. *Slovenský slovník z literatury aj nárečí* (Banská Bystrica, 1924).

Karcevski, S. *Système du verbe russe* (Prague, 1927).

Karskij, E. *Bělorussy* (Varšava, I, 1903; II-1, 1908).

Kock, A. "Die alt- und neuschwedische Akzentierung." *Quellen u. Forschungen zur Sprach- und Kulturgeschichte der germanischen Völker*, 87 (1901).

Kokorev", Iv. "Savvuška." *Očerki i razskazy* (M., 1857).

Korš", F. "O zvukax" *e* i *o* v" grečeskom" jazykě." *ŽMNP*, No. 3 (1881), 107–156.

Kryms'kij (and Šaxmatov). Narysy z istorii ukrajins'koji movy ta xrestomatija z pam'jatnykiv pysmens'koji staro-ukrajinščyny (Kyjiv, 1924).

Kul'bakin, S. a) "Du classement des manuscripts dits moyen-bulgares: manuscrits à *u* valant ъ." *Revue d. ét. slaves*, IV (1924), 24–52.

b) *Mluvnice jazyka staroslověnského* (Praha, 1928).

c) *Paleografska i jezička ispitavanja o Miroslavljevom jevanđeljy* (Sremski Karlovci, 1925).

Kurylo, O. a) "Do xarakterystyky i procesu monoftonhizaciji černihivs'kix diftonhičnyx zvukiv." *Ukrajina*, V (1925), 14–38.

b) "Do pytannja pro umovy rozvytku dysymiljatyvnoho akannja." *Ukr. A. N., Zapiski Ist–Fil. Vidd.*, XVI, 48–73.

c) *Sproba pojasnyty proces zminy o, e v novyx zakrytyx skladax u pivdennij hrupi ukrajins'kyx dijalektiv* (K., 1928).

Kurschat, F. *Grammatik der litauischen Sprache* (Halle, 1876).

Larin, B. "Materialy po litovskoj dialektologii." *Jazyk i literatura*, I (1926), 93–170.

Lehr-Spławiński, T. "De la stabilisation de l'accent dans les langues slaves de l'ouest." *Revue d. ét. slaves*, III (1923), 173–192.

Leskien, A. "Litauische Volkslieder aus der Gegend von Wilkischken. Vorbemerkungen." *Litauische Volkslieder u. Märchen*, gesammelt von A. Leskien u. K. Brugmann (Strassburg, 1882), 3–12.

Lorentz, F. a) *Geschichte der pomoranischen (kaschubischen) Sprache* (Berlin u. Leipzig, 1925).

b) *Slovinzische Grammatik* (SPb., 1903).

Marr, N. "Po povodu russkogo slova «salo» v drevnearmjanskom opisanii xazarskoj trapezy VII veka." *Teksty i razyskanija po kavkazskoj filologii*, I (1925), 66–125.

Meillet, A. a) *Introduction à l'étude comparative des langues indo-européennes* (Paris, 1912).

b) *La méthode comparative en linguistique historique* (Oslo, 1925).

c) *Le slave commun* (Paris, 1924).

d) "R. Ekblom. Zur Entwicklung der Liquidaverbindung im Slavischen." *Bull. de la Soc. de Linguist. de Paris*, XXIX (1929), 208–209.

Meyer, K. H. *Untersuchungen zur Čakavština der Insel Krk (Veglia)* (Leipzig, 1928).

Miletič, Lj. a) *Das Ostbulgarische* (Wien, 1903).

b) *Die Rhodopemundarten der bulgarischen Sprache* (Wien, 1912).

Mladenov", S. a) "Dva văprosa izǎ staro-bǎlgarskata gramatika." *Spisanie na Bǎlg. Akad. na Naukite*, XXXV (1926), 37–59.

b) "Mekost'ta na săglasnitě vă bălgarskitě govori." *Godišnikǎ na Sofijskija Universitetǎ*, X–XI (1915), 1–12.

Mucke (Muka), K. E. a) *Historische Laut- und Formenlehre der niedersorbischen Sprache* (Leipzig, 1891).

Muka, E. b) Słownik dolnoserbskeje rěcy a jeje narěčow, I (Petrohrad-Praha, 1911–1926).

Obnorskij, S. "Durnovo, N. Dialektologičeskija razyskanija v" oblasti veliko-russkix" govorov", I." *Zeitschr. f. slav. Phil.*, I (1925), 240–251.

Opyt" dialektologičeskoj karty russkago jazyka v" Evropě s" priloženiem" Očerka russkoj dialektologii. Sostavili N. Durnovo, N. Sokolov", i D. Ušakov" (M., 1915).

Otčet" (Kratkij) o dialektologičeskix" ěkskursijax" 1916 goda." *Trudy Moskovskoj Dialektologičeskoj Komissii*, VIII (1919), 24–36.

Paul, N. *Prinzipien der Sprachgeschichte* (Halle a. S., 1909).

Polivanov, E. *Vvedenie v jazykoznanie dlja vostokovednyx vuzov* (L., 1928).

Porzeziński, W. "Rzekome pierwiastki lechickie w językach wschodniosłowiańskich." *Prace filologiczne*, X (1926), 86–104.

Rastorguev, P. a) "K voprosu o ljašskix čertax v belorusskoj fonetike." *Trudy Postojannoj Komissii po dialektologii russk. jazyka*, IX (1927), 35–48.

b) *Seversko-belorusskij govor. Issledovanie v oblasti dialektologii i istorii belorusskix govorov* (L., 1927).

Rozwadowski, J. a) "Historyczna fonetyka czyli glosownia." Benni, Łoś, Nitsch, Rozwadowski, Ułaszyn: *Gramatyka języka polskiego* (Kraków, 1923).

b) "Kul'bakin" S., K" voprosu o pol'skom" ro." *Rocznik slawistyczny*, II (1909), 186–188.

Saussure, F. de. *Cours de linguistique générale* (Paris, 1922).

Savickij, P. *Geografičeskie osobennosti Rossii*, I (Praga, 1927).

Schleicher, A. *Sprachvergleichende Untersuchungen* (Bonn, 1848).

Seliščev, A. a) "Kritičeskie zamečanija o rekonstrukcii drevnejšej sud'by russkix dialektov." *Slavia*, VII (1928), 33–43.

b) *Očerki po makedonskoj dialektologii*, I (Kazan', 1918).

Smal-Stockyj, S., and Gartner, Th. *Grammatik der ruthenischen (ukrainischen) Sprache* (Wien, 1913).

Sobolevskij, A. a) *Lekcii po istorii russkago jazyka* (M., 1907).

b) *Opyt" russkoj dialektologii* (SPb., 1897).

Sommerfelt, A. "Sur la nature du phonème." *Norsk Tidsskrift for Sprógvidenskap*, I (1928), 22–26.

Stumpf, S. a) *Die Sprachlaute* (Berlin, 1926).

b) *Tonpsychologie*, II (Leipzig, 1890).

Sweet, Henry "Russian pronunciation." In *Collected papers of Henry Sweet*, arranged by H. C. Wyld, 448–464. Oxford: Oxford University Press (1913).

Šaxmatov", A. a) "Historická mluvnice jazyka českého. Napsal Jan Gebauer. Kritičeskij otzyv"." Excerpted from *Otčet" o prisuždenii premij prof. Kotljarevskago v" 1898 g.*

b) "K" istorii zvukov" russkago jazyka. I." Excerpted from *Izv. II. Otd. I. A. N.* (1896), 1–4.

c) *Očerk" drevnějšago perioda istorii russkago jazyka* (P., 1915).

d) *Očerk sovremennogo russkogo literaturnogo jazyka* (L., 1925).

e) "Opisanie Lěkinskago govora Egor'evskago uězda Rjazanskoj gub." *Izv. P. Otd. I. A. N.*, XVIII-4 (1913), 173–220.

f) "Zamětki po istorii zvukov" lužickix" jazykov"." Excerpted from *Izv. 11. Otd. I. A. N.* (1916), XXI-2.

Šaraf, G. "Paljatogrammy zvukov tatarskogo jazyka sravnitel'no s russkimi." *Vestnik naučnogo obščestva tatarovedenija*, No. 7 (1927), 65–102.

Ščepkin", V. a) *Bolonskaja psaltyr'* (SPb., 1906).

b) *Razsuždenie o jazykě Savvinoj knigi* (SPb., 1899).

c) *Učebnik" bolgarskago jazyka* (M., 1909).

Ščerba, L. *Russkie glasnye v'' kačestvennom" i količestvennom" otnošenii* (SPb., 1912).

Šembera, A. *Mistra Jana Husi ortografie česká* (Víděň, 1857).

Špet, G. *Vvedenie v ètničeskuju psixologiju* (M., 1927).

Tanfil'ev, G. *Geografija Rossii, Ukrainy i primykajuščix k nim s zapada territorij*, II-3 (1924).

Tesnière, L. "Buzuk, Sproba lingvistyčnae heohrafii Belarusi." *Slavische Rundschau*, I (1929), 228–285.

Thomson, A. a) "Die Erweichung und Erhärtung der Labiale im Ukrainischen." *Ukr. A. N. Zapiski Ist.-Fil. Vidd.*, XIII–XIV (1927), 253–263.

b) *Obščee jazykověděnie* (Odessa, 1910).

Torbiörnsson, T. a) "Die altbulgarische Umbildung der Partizipialformen." *Slavia*, I (1922), 208–214.

b) "Eine altpolnische Neubildung." *Archiv f. slav. Phil.*, XXXVIII (1922), 120–127.

Trubetzkoy, N. a) "De la valeur primitive des intonations du slave commun." *Revue d. ét. slaves*, I (1921), 171–187.

b) "Die Behandlung der Lautverbindungen *dl*, *tl* in den slavischen Sprachen." *Zeitschr. f. slav. Phil.*, II (1925), 117–120.

c) "Essai sur la chronologie de certains faits phonétiques du slave commun." *Revue d. ét. slaves*, II (1922), 217–234.

d) "Einiges über die russische Lautentwicklung und die Auflösung der gemeinrussischen Spracheinheit." *Zeitschr. f. slav. Phil.*, I (1925), 287–319.

e) "K voprosu o xronologii stjaženija glasnyx v zapadnoslavjanskix jazykax." *Slavia*, VII (1929), 805–807.

f) "Les voyelles nasales des langues léchites." *Revue d. ét. slaves*, V (1925), 24–37.

g) "Ob otraženijax obščeslavjanskogo ę v češskom jazyke." *Slavia*, VI (1928), 661–684.

h) "Obščeslavjanskij èlement v russkoj kul'ture." *K probleme russkogo samopoznanija*. Sborn. statej (1927), 54–94.

i) "Otraženija obščeslavjanskago *o* v" polabskom" jazykě." *Slavia*, IV (1925), 228–237.

Ušakov, D. "Zvuk *g* frikativnyj v russkom jazyke v nastojaščee vremja." *Sb. II. Otd. A. N. SSSR*, CI-No. 3 (1928), 238–240.

Van Wijk, N. "Zur Entwicklung der partizipialen Nominativendung -*onts* in den slav. Sprachen." *Zeitschr. f. slav. Phil.*, I (1925), 279–286.

Vasil'ev", L. a) *O značenii kamory v nekotoryx drevne-russkix pamjatnnkax XVI-XVII vekov. K voprosu o proiznošenii zvuka o v velikorusskom narečii* (L., 1929).

b) "S" kakim" zvukom" mogla associirovat'sja bukva 'neiotirovannyj jus" malyj' v" soznanii piscov" někotoryx" drevnějšix" russkix" pamjatnikov"." *Rus. fil. věstn.*, LXIX (1913), 181–206.

Wundt, W. *Logik*, I (1906₃).

Zelenin", D. *Opisanie rukopisej učenago arxiva I. Rus. Geogr. O-va*, I (P., 1914).

Zernov", V. *Absoljutnyja izměrenija sily zvuka* (M., 1909).

Annotation References

Andersen, Henning. 1973. "Kil'kisni zminy ta rozvytok spoluk *(t)ort* u spil'noslov'jans'kij movi." In *Streszczenia referatów i komunikatów: VII Międzynarodowy Kongres Slawistów*, Warszawa, 21–27 VIII 1973, edited by Janusz Siatkowski, 10–11. Warsaw: PWN.

—. "Slavic." 1998. In *The Indo-European Languages*, edited by Anna Giacalone Ramat and Paolo Ramat, 415–453. London: Routledge.

Čermák, František. 1997. "Synchrony and Diachrony Revisited: Was R. Jakobson and the Prague Circle Right in Their Criticism of de Saussure?" *Folia linguistica historica* 17 (1–2): 29–40.

Eramian, Gregory. 1978. "Some Notes on Trubetzkoy's Abandonment of Disjunctive Oppositions." *Historiographia linguistica* 5 (3): 275–288.

Feldstein, Ronald F. 1980. "The Phonological Background of Ukrainian Consonant Dispalatalization." *Die Welt der Slaven* 25 (1): 135–152.

—. 2003. "The Unified Monophthongization Rule of Common Slavic." *Journal of Slavic Linguistics* 11 (2): 247–281.

—. 2006. "Polish *trot* Reflexes and the Segmental Properties of Metathesis." In *Jezikovna predanost: Akademiku prof. dr. Jožetu Toporišiču ob 80-letnici*, edited by Marko Jesenšek and Zinka Zorko, 205–213. Maribor: Slavistično društvo.

Halle, Morris. 1986. "Remarks on the Scientific Revolution in Linguistics 1926–1929." *Săpostavitelno ezikoznanie* 11 (5): 31–43.

Harris, Roy. 2001. *Saussure and His Interpreters*. Edinburgh: Edinburgh University Press.

Ivić, Pavle. 1958. *Die serbokroatischen Dialekte*. Mouton: The Hague.

—. (1965) 2001. "Roman Jakobson and the Growth of Phonology." In *Phonology*. Vol. 1, *Critical Concepts*, edited by Charles W. Kreidler, 69–107. London: Routledge.

Jakobson, Roman. (1923) 1969. *O češskom stixe preimuščestvenno v sopostavlenii s russkim*. Providence, RI: Brown University Press.

—. (1928) 1962a. "The Concept of Sound Law and the Teleological Criterion." In *Selected Writings I: Phonological Studies*, 1–3. The Hague: Mouton.

—. (1928) 1962b. "Proposition au Premier Congrès International des Linguistes: Quelles sont les méthodes les mieux appropriées à un exposé complet et pratique de la phonologie d'une langue quelconque?" In *Selected Writings I: Phonological Studies*, 3–6. The Hague: Mouton.

— 1931. "Prinzipien der historischen Phonologie." *Travaux du Cercle Linguistique de Prague* 4: 247–267.

— (1936) 1962. "Spornyj vopros russkogo pravopisanija (*dьžgъ, dъžčь*)." In *Selected Writings I: Phonological Studies*, 247–253. The Hague: Mouton.

—. (1938) 1962. "Observations sur le classement phonologique des consonnes." In *Selected Writings I: Phonological Studies*, 272–279. The Hague: Mouton.

—. 1952. "On Slavic Diphthongs Ending in a Liquid." *Word* 8 (4): 306–310.

—. 1955. *Slavic Languages: A Condensed Survey*. 2nd ed. London: King's Crown Press.

—. 1962. *Selected Writings I: Phonological Studies*. The Hague: Mouton.

—. (1963) 1971. "Opyt fonologičeskogo podxoda k istoričeskim voprosam slavjanskoj akcentologii." In *Selected Writings I: Phonological Studies*, 664–689. 2nd exp. ed. The Hague: Mouton.

—. 1985. "Sign and System of Language: A Reassessment of Saussure's Doctrine." In *Verbal Art, Verbal Sign, Verbal Time*, edited by Roman Jakobson, Krystyna Pomorska, and Stephen Rudy, 28–36. Minneapolis: University of Minnesota Press.

—. 1989. "O foneme." *Săpostavitelno ezikoznanie* 14 (2): 26–39.

Jakobson, Roman, C. Gunnar M. Fant, and Morris Halle. 1951. *Preliminaries to Speech Analysis: The Distinctive Features and Their Correlates*. Cambridge, MA: MIT Press.

Jakobson, Roman, and Morris Halle. 1956. *Fundamentals of Language*. The Hague: Mouton.

Jakobson, Roman, and Linda R. Waugh. 1979. *The Sound Shape of Language*. Bloomington: Indiana University Press.

Joseph, John E. 2000. *Limiting the Arbitrary*. Amsterdam: John Benjamins.

Lunt, Horace. 1956. "On the Origins of Phonemic Palatalization in Slavic." In *For Roman Jakobson: Essays on the Occasion of His Sixtieth Birthday, 11 October 1956*, compiled by Morris Halle, Horace G. Lunt, Hugh McLean, et al., 306–315. Mouton: The Hague.

—. 1966. Review of *The Historical Phonology of Common Slavic*, by George Y. Shevelov. *Slavic and East European Journal* 10 (1): 85–92.

—. 2001. *Old Church Slavonic Grammar*. 7th rev. ed. The Hague: Mouton.

Rigler, Jakob. 1986. "Pregled osnovnih razvojnih etap v slovenskem vokalizmu." In *Razprave o slovenskem jeziku*, 139–187. Ljubljana: Slovenska Matica.

Saussure, Ferdinand de. 1959. *Course in General Linguistics*. Translated, with an introduction and notes, by Wade Baskin. New York: McGraw Hill.

Šaxmatov, A. A. (1915) 2002. *Očerk drevnejšego perioda istorii russkogo jazyka*. Moscow: Indrik.

Stieber, Zdzislaw. 1962. *Rozwój fonologiczny języka polskiego*. Warsaw: PWN.

—. 1969. *Zarys gramatyki porównawczej języków słowiańskich. Fonologia.* Warsaw: PWN.

Townsend, Charles E., and Laura A. Janda. 1996. *Common and Comparative Slavic: Phonology and Inflection.* Columbus, OH: Slavica.

Trubetzkoy, N. S. 1922. "Essai sur la chronologie de certains faits phonétiques du slave commun." *Revue des études slaves* 2 (3–4): 217–234.

—. 1925. "Einiges über die russische Lautentwicklung und die Auflösung der gemein-russischen Spracheinheit." *Zeitschrift für slavische Philologie* 1 (3/4): 287–319.

Trubetzkoy, N. S., and Roman Jakobson. 1975. *N. S. Trubetzkoy's Letters and Notes.* Prepared for publication by Roman Jakobson with the assistance of H. Baran, O. Ronen, and Martha Taylor. The Hague: Mouton.

Notes

Chapter 1

1. Saussure describes phonemes as "the first units obtained by cutting the spoken chain" (65) and "above all else, opposing, relative, and negative entities" (164). Polivanov (217), following Ščerba (14), defines the phoneme as "the shortest generic phonetic representation of the given language, capable of being associated with semantic representations and serving to differentiate words." Jakovlev: "We should recognize as phonemes those phonetic properties that are delimited in speech as the shortest elements that can serve to differentiate meaningful elements of a language" (*a* 46). Cf. Jones 19, Sommerfelt.

2. Cf. Wundt 126.

3. Here and below, I use the traditional term "linguistic consciousness," although it is more precise to speak of "linguistic ideology," since we are dealing not with psychic processes but with phenomena of an ideological order, notably signs that constitute social values.

4. Finally, in still other languages the very same vowel length differences can be an extragrammatical fact, either combinatory or stylistic (cf. §1.5). We find both of these uses in Russian, for example (Jakobson, *c* 23, 44).

5. In the phonological systems of the Slavic languages, the oppositions "voiced—voiceless consonant" and "lax—tense consonant" are merged. It would be interesting to examine which of these oppositions is evaluated as phonological and which only appears as a concomitant extragrammatical difference, susceptible of distortion.

6. I use the terms "unaccented," "atonic," "pretonic," and so on, without specifying whether we are dealing with relations of high pitch or of intensity. In each specific case, this follows from the context.

7. The archiphoneme and the phoneme are frequently confused in the linguistic literature. Two correlative phonemes of a given language (e.g., accented vowel—unaccented vowel, long vowel—short vowel) are treated as if they constituted just one phoneme, contrary to the usual definition of the phoneme.

8. Baudouin de Courtenay and his students speak of "optional variants" in this case (cf., e.g., Polivanov 217). The term "stylistic variant" seems clearer and more precise to me (cf. Jakobson, *c* 74–75).

9. For example, the quantitative relations of Russian (see note 4).

10. The fact that *i* and *y* are merely variants of the same phoneme (called "mutable *i*") was emphasized by Baudouin de Courtenay (§44). Regarding the degree of independence of *y* in the phonological system of Russian, it should be observed that if this combinatory variant of *i* is more individualized in the linguistic consciousness than the combinatory variants of the other vowel phonemes, it is because all of the other back vowels represent basic variants of phonemes in Russian and that the corresponding front vowels are combinatory variants, while the relation of *y* and *i* is the opposite: *i* appears at the beginning of a syllable and *y* occurs only after hard consonants.

11. It would perhaps be more precise to interpret the voiced velar fricative γ as a complementary correlative variant in relation to *x*. Cf. *l'éž'by* 'would lie down', *izdóγby* 'would die'. As for γ in *γospodi* 'Lord', *boγa* 'God, gen. sg.', and so on, these words with γ are felt to occupy a special stylistic stratum. Insofar as they merge from the stylistic point of view, in the global vocabulary of the language γ loses its reason for being and is replaced by *g*. Cf. the interesting observations of Ušakov.

Chapter 2

1. I follow the terminology of the Saussurean school, which distinguishes *phonology*—the science of acoustic-motor images that are part of a system of significant values, and *phonetics*—the science of phonic phenomena, treated independently of their relation to said system. According to the ideas of this school, phonology is a synchronic discipline and phonetics is a diachronic discipline. The system of significant values is, from my point of view, the cornerstone not only of synchronic linguistics, but also of diachronic linguistics. That is why, along with synchronic phonology, I study diachronic phonology on an equal basis. Thus, I infer that the term *phonetics* means, on the one hand, a science of sounds used in speech, a science of sounds considered as articulatory and acoustic (objective phonetic) reality, and, on the other hand, a science of corresponding (subjective phonetic) acoustic-motor representations. It is a science contiguous to the science of language in the proper sense of the word. By *phonology*, I infer the part of linguistics that deals with "semanticized" acoustic-motor representations and examines the ideas of sounds from the point of view of their function in the given language. I designate as *phonic* all of the elements that directly relate to the phonatory activity of a human being, to the perception of this activity, to its psychic correlates, and thus to the social values produced by it. Among the phonic elements, I make a distinction between *phonological* elements, capable of differentiating meanings in intellectual speech, and *phonetic* (extragrammatical) elements, which are unable to perform this role and which can, in turn, be subdivided into combinatory and stylistic elements. All of the aforementioned elements can be considered both from a diachronic and from a synchronic point of view.

What is conventionally called *phonology* is called *phonemology* by Jakovlev (*b* 64ff.); the term *phonematics* is equally current; Baudouin de Courtenay and his students use the term *psychophonetics* in the same meaning (cf., e.g., Polivanov 213ff.). The latter term is inexact, since psychophonetics (i.e., phonology) is not distinguished from phonetics at all by a greater degree of psychologism. On the contrary, it is phonetics that is psychological par excellence, and phonetics operates with acoustic-motor representations, on the perception of sounds and the role of memory and attention, whereas phonology can be completely abstracted from psychology, and whereas it is arbitrary values with an existence in the community that are its object. Špet is fully justified in emphasizing that "power," "family," "economy," "language," "ministry," "police commissioner," and so on, are relationships within a dynamic collective, that these are social definitions, not psychological ones, and that in "objectivizing" them, we commit less of an error than when we treat the psychology of "pairs" that realize these relationships (104).

2. This is an expanded statement of the law established by Trubetzkoy (d 303ff.).

3. This law is formulated and interpreted in Jakobson, c 23ff. Cf. Trubetzkoy, d 303ff. Regarding the psychological explanation of this law and Trubetzkoy's (see note 2), see de Groot.

4. This law is formulated in Jakobson, c note 25.

5. And, naturally, the reverse: if the latter correlation exists, the former is absent.

6. A similar typology of systems is equally possible with respect to other areas of language. Thus, Brøndal makes a very interesting attempt to establish the possible simultaneous combinations of word classes. He states that certain groups of classes are interdependent in the sense that the existence of a given class causes the nonexistence of certain others (29).

7. The priority of acoustics over the physiology of sounds has been admitted more than once in the scholarly literature, for example, by Saussure: "The auditory impression is not only sensed as directly as the motor image of the organs of articulation—it is the natural basis of any theory" (63). Also see Stumpf (a 1–2; and the bibliography of the subject found there). In certain places in the present work, I use terms borrowed from the physiology of sounds because they are current, but it would be more rational to resort to acoustic terminology and classification.

Chapter 3

1. My interpretation of the history of front vowels preceding l in the same syllable is borrowed from a work of Trubetzkoy that is as yet unpublished. The references to Trubetzkoy without an indication of the source refer to his unpublished work and oral communications.

2. Since my sketch of the history of the diphthongs o, $e + r$, l, i is just a modification of Trubetzkoy's theory, formulated by him in a private letter written at the beginning of 1928, I find it necessary to cite it here in its original form:

In the diphthongs under acute intonation, the first component was longer than the second; it was the opposite in the case of circumflex diphthongs (as in Lithuanian). I designate the element that is shorter than half of a normal long by $_1$ (o_1, r_1, etc.) and the element that exceeds the duration of half the normal long by $_2$ (o_2, r_2, etc.); finally, I designate the length of a normal long by $_3$ (o_3); vowels of normal short duration were of length $_2$ (o_2).

At the beginning of the word, preceding liquids of the same syllable, o was lengthened to a normal short in those cases where it was ultrashort ($o_1 r_2 st\check{\textit{b}} > o_2 r_2 st\check{\textit{b}}$) and to a long when it was a normal short ($o_2 r_1 dlo > o_3 r_1 dlo$).

The quantitative difference between $o_2 r_1$ under the acute and circumflex intonations, in the environment between consonants, was eliminated: in South Slavic and Czecho-Slovak $o_2 r_1$ was generalized, but in the other dialects it was $o_1 r_2$.

The ultralong groups o_2r_2 and o_3r_1 at the beginning of the word were transformed by r_2 shortening to r_1 and by the liquids leaving the syllabic melody.

$o_2r_1 > o_3r_1$. This process occurred in Czech before the aforementioned process, but after it in Slovak and South Slavic.

In Russian, the groups o_1r_2, etc., became disyllabic ($o_1r_2 > or\ ŗ$).

In all dialects and all word positions, the groups e, o (long and short) + liquid, preceding a consonant, underwent a metathesis, with the intonation of the entire group nevertheless being preserved, as well as the quantity of each component of the group.

It is possible that parallel to the evolution of $oo_2ȓdlo > o_3ȓdlo > o_3rdlo > ro_3dlo$, the evolution $o_2i_1s(k)nъ > o_3i_1s(k)nъ > o_3js(k)nъ > jo_3s(k)nъ$ took place; cf. Lithuanian *aiskus*.

I think that the modifications of this ingenious theory presented here do the following: (1) give a simpler interpretation of the difference in the treatment of initial diphthongs in Czech vs. Slovak and South Slavic; (2) explain the coincidence of the dialect isogloss of *tort*, etc., with the dialect isogloss of *turt*, etc.; (3) present a more synthetic formula for the changes of *tort*, etc., in the West and Northeast of the Slavic world; (4) more systematically identify the fate of the diphthong *oi* with the evolution of liquid diphthongs.

3. I leave aside the question whether the desinence -*ən* was formed by means of contamination of the desinence -*y* with that of the participles of verbs of other classes: -*en'* (cf. Ščepkin, *b* 89), or even by means of the contamination of masculine and neuter participles, as suggested by Trubetzkoy, or, finally, if the variation of the desinences -*y*, -*en'* was originally conditioned by a difference of intonation (cf. the difference between *syny* 'sons, acc. pl.'—*berę* 'taking, pres. act. part.' and the Old East Slavic *koně* 'horses, acc. pl.'—*plača* 'crying, pres. act. part.', on the one hand, and the difference between the treatment of the accusative plural -*ůs*, -*us* and that of participles of the type *vedãs* 'lead' in Lithuanian, on the other hand; cf. Fortunatov, *a* 180. In any case, I do not see any obstacles to relating the forms in -*en* to the Proto-Slavic period. Its reflexes are systemically regular. The objections of Torbiörnsson (*b*) to the existence of a Proto-Slavic prototype of forms like Russian *nesa*, etc., assumed by Ekblom (*b*), only have value if we, along with Ščepkin (loc. cit.), reduce the difference between the phonic forms *nesę* (несѧ) and *nosę* (носѧ) 'carrying' of Zographensis to the fact that the consonant preceding the desinence is soft in the latter case and hard in the former, and if we interpret the corresponding difference in Proto-Slavic in the same way. However, a similar interpretation is not very likely. Once we admit the group "hard consonant + back vowel" for the forms of Zographensis *nesę* (несѧ), etc., and for the corresponding forms of the other Proto-Slavic dialects, the aforementioned objections lose their force. Van Wijk confronts the forms of Russian and Czech present active participles *nesa* 'carrying' with *rzeka* 'speaking' of Old Polish and treats the -*a* desinence of these forms as going back to an original -*onts*. However, the loss of the nasal element in the form *rzeka* (which, by the way, occurs in only one text; cf. Van Wijk 280) is easily explained by the fact that it is a *verbum dicendi* 'verb of speaking', with a subsidiary role, and by the fact that forms of this type tend to be pronounced in a rapid manner, not carefully, and are often reduced and abbreviated in various ways.

4. I designate this correlation conventionally as "soft group ~ hard group."

5. Cf. Šaxmatov, *f* 30.

Chapter 4

1. After the detailed argumentation of Durnovo (*j*) and Ekblom (*a*), one can consider that the theory that initial *o* does not go back to Proto-Slavic *e*, and was only a vestige of the Indo-European *e* ~ *o* alternation (see Il'inskij, *a, b*), has been definitively discredited.

2. Now Durnovo has accepted my point of view (*k* 225).

3. The only suspicious one is Czech *jezero*; because if we assume Proto-Czecho-Slovak *jäzero*, we would have no reason to expect an *e*, in view of the fact that the following *e*, preceding a hard dental, should have changed to a back vowel and thus caused a hardening of the preceding *z* (cf. §6.4). The specific question of whether phonetic forms of the type *jäzero, jälito* equally applied to the Czech area needs to be clarified.

Chapter 5

1. The change of *dl* to *l* belongs to the preliterary period of Russian. Thus, in an Arabic text from the middle of the tenth century, we find the form *dulâbe* = *duleby* 'Dulebs (early East Slavic tribe)' (cf. Kryms'kyj 132); in an even older Armenian text, the Russian word *salo* 'lard' appears without *d*, as Marr indicates. Forms with *gl* (< *dl*) are vestiges of a feature of certain peripheral Northern Russian dialects. Contrary to the fusion of affricates, this feature has nothing to do with the influence of Novgorod as a center; it is completely absent in the Novgorod monuments. Rather, it is the elimination of this feature that was due to the influence of Novgorod.

Chapter 6

1. For the forms *kъgda* 'when', *jegda* 'when', etc., see Fortunatov, *b* 23ff. For the form *tъkmo* 'only', see Durnovo, *i* 116.

2. The tendency to avoid the coexistence of the correlation "one ~ another intonational structure" and the correlation "soft ~ hard consonant" in the same system can easily be interpreted from the psychological point of view. It is difficult to simultaneously pay attention to heterogeneous elements of tonality (cf. Stumpf, *b* 30ff.). Attention is directed either toward the distinction in vowel tonality or toward the distinction in the fundamental tone of consonants. The tendency to avoid the coexistence of the afore-mentioned correlations, regular in the Slavic languages, would seem to have a larger field of application; but we cannot deduce a general law, since Japanese dialects simul-taneously admit both correlations (cf. Polivanov 28, 169ff.).

3. In this connection, let me mention several cases of the coincidence of isoglosses that require a linguistic interpretation. The Slavic languages that changed *tort* to *tort* did not shorten long accented vowels. The Slavic languages that make greater use of long vowels than others give evidence of a stronger tendency to preserve the quantita-tive correlation. In this regard, it is curious to confront two typical languages that both have fixed accent, namely, Czech, where *tort* > *trōt* and where the old accented long vowels survived under certain conditions, and Polish, where *tort* > *trot* and where accented long vowels were shortened. In the first case, the quantitative correlation has been preserved, while in the second case, it has been eliminated. This is how one can

interpret the relationship stated by Meillet between "the treatment *trat, trět*" and the fate of quantitative distinctions (*d*, 209).

4. "Sometimes, in their encounter, words destroy each other. This is the case for *épi* 'ear of grain' and *épine* 'thorn', which have literally and reciprocally collided with each other in Gascony" (Dauzat 66).

5. The present work was almost finished when I became acquainted with Trubetzkoy's study of the structure of vowel systems, which will appear in volume I of the *Travaux du Cercle Linguistique de Prague* and which opens up vast perspectives for comparative phonology. It is only in §6.4 and in §§7.6 and 7.9 that I was able to make use of the productive procedures that Trubetzkoy uses to establish the patterns of vowel systems.

6. Cf. Šaxmatov, *a* 80ff.

7. Trubetzkoy (*e*) has demonstrated that in the West Slavic languages, the loss of intervocalic *j* and the contraction of vowels preceded the loss of weak *jers*, while in the South Slavic languages, the changes took place in the reverse order.

8. Hujer states that *uo* is attested by texts, mainly after labials and velars (89). Cf. also the change of *o* to *u* that occurs in those Moravian dialects where short mid vowels have shared the fate of the corresponding long vowels. It is highly possible that the composite vowel *uo*, after labials and velars, spread throughout an area in Old Czech that was larger than the written records allow us to assume. It would be more logical to ask what motive impelled the scribe to note the extragrammatical difference between the variants of the same phoneme—*o* and *uo*—than to ask the opposite question of why the scribes so rarely represented this distinction. The phonetic testimony of Jan Hus is very interesting: "*Quid enim noceret sine difficultate scribere sic: koniam et non sic quoniam, similiter kvam et non quam, et kve, non que, similiter linko et non linquo etc.*" [What harm would it do to write thus without any difficulty: *koniam* and not *quoniam*, similarly, *kvam* and not *quam*, and *kve*, not *que*, *linko* and not *linquo*, etc.—RF] (Šembera 18).

9. An analysis of the evolution of Proto-Slavic intonations leads Trubetzkoy (*a* 179) to establish a classification of dialects that is close to mine; he distinguishes the representatives of the northeastern tendency (Russian, Polish, and Sorbian), the representatives of the southwestern tendency (Serbo-Croatian and Slovene), and, finally, the dialects that occupy an intermediate position and participate in these two tendencies at the same time (Bulgarian and Czech).

10. Korš has maintained that if long and short vowels exist in a language at the same time as an intensity accent, the longs tend to be high and the shorts to be low (147).

11. Between Polish and the Northern Kashubian dialects that have pitch oppositions, there is an intermediate area of Kashubian dialects that resembles the zone of Western Bulgarian and Macedonian. These dialects lack both the pitch correlation and the correlation "soft ~ hard consonants." In one part of this zone, we observe fixed accent.

Chapter 7

1. An entire series of written Russian texts from the period preceding the fall of weak *jers* (including original texts that do not reproduce South Slavic models) maintains the

distinction of palatalized *l* and *n*, on the one hand, and palatal *l* and *n*, on the other, preceding *e* and *ä*. Cf. Vasil'ev (*b*) and Durnovo (*d*). The opinion of the former, who views this distinction as a reflection of spoken Russian, seems more convincing to me than Durnovo's assumption, which refuses to view this as anything other than an artificial pronunciation of Church Slavonic, as represented by these Russian letters.

2. Conev 16; Mladenov, *b*.

3. The only exception to this is the Slovak dialect pair *ä—a*. For a description of *ä* and its spread, see Hála 96ff. Unfortunately, the author does not provide either a palatogram or a description of the *a* precisely in the pronunciation of those Slovak subjects who also possess an *ä* in their dialect. My own fleeting observations in Slovakia have given me the impression that the tonality of *a*, in the dialects that have *ä*, is lower than its tonality in Czech. In languages where *a* has a front partner, it generally tends to be more of a back vowel; cf. for example the back *a* of Turkish. One can assume the same phenomenon for the Proto-Slavic dialects that had the opposition "paired soft consonant + *ä*—paired hard consonant + *a*."

4. Broch points out that in Russian, the vowel becomes quite variable, depending on whether it is surrounded by hard or soft consonants. He states that one can examine several "points" along the trajectory of this range (*a—á—ä*), and that one can define the limits of this range, although the specific cases can deviate from it. Broch, following Sweet (456), defines the vowels in question as "very fluctuating" in this regard.

5. I only managed to become acquainted with Thomson's (*a*) interesting study at the very moment when my work was delivered to the typesetter. The distinction that I make between consonants with adjusted softness and those with autonomous softness generally corresponds to Thomson's distinction between "semisoft" consonants, which were pronounced with anticipation of the following vowel, and "softs," which themselves possessed softness, that is, a higher fundamental tonality than that of the following vowel (261). Thomson is correct to reject the hypothesis of the change of the former category to the latter in Common East Slavic (loc. cit.). Ukrainian identified the "semisoft" consonants with the "hards," while the other East Slavic dialects identified them with the "softs." Thomson proposes the following explanation of this divergent evolution: "In northern East Slavic, the degree of softness of soft consonants that derived from Common East Slavic became more moderate. Those who wish to view this as an influence of the Finnish base of articulation can find arguments to support their thesis" (252). It is from this objective realignment between softs and semisofts that Thomson deduces the fusion of the two categories. The lowering of the degree of softness, to the extent that it is not connected to the entire phonological evolution of East Slavic, seems to be a *deus ex machina* that comes to the rescue, just like the previous explanations of the divergence between Ukrainian *ï* and *t'i* of other East Slavic dialects, which Thomson rejects. We do not have any data that permit us to attribute a more elevated degree of consonant softness to Ukrainian than we observe in the *akan'e* dialects. The possibility of a Finnicism, with an isogloss that covers both Southern Russian and Belarusian, is doubtful, especially since the evolution of Polish is parallel to that of Russian. The very need to alter the adjusted softness in one direction or the other is not explained by Thomson. That is why it seems more probable to me to derive the change in adjusted softness from the institution of the autonomous correlation "soft ~ hard consonants," which, in turn, was caused by the loss of weak *jers*. Subsequently,

I connect the difference between the treatment of adjusted softs, in both Ukrainian and the other East Slavic dialects, with the repertoire of correlations that differentiated these two dialect types at the moment of weak *jer*-fall.

6. As we read in Ščerba's work, "The oldest generation, it seems, did not as yet confuse *e* and *i* (pretonic). That is why my mother clearly distinguishes *mela* and *mila*, while my generation—that is, people 30 years old or less—pronounces *m'ьla* in both cases [the symbol ь is described by Ščerba as resembling an English short lax [i], suggesting [m'ɪła]—RF], which incidentally does not prevent us from psychically differentiating *e* and *i* in this position, since we have heard this difference in the speech of our elders. Thus, we seem to find ourselves on the border of two phonetic states" (97–98).

7. This question is treated in the suggestive study by Savickij that will appear in volume I of the *Travaux du Cercle Linguistique de Prague*.

8. What has just been said about the *dzekan'e* of Belarusian [palatalized *d'* pronounced as *dz'*—RF] probably can equally apply to a similar trait in the neighboring Lithuanian dialects (see Kurschat §118).

9. Following Šaxmatov, I conventionally use the symbol *ô* to designate the reflexes of *o* under acute intonation in those Russian dialects where its reflexes differ from *o* of other origins.

10. Concerning the *ă* (ъ) of Bulgarian, Broch observes that "with respect to the position of the tongue, *ă* varies more than the other vowels do; it seems that the tongue position is generally high and corresponds to the position required by the pronunciation of rounded *u*, but it often happens that it is lower, on a mid level, and corresponds rather more to the position of *o*" (*b* 81; cf. 83).

11. Here, I leave aside Kashubian, which was discussed in §6.6.

It is interesting to note that for the Slavic languages, there is a limit on the impoverishment of the inventory of correlations. Besides the correlation "voiced ~ voiceless consonant," each Slavic language, except for some isolated transitional dialects used locally (e.g., Laština, Eastern Slovak, Rusnak, Macedonian with fixed accent, Southern Kashubian), has preserved at least one additional correlation; thus, Czech and Slovak have preserved the quantitative correlation, Eastern Bulgarian has the intensity correlation, and Polish has the correlation "soft ~ hard consonant."

12. The zone of a given inventory of phonological correlations usually takes in a complex of contiguous languages, whether genetically related or not (cf. §6.6). Thus, Hungarian adheres to the western domain (cf. §6.3), the second of the zones of the Slavic world that have been examined (the quantitative correlation occupies the same place in the Hungarian phonological system as in Czech and Slovak); and, with its phonological intensity accent, Greek adheres to the eastern domain of the same zone (Eastern Bulgarian). Romanian, which forms an enclave between Eastern Bulgarian and Ukrainian, matches these languages with its correlations "soft ~ hard consonant" and "intensity accent ~ unaccented." In an unpublished work, Bubrix emphasizes the intimate structural commonality between Mordvin and Russian. The isoglosses of correlations are a current issue for linguistic geography. It would be important to highlight the "areas of development" of such complexes of correlations, without regard for the genetic relationships of languages that are part of a common complex.

Chapter 8

1. It should be noted that a very rare dialect of Northern Russian (Jarensk district, Vologda *gubernija*) has the forms *umyjus'*, *šyju*, etc., and, at the same time, has forms of the type *suddja* (cf. *Otčet*).

Chapter 9

1. At present, Durnovo has already abandoned this theory (*g* 270).

2. Zernov unites these two categories into a single "group of strong vowels," which he opposes to the clearly delimited "group of weak vowels" (50).

3. For the list of *akan'e* types, see Durnovo, *h* §91, *k* §63, or Obnorskij 243–244.

4. Kurylo rejects the hypotheses that derive dissimilative *akan'e* from quantitative relations, and attempts to find another explanation. The fact that accented vowels became high and unaccented vowels were reduced in the direction of short *a* introduced the dissimilative principle into the vowel system. High vowels become predominant in accented syllables, and low vowels in unaccented syllables. The most pronounced manifestation of this dissimilative principle is the fact that low pretonic vowels attained their maximum low position when preceding a high unaccented vowel (*b* 69).

Chapter 10

1. On the political plane, corresponding to this, one can observe a clear consciousness of Russian unity, frequently noted by literary historians in the works of various Russian authors of the eleventh and twelfth centuries.

2. I omit modern literary theory, which is tightly linked to linguistics, even in its origins. The history of literature (especially in the works of the Russian "Formalist" school) is shedding its previous accidental and eclectic nature, and its multiplicity of topics. Rather than appearing to be a series of isolated anecdotes, it is becoming a structural science that studies literature as a functional system and seeks to establish its static and dynamic laws.

Index

Page locators for the editorial material (foreword, chapter annotations, and appendices B and C) are italicized. Locators for endnotes are of the form *000n00.00*, where *000* is the page number on which the note occurs, the following *00* is the chapter number, and the final *00* is the note number.